^{THE}ART & SCIENCE
OF
FINANCIAL RISK
ANALYSIS

D1563322

National Association of Credit Management

THE ART & SCIENCE OF

OF

FINANCIAL RISK ANALYSIS

THIRD EDITION

THE ANALYST'S GUIDE TO DETERMINING A COMPANY'S FINANCIAL STRENGTH AND CREDITWORTHINESS

By

Jerry F. Dean, CCE

National Association of Credit Management

To

My wife Lois, my daughters Michelle and Jennifer,
and son Greg.

You have been and continue to be my sources of inspiration and encouragement. Thank you for your love, patience and support.

Thanks also to my sons-in-law, Matt Benn and Darren Domilise for their love and support.

Special thanks to our grandkids Blake, Zachary and Mackenzie Benn, and Dean Domilise. Lois and I are truly blessed with your presence and we pray that all your dreams come true.

Table of Contents

Summary of Exhibits, Figures, and Tables xiii

Introduction xv

Chapter 1 Preliminary Financial Statement Review   1
           Accounting Policy   3
           Adjustment of Items   4
           Auditor's Opinion   4
           Management's Opinion   4
           Cash Flow Statement   5
           Types of Financial Statements   5

Chapter 2 Preliminary Adjustments to Book Net Worth
           and Fixed Assets   8
           Book Net Worth   8
           Adjusted Net Worth   8
           Fixed Asset Adjustments 10

Chapter 3 Additional Steps in Determining a Company's
           Credit Line 16
           Personal Net Worth Analysis 16
           Footnotes 18
           Credit Agency Reports 18
           Bank Reference Information 18
           Trade Reference Information 19
           Final Determination of Credit Lines 20
           Internal Analysis (Eye-Ball Analysis) 21

Chapter 4 Ratios 25
           Balance Sheet Ratios 25
           Liquidity Ratios 26
           Turnover Ratios 27
           DSO Calculations 28
           Profitability Ratios 29

Chapter 5 Appraising the Use of Ratios 34
           Cash Conversion Cycle 35
           Defensive Interval (DI) 38

Chapter 6 Cash Flow Analysis 42
           Sources and Uses of Funds 44
           Developing a Statement of Cash Flows 45
           Statement of Cash Flows 48
           What Should the Analyst Do? 54
           What Have We Learned? 56

Chapter 7	**Profitability Analysis Using the Extended DuPont Model**	**57**
	Analysis of Return on Sales	61
	Efficiency in Managing Assets	63
Chapter 8	**Financial Planning and Sustainable Growth**	**71**
	LTSGR Formula	71
Chapter 9	**Predicting a Company's Sustainable Growth** ...	**73**
	Steps in Projecting Financial Statements	75
Chapter 10	**Derivatives Risk Analysis**	**78**
	Introduction	78
	Where Does Risk Lie—Forwards	80
	Where Does Risk Lie—Swaps	85
	Swaps Terminology	86
	Marking Swaps to Market	86
	Evaluating Potential Swaps Risk	89
	How Is Potential Risk Quantified?	89
	Controlling Swaps Credit Risk	89
	Setting Trading Limits	89
	Margin/Collateral	90
	Standard Credit Terms	91
	Swaps Flexibility	93
	Keys to Swaps Risk	94
	Basis Risk	94
	Risk Categories and Definitions	96
	Suggested Principles for the Assessment of Derivatives	97
	Questions We Should Ask Ourselves in Order to Mitigate Credit Risk	99
	Oil and Natural Gas Markets: A Growing Role for Derivatives	102
	Condensed Summary Sheet of Options, Futures and Swaps	102
Chapter 11	**Evaluating HLCs, LBOs, LLCs and Subchapter "S" Corporations**	**107**
	The Various Forms of Business Entities	107
	Evaluating the Various Forms of Business Entities .	109
	Limited Liability Company Analysis—LLCs	115
	Subchapter S Corporation Analysis	116
Chapter 12	**International Credit Risk**	**118**
	Country Risk	119
	Insuring Credit Risk	121
Chapter 13	**Bank Analysis**	**122**

Chapter 14   **Security Instruments** **125**

What Is an LC? 125

Types of LCs 126

Guarantees 132

Other Methods to Secure Accounts 135

Letter of Credit Format 136

Chapter 15   **Credit Scoring Models** **138**

Introduction 138

Scoring Model Parameters 140

Spread Types 144

Altman Z Score 145

Lambda 147

Bond Rating 150

Model Formats 151

Chapter 16   **Rating Agencies and Default Probabilities** **152**

Measuring Default Probability: A Practical

Approach 153

Chapter 17   **Portfolio Risk Analysis** **160**

Probability Distribution 162

Key Risk Parameters 164

Risk and Capital Allocation 165

Default Model Paradigms 168

Potential Future Exposure (PFE) 171

Chapter 18   **FASB Updates and the Sarbanes-Oxley Act** **179**

FAS-105 179

FAS-133 181

The Sarbanes-Oxley Act of 2002 182

Chapter 19   **Financial Planning** **183**

Overview 183

Break Even Analysis 183

Sustainable Growth 185

Sustainable Growth and the DuPont Model 191

Building a Financial Plan 192

Chapter 20   **Economic Value Added (EVA) and**

Risk Adjusted Return on Capital (RAROC) **193**

The EVA Message 197

The Incentive to Turn Receivables for Credit

Management 198

Conclusion 201

What EVA Is 202

What EVA Is Not 202

Risk Capital and RAROC 203

Chapter 21   **Warning Signs and Financial Shenanigans** **207**
Always Look for the Warning Signs 207
Accruals and Structured Finance 209
Financial Shenanigans 213

Chapter 22   **Bankruptcy** **217**
The Bankruptcy Abuse Prevention and Consumer
Protection Act of 2005 217
Chapter 7 220
Chapter 11 221
Critical First Days 222
Financial Crisis Event Response Plan 223
Preference Payments 224
Frequently Referenced Glossary of Terms 225

Chapter 23   **Serving on a Creditors' Committee:**
What to Know **226**
Why Serve on the Committee? 226
Committee Powers and Duties 227
Committee Organization and Operation 228
Conclusion 229

Chapter 24   **Collateral Document Guidelines** **230**
When Is Collateral Necessary or When Should It Be
Considered? 230
Risk Mitigation Instruments 230
Trade Credit Insurance 241
Securitization of Trade Receivables 241
Credit Default Swap Transactions 242

Chapter 25   **Credit Derivatives** **243**
What Are Credit Derivatives 243
Limitations on the Use of Credit Derivatives 247
How to Make the Best Use of the Credit Derivative
Market 248

Chapter 26   **How to Write a Credit Analysis** **249**
The Elements of Style 249
Six Rules for Good Analysis 249
Outline for Credit Analysis 252
Summary 254

Chapter 27   **Author's Viewpoint** **255**
Opportunities to Shine 256

Chapter 28   **How to Read Financial Statements from an**
Investor's Viewpoint **258**
The Balance Sheet 258
The Income Statement 259

The Statement of Cash Flows 260
Don't Ignore the Footnotes 261
Write-Downs and Reversals 265
Goodwill Games 266
Stock Options 266
Special-Purpose Entities (SPEs) 267
Investor Measures 269
Appendix A Glossary of Letter of Credit Terms 273
Appendix B Export Letter of Credit Checklist 277
References Useful for Further Reading 278
Special Thanks 278
Index 279

Summary of Exhibits, Figures, and Tables

Exhibit 1	Extended DuPont Model	60
Exhibit 2	Crude Oil Swap Contract Between Oil Producer and Refiner	84
Exhibit 3	Acquisition Cost for 10,000 Barrels (Dollars)	85
Exhibit 4	Marking Swaps to Market	87
Exhibit 5	Derivatives Risk Tracking Report	88
Exhibit 6	Analyzing Energy Transaction Risk	105
Exhibit 7	Bank Analysis Format	123
Exhibit 8	Ratio Weighting Percentage	124
Exhibit 9	Standby Letter of Credit Format	133
Exhibit 10	Letter of Credit Format	136

Figure 6-1	Balance Sheet Analysis of Sources/Uses	45
Figure 6-2	Indirect Statement of Cash Flows	51
Figure 6-3	Direct Statement of Cash Flows	55
Figure 7-1	Using DuPont Model to Uncover Asset Turnover Slowdown	58
Figure 7-2	Common Size Income Statement Analysis	62
Figure 7-3	Management of Assets Analysis	63
Figure 10-1	Example of an Oil Future Contract	81
Figure 10-2	Petroleum and Natural Gas Price Risks and Risk Management Strategies	101
Figure 17-1	Levels of Risk Measurement Methodologies	161
Figure 17-2	Risk Capital	162
Figure 17-3	Risk Capital (credit risk)	163
Figure 17-4	Credit Exposure Normal Distribution	165
Figure 17-5	Counterparty Credit Exposure	165
Figure 17-6	Risk Categories	169
Figure 17-7	PFE Profile — Forward Contract	172
Figure 17-8	PFE Profile — Swap Contract	173
Figure 17-9	Credit Management Process	174
Figure 17-10	PFE Distribution Across a Range of Confidence Levels	175
Figure 17-11	Principal Component Analysis	176
Figure 17-12	PFE Modelling Using Monte Carlo Simulation	177
Figure 17-13	D&B Financial Stress Score v. S&P Default Rates	178
Figure 17-14	Comparison of Three Credit Rating Agencies	178
Figure 20-1	Calculating EVA	195
Figure 20-2	Weighted Average Cost of Capital	196
Figure 20-3	Modified DuPont Formula	204

Credit Limit Worksheet 23
Credit Limit Formula 24
Checklist of Financial Indicators 32
Cash Conversion Cycle Breakdown 38
TAT Decomposition 69
NPM Decomposition 69
Financial Leverage Multiplier Decomposition 70
ROE Decomposition 70
Relationship between Assets and Sales 187
Building a Financial Plan 192
Investor Measures 272

Introduction

Financial risk analysis can be described as both an Art and a Science.

Ratio calculations and various number crunching exercises represent the science. The art is the actual interpretation and decision making process whereby all types of company information are reviewed and based on the analyst's past experience and industry knowledge, then a decision is made which may include a "gut feel" about the risk/reward of doing a particular deal.

This book is intended to help the reader develop the art and science of financial risk analysis. It will satisfy the needs of credit analysts looking for the basics as well as those wanting a more in-depth understanding of financial analysis techniques. Instructional in nature, it provides an understanding of how to arrive at a final credit decision, as well as how to write a final recommendation. The explanations provided and concepts introduced will be useful to the many persons in credit, finance, derivatives trading and accounting employed in all types of industries.

The book was formatted to first step through an understanding of basic credit concepts and then build from there. As a result, topics for discussion following the basic concepts will include Cash Flow Analysis, Profitability Analysis using the DuPont Model, Break Even Analysis, Economic Value Added (EVA), Bank Analysis, and Derivatives Risk Analysis. A thorough explanation will be provided with regards to the concepts of Sustainable Growth, Point Scoring, Distress or Default Probability Modeling. In addition, it will cover Bank Letters of Credit, Guarantees, discuss Financial Shenanigans and Financial Warning Signs and provide an overview of various business structures such as LLCs and Subchapter S Corporations. Instructional in nature, it gives the reader practical tools and concepts that can be applied immediately to improve upon the internal decision making process. In addition, it will provide a framework of how to effectively write a narrative interpretation and recommendation of findings. In my opinion, the last step of writing a narrative interpretation of all the findings is the most important exercise of the entire analytical process.

The sudden collapse of Enron worth $80 billion in less than a year has brought to light that the manipulation of data is possible even in some of the strongest and largest companies in corporate America. Making matters worse was the fact that Arthur Andersen, the outside auditors, was a part of this conspiracy. It took the terrorist attacks on September 11, 2001 to prove that our nations security measures were inadequate. It took the Enron bankruptcy in late 2001 to prove that the fundamental auditing processes were not up to the task of protecting those who read financial statements.

The pressure builds for financial managers to sharpen their skills in reading financial statements and to completely understand what's behind them. Doing a few standard liquidity ratios is not enough. You must pour over footnotes, track on trends and ask questions when anomalies are discovered. The alert financial analyst becomes a detective and each set of financials is a story that needs to be understood. Financials that have been manipulated to make the company look better than they are usually contain clues that financial analysts can spot to get to the truth.

In the case of Enron, the truth is that the published 10K report for the year ending 2000 suggests the company's cash flows were insufficient to meet its operating needs. A close look at the investing activities would have revealed Enron used $11.7 billion of cash that created a deficit in excess of $4.0 billion. A further review of the financial activities reflects Enron increased its long-term borrowing and issued new stock of approximately $2.0 billion to bridge its cash deficit.

Enron was far from being a best in class type of company. In addition to the company's cash deficit, there were other subtle distress signals coming to the surface. The company began to venture away from its core business into more speculative and volatile activity. Turnover at key senior management positions was very high. An unethical environment surrounded by greed led to unethical accounting practices. Add to this mess the company's off-balance sheet partnership activity, and the fall of the seventeenth largest market capitalized company in the country was only a matter of time. This book will show you where to look for the warning signs and will emphasize that cash flow analysis is still the most reliable tool to determine a company's financial condition.

Chapter 1

PRELIMINARY FINANCIAL
STATEMENT REVIEW

The evaluation of a new customer for the extension of credit is, for the most part, a fairly subjective exercise. This exercise is best underscored by applying the five "Cs" of credit (character, capacity, capital, conditions, collateral). Of these five items, capital is the only one that can truly be looked at on a quantitative level, through analysis of a company's financial statements.

A customer's current financial statement is defined as their fiscal or calendar year-end statement. Prior to "crunching" the numbers, you should complete an overview by briefly examining various sections of the published financial statement in order to develop a feel about the company's direction, accounting policies and profitability. Crunching the numbers will uncover more of the mystery novel but initially look at things from a higher level. The following outlines a step approach before pushing the numbers.

*Step One: **Read for an Understanding***

- Read footnotes, auditor's opinion, accounting policies, presidents message before "pushing" the numbers
- Don't accept the written word as gospel
- Read "between the lines"
- Look for confirmation elsewhere in the statements
- Look for changes in accounting policies and ask why
- Be a detective trying to solve a mystery

*Step Two: **Review Cash Flow Statement***
*Step Three: **Crunch the Numbers***
*Step Four: **Do a Quick Eye-Ball Analysis***, make notes and get answers to questions raised by calling the firm's CPA or owner for further explanation!

Although analysis is a key factor in determining a customer's credit limit, the final credit decision involves value judgments made by weighing the importance of various factors present in each case. Probably the most important key to making good credit decisions, outside of the aforementioned financial statement and trend analysis, is the proper evaluation of the character, reputation, and experience of the company, as well as the individuals responsible for day-to-day management. As a result, every customer credit evaluation and the assignment of a credit limit should include the examination of factors referred to as the "Cs" of credit:

- Character
- Capacity
- Capital
- Conditions
- Collateral

Character. The willingness of the debtor to pay obligations promptly. It consists of an account's reputation for honesty and dependability.

Capacity. The ability of the account to conduct its business successfully. It includes management ability and technical know-how.

Capital. The most important source of information on capital is the financial statement and its analysis to determine whether the account will be able to pay its obligations. This factor highlights the financial condition and trend of operations.

Conditions. The external influences not traceable to any of the credit factors fall under the conditions category. General economic conditions in the nation, in the community, and in the industry will exert a modifying influence on the final analysis of the account.

Collateral. To ensure payment and avoid the loss of a sale, special written legal arrangements are made when an account appears weak and unacceptable after an evaluation of character, capacity, capital and conditions.

Methods of analysis may be divided into two general categories: internal and comparative. With internal analysis, we use figures from the financial statements of any one date or period to gain an understanding of the company. Comparative analysis may be used to determine trends where two or more successive sets of figures are reviewed, or may be used to evaluate a given company's financial statement against the industry standards of similar asset-sized companies.

The principle sources of credit information are listed below:

- Financial statements
- Credit agency reports
- Bank reference information
- Trade reference information
- Newspapers, publications and specialized services

ACCOUNTING POLICY

Before beginning the analysis of a financial statement, make some general observations that will let you know about the type of accounting policy used by the customer. A conservative accounting policy, for example, tends to understate assets, overstate liabilities, and understate the reported net profit and net worth.

Practices that understate assets and reduce reported earnings include:

- Large allowances for uncollectibles
- Conservative inventory valuations
- Heavy depreciation changes
- Expensing of research and development costs
- Heavy liabilities contingency reserves

Practices that overstate assets and inflate reported earnings include:

- Minimal allowances for uncollectibles
- Liberal inventory valuations
- Stretched-out depreciation schedules
- Capitalization of research and development costs
- Inadequate provisions for contingencies

You should review the financial statement and examine the footnotes to determine the following:

- Inventory valuation method (LIFO vs. FIFO)
- Plant and equipment depreciation method (Accelerated depreciation vs. Straight line)
- Method of accounting for drilling operations (Full cost vs. Successful efforts)
- Size of allowance for uncollectibles in relation to receivables

ADJUSTMENT OF ITEMS

If you do not agree with the auditor's classification of an item as current or non-current, then an adjustment should be made. This would not affect the totals for assets, liabilities, or net worth but may change several financial ratios.

Another adjustment would occur if a scaling down of assets were needed on items that are judged to be inflated or classified as intangibles. This adjustment is made directly to the company's net worth prior to the final credit line calculations.

Other adjustment items made directly to the company's net worth would be prepaid expenses (money already spent which a creditor does not have access to), investments that have not been footnoted (call the customers to determine their nature), receivables from stockholders, and investments in subsidiaries (one must determine the financial condition of the subsidiary in order to judge if the asset is worthy of listing and this information may not be readily available).

AUDITOR'S OPINION

As an important first step in internal analysis, the financial statement should be examined for validity and general correctness. If there is an auditor's opinion, be certain to note whether the auditor's letter contains language indicating that they "examined" the financial statements and that an "opinion" is given that the financial statements are "in conformity with generally accepted accounting principles." An audited statement may be "qualified," which means the accounting firm has identified an accounting irregularity. This should obviously be a "red flag."

Frequently, customers provide financial statements printed on an auditor's letterhead or accompanied by a letter from a certified public accountant. If this letter is merely a transmittal document and does not include the language described above, the report cannot be considered as reliable as audited statements. It is up to the discretion of the Credit Manager to lower the percentage a company might qualify for as a result of the fact that the statement is unaudited.

MANAGEMENT'S OPINION

Make sure you read through any and all comments associated with the past year from management's perspective. Ask the question if previous year's goals and objectives were achieved. If not, what caused the problem? What steps have been identified to correct or improve upon a given situation? Do they make sense and are they achievable short or long-term? A wealth of knowledge and accountability can come from a critical reading of this report.

CASH FLOW STATEMENT

Review this statement thoroughly and develop questions that hopefully will be answered during the number crunching exercise. This statement uncovers the heart and soul of the company. Familiarize yourself with the format and learn how to spot trends. It tells how the company made money and specifically how it was spent. The forthcoming chapter on Cash Flow Analysis will complement this preliminary review process.

TYPES OF FINANCIAL STATEMENTS

Financial statements reflect varying degrees of integrity in how they were developed and prepared. Listed below are brief descriptions of different types of financial statements used for credit analysis purposes.

Audited

- Auditors have reviewed documents, transactions, bank statements and tested cash transactions. Confirmations have been sent to banks, receivable customers, payable vendors and suppliers to verify balances.
- Inventories have been tested and fixed assets inventoried. Sales have been tested with random sampling. Attorney representation letters have been obtained.
- When auditing has been completed, the CPA/audit firm has to be assured the financial statements are materially correct, prepared, and presented in accordance with Generally Accepted Accounting Principles (GAAP) before stating their opinion.
- Audited financial settlements are very costly. For a medium-sized publicly held firm (300 employees, $20 million annual sales), the cost may be in the $40,000 to $100,000 range.
- All publicly held corporations must have annual audited financial statements.
- A D&B full capital and composite first line rated company (i.e., 5A1, 4A1) assumes that three years of annual audited financial statements have been received and reviewed.

Reviewed

- Financial statement is partially audited, with all testing and audit work scaled down. There are not as many assurances as with an audited statement and you have lesser reliance on statement accuracy.
- Accountant's statement that it was prepared in accordance with GAAP may or may not be included. This inclusion will depend on the degree of testing, auditing, and sampling conducted.
- The cost of a review for medium-sized, closely held, corporations may range from $20,000 to $50,000 per year. A closely held corporation is one which is private. They do not have to file 10Ks or 10Qs. Stock certificates are issued to shareholders but cannot be traded.

Compiled

- Management presents the company's financial statement. An accountant looks at the data, and should be aware of the client's professional integrity and particular industry, and is then responsible for preparing the data submitted in a proper financial statement form.
- If the accountant identifies errors with the data submitted, management must correct them or they must be disclosed in the opinion statement. The cost of a compiled statement may range from $5,000 to $10,000, depending on the firm's size and other factors.

Management Prepared

- This statement has a far lower degree of integrity than those mentioned above. They do not include any outside accountant's involvement.
- Reliability of the figures presented coincides with the perceived reliability of the owners and officers. They do have value for credit analysis and should be used as a starting point and correlation with other information gained during the analysis process.

Tax Returns

- A customer's tax return is another good source for analysis. In many instances, these are the best and most reliable financial statements.

- The customer should be requested to certify the accuracy of their tax returns by signing and attaching a statement such as: "This verifies that the attached tax returns are true, accurate, and complete copies of original tax returns submitted to the IRS and all State Tax Return Schedules are enclosed."

Chapter 2

PRELIMINARY ADJUSTMENTS TO BOOK NET WORTH AND FIXED ASSETS

BOOK NET WORTH

Book Net Worth is the net or sum of the components of the owner's equity on the balance sheet. Generally, the credit limit will be determined as a percentage of net worth. Adjustments may be made to net worth prior to calculations of the credit limit.

ADJUSTED NET WORTH

Adjusted Net Worth is used for credit purposes to determine the actual financial strength of a company. A discussion of significant adjustments follows.

Inventory Adjustments

Valuation of inventories is generally on a first in, first out (FIFO) basis or a last in, first out (LIFO) basis. During a period of increasing prices the LIFO method results in balance sheet inventory values lower than current market values. Conversely, during a period of declining prices, the LIFO method may overstate the value of inventories. It will be necessary to adjust the working capital and net worth to reflect adjustments to inventory based upon market values. The following is recommended for the adjustment procedure during increasing price periods; add to the LIFO value the "LIFO Reserve" multiplied by 50 percent. The amount of LIFO reserve is stated in the financial statement footnotes.

Only 50 percent of the reserve is to be added to working capital and net worth in recognition of the possible adjustment upon liquidation of LIFO-valued inventories.

Example:

Net Worth per Balance Sheet	$200,000
LIFO Reserve: ($40,000 × 50%)	20,000
Adjusted Net Worth	$220,000

During substantial *declines* in market values it may be necessary to discount the FIFO or adjusted LIFO inventory values downward to estimate the market value.

Example:

Inventory @ LIFO Value	$100,000
LIFO Reserve	40,000
Inventory @ FIFO Value	$140,000
Less Market Decline @ 20%	28,000
	$112,000

Adjustments on Market vs. LIFO 6,000	
Value: $ 112,000	
– 100,000	
$12,000 × 50%	– 6,000
	$106,000

Intercompany Receivables and Payables

Accounts receivable by a subsidiary from its parent entity, other companies that are related, or receivables from principal officers, may not be collectable. Although legally due, an intercompany receivable is no better than the financial strength of the owing company.

Intercompany receivables may also be offset by intercompany payables. Sometimes, the net amount of intercompany receivables and payables should be subtracted from net worth and working capital. However, before deducting these items, an attempt should be made to determine their true value. In cases where a large parent company is involved, no deduction may be the correct decision.

Pensions

Beginning in 1987, companies with large unfunded pension liabilities were required to show that liability on their balance sheet. To prevent an impact on earnings, companies may offset this liability with a "valueless" asset. This valueless asset should be eliminated and the net worth reduced accordingly.

Redeemable Preferred Stock

This stock also may need to be deducted if included in the stockholders' equity section. Preferred stock which is redeemable should be considered long-term debt and not stockholders' equity. This type of preferred stock, also referred to as Callable Preferred Stock, carries the provision that the issuer has the right to call in the stock at a certain price and retire it.

Other Deductions

Intangible assets have no value to a creditor, and therefore, should be deducted from net worth. The following are considered to be intangible assets:

- Goodwill
- Covenant not to compete
- Organizational costs
- Patents
- Real estate in excess of fair market value
- Franchise fees
- Customer lists

Deferred income tax benefits may have no value to the company for which expected future profits are doubtful. In such a case, it is recommended that this asset value be deducted from net worth.

FIXED ASSET ADJUSTMENTS

Refineries

It is important to evaluate the net book value of a refinery, particularly the smaller refineries carried on the balance sheet. In some cases, this value is listed separately in the fixed asset section or in the notes of the financial statements. More often however, this value does not appear separately but can be fairly accurately determined using the following formula:

1. % of Refinery to Fixed Assets = $\dfrac{\text{Gross Refinery Value}}{\text{Total Fixed Assets}}$

2. Refinery Depreciation =
   % of Refinery Asset to Fixed Assets × Total Depreciation

3. Net Book Value Refinery =
   Gross Refinery Assets − Refinery Depreciation

This equation provides an appropriate useful life of the refinery.

This information should be noted in the credit file. In some instances, such as during periods of low refining margins, the net book value of a refinery will be deducted from a company's net worth before the credit line is determined.

Oil and Gas Reserves

Another fixed asset, which must be evaluated is a company's oil and gas reserves. One of two accounting methods is used for valuing oil and gas reserves. They are the Full Cost and the Successful Efforts methods. Generally, the method followed will be reflected on the balance sheet or in the notes to the financial statements.

The full cost method capitalizes all costs of drilling both successful and unsuccessful wells. These costs are subsequently written off pro rata against units of production from the successful wells. The balance sheet effect is to state fixed assets at an amount that may be greater than the actual value of the reserves discovered.

Under the successful efforts method, only the costs of successful wells are capitalized and the costs of unsuccessful wells are expensed currently. This method presents fixed assets, and thus net worth, at conservatively lower values than the full cost method.

Net worth based upon either the full cost or successful efforts method should be adjusted to reflect current market values. This adjustment can be accomplished by simply multiplying the company's proven crude oil reserves plus the total proven natural gas reserves (found in the notes to the audited statement) by the dollar amount which management feels is a realistic market value. This total is then compared to the net book value of oil and gas reserves (often referred to as the net capitalized costs) on a company's balance sheet. The net worth can then be adjusted either up or down to reflect the current market value of the reserves.

Also, larger petroleum companies provide a footnote reflecting the "standardized measure of discounted future net cash flows" or the "present value of estimated future net revenue." This is determined by the excess of future cash inflows from proved reserves less the future costs of producing and developing the reserves, future income taxes, and discount factor. This amount may also be compared with net capitalized cost of oil and gas reserves on the balance sheet to determine if reserves are over or understated.

Having useful and reliable information on oil and gas reserves is enormously important to risk managers, investors, and the public. Over 150 publicly owned U.S. oil and gas producers file reserves data in their

10-K, and their reported total reserves of oil and gas is valued at over $3 trillion. Financial analysts covering the industry generally find that for energy companies, over 70 percent of the total market value is determined by the amount of proved reserves the company has.

Companies are currently required to provide *unaudited* estimates of proved reserves to the Securities and Exchange Commission (SEC), using strict and conservative definitions provided in the SEC regulations for proved and proved developed reserves. In theory, given these strict definitions, and in this era of rising oil and gas prices and improving recovery techniques, it is hard to envision scenarios where companies could report significant downward "technical revisions" in proved reserves. In practice, however, recent large downward revisions in proved reserves by Shell (20 percent reduction of proved oil and gas reserves in 2004) and El Paso (41 percent reduction of proved gas reserves), and smaller restatements by a handful of other companies has shown that the reserves data are indeed vulnerable to disclosure quality risk.

These events confirm that despite their overall reliability, the current unaudited reserves data are viewed by investors and analysts as just not reliable enough. In fact, as investors learn more about how reserves are estimated and reported, it might come as surprising to them that items on a company's balance sheet, such as cash and accounts receivable, which contribute to only a small part of the total value of the company, are subject to far more external audit and internal controls than proved reserves estimates despite the reserves being the main driver of an energy company's upstream value.

Current Disclosure Requirements

Given the strategic importance of reliable oil and gas reserves estimates, all major U.S. energy producers with significant oil and gas reserves are currently required by the Securities and Exchange Commission to report their estimates of proved developed reserves and proved undeveloped reserves in their annual filings with the SEC. The SEC disclosure regulations (Reg. § 210.4-10) on reserves date back to the energy crisis of the late 1970s. Even though the reserves data are disclosed in the annual filings as footnotes to audited financial statements, the footnotes themselves are not audited by the auditing firms and are clearly labeled in the 10-K filings as "unaudited."

The SEC disclosure rules on reserves are highly respected. The SEC uses strict definitions of the terms "proved" and "proved developed" reserves, and there is general consensus in the industry and among analysts that the SEC's definitions are quite conservative, if not too restrictive. Under SEC definitions, reserves can only go in the "proved" category reporting if there is "reasonable certainty" that they can be developed at current prices. In Reg. § 210.4-10, the SEC defines proved oil and gas reserves as "the estimated quantities of crude oil, natural gas, and natural gas liquids which geological and engineering data demonstrate with **reasonable certainty** to be **recoverable** in future years from **known reservoirs** under **existing economic and operating conditions**." (Emphasis added.) As noted, the key highlighted phrase in the above definition is "reasonable certainty." The SEC has interpreted this phrase especially quite strictly and appropriately so, and has generally required evidence from test wells, rather than allowing companies to rely on newer technologies for estimating reserves. Specifically, the SEC requires that "Reservoirs are considered proved if economic producibility is supported by either **actual production or conclusive formation test**."

U.S. energy companies are required to provide a considerable amount of disclosures covering both financial and non-financial aspects of their business. However, the list also indicates that all disclosure related reserves (quantity as well as the standardized measure of cash flows) are unaudited. Therefore, investors and regulators looking to find the cause of the credibility gap in reserves disclosures should naturally focus first on the quality of data and reporting standards of current disclosures rather than on potential additional disclosures.

Importance of Reserves Disclosures

As a result of an unaudited position regarding quantity and measure of cash flows, surveys of investors and petroleum industry managers show that investors and financial analysts *want* to believe the reserves numbers, but *do not,* for the most part, rely on them. Unaudited reserves disclosures of companies are not viewed by investors as adequately reliable for valuation purposes, unless the data are also supported by other audited financial disclosures of the company.

In 2004, Shell's reserves restatement shocked the markets and the industry for the magnitude of the downward restatement. About 20 percent of Shell's total proved reserves (3.9 billion barrels of oil equivalent) were reclassified as a result of the restatement from proved category to other categories. Apart from Shell, however, there have been few reserve restatements by major U.S. companies. As noted, only a handful of other companies have restated their proved reserves estimates. Still, many analysts and investors are surprised and confused by the revisions. After all, investors have a right to think that the reported proved reserves numbers are technically determined and should be reliable and not fuzzy.

As noted above, the SEC does have a strict and conservative definition of what can be classified as proved reserves. It is no wonder that investors and regulators are asking whether there may be fundamental estimation and reporting issues related to reserves estimation that need to be addressed. Shell's internal investigations have shown that the problem of overvaluation of proved reserves was limited to just two or three geographic areas. The other cases of reserves restatements may well have been exposed from the process of implementing the Sarbanes-Oxley Act's internal control certification requirement

Verifiable Reserves Data: Lack of Audit and Certification

Given the importance of the reserves disclosures for investors and regulators, it is surprising that there has been very little focus in the financial media on how the reserves data are prepared and reported by companies. Currently, reserves disclosures in the financial statements are not audited by independent public accountants, nor are they audited by any petroleum industry-designated independent evaluators. Performing the critical "reserves evaluator" function also does not currently require any recognized certification program or other mandatory industry-wide training requirements. There is also no industry-wide peer review or monitoring program of the work.

An industry standard approved by the Society of Petroleum Engineers (SPE), titled "Standards Pertaining to the Estimating and Auditing of Oil and Gas Reserves Information," provides guidance to reserves evaluators. However, there is no industry-wide system to enforce the standards.

Making reserves disclosures more useful to investors would require addressing the credibility gap issues by improving both the relevance and reliability of the disclosures, which in turn requires significant improvements to the processes by which reserves data are currently estimated, audited and reported. Both the industry and the SEC need to take concrete steps that will result in the end-users perceiving the reserves data as reliable and useful for valuation purposes. While the Sarbanes-Oxley Act has made companies pay serious attention to these conflicts by requiring companies to have their internal control processes certified, there is still a potential need to require external audits of the reserves estimation process to fully address the reporting credibility.

Rather than relying on continued luck, it is preferable for the SEC and the industry to seriously consider proposals for certification and external reserves audit, and other proposals affecting the quality of reserves disclosures and regulations.

Market Appraisals

Occasionally, companies will provide market appraisals of fixed assets. The use of market appraisals to substantiate greater net worth than reflected on the balance sheet is not acceptable for credit purposes. Although assets may indeed have a market value greater than the net book value, the reliability of market appraisals is questionable. Particularly of little use are estimates of replacement costs. Somewhat more reliable is an economic valuation based upon the discounted cash flows from projected future operations.

Chapter 3

ADDITIONAL STEPS IN DETERMINING A COMPANY'S CREDIT LINE

PERSONAL NET WORTH ANALYSIS

Occasionally, a company's credit line is supported by the strength of an individual's personal guarantee, which is supported by that individual's personal net worth. The individual's net worth must be evaluated just as if it was the customer. To arrive at an adjusted personal net worth, the Credit Analyst must first determine the net worth or equity of the individual from the financial statements and then make the following deductions:

1. Company Stock

Many times, stock in the company an individual is guaranteeing will be listed as an asset on their personal financial statement. This asset should be deducted to avoid any magnification of worth. This would occur when a credit line is based on a combination of both the company's and the individual's net worth.

2. Notes Receivable from the Company

Receivables from the company an individual is guaranteeing should always be deducted from personal worth. Normally, personal guarantees are received from the sole owner or majority stockholder of a company. Should that company begin to experience cash flow problems, a debt to the owner can easily be deferred.

3. Book Value of the Individual's Home

The asset value of a home, less any mortgages outstanding on that home, is considered the book value. Normally, this asset is not available to the unsecured creditor. However, individuals may be required to liquidate their primary residence in a bankruptcy case. To determine this, a number of factors need to be examined: did the individual file Chapter 7, 11 or 13; does the individual have the capacity to generate current income; is the individual married and, if yes, did the spouse file for bankruptcy; did the individual take the federal or state exemptions, if a Chapter 7 and if the state exemptions were taken, in what state does the individual reside (Texas and Florida have either unlimited or substantial homestead exemptions whereas New Jersey's homestead exemption is less than $20,000); what is the equity value of the home, etc.?

4. Book Value of Automobiles/Value of Personal Items

Depending on the same factors mentioned above, an individual entering bankruptcy may be allowed to keep one automobile.

Personal items such as paintings, jewelry, furniture, coins and boats can easily be liquidated and should not be considered part of the personal net worth. However, some items also may not be considered part of the bankruptcy estate. For instance, if the case is a Chapter 7, the trustee may not be able to liquidate a family heirloom. Again, the factors listed above would come into play.

5. Questionable Investments

Assets that are questionable, such as stock in a bankrupt company, should be considered valueless and deducted from personal worth.

6. Personal Retirement Accounts

IRAs and KEOGHs are not considered part of the bankruptcy estate under the current bankruptcy laws. As such, these would not be available to unsecured creditors in a bankruptcy. The cash value of any life insurance policy also falls in this category.

To be more specific with regards to retirement plans and insurance policies: funds in retirement plans, such as IRAs and KEOGHs, are exempt from the bankruptcy estate to the extent that said funds are reasonably necessary for the debtor's support. This is generally interpreted to provide the debtor with sufficient funds to maintain the debtor's current lifestyle post-retirement. In making the determination, courts look to a number of factors such as the amount in the retirement account, current income, years to retirement, and if any extraordinary contributions were made just before filing for bankruptcy, etc. It is very unusual, however, for a trustee to challenge the funds in a retirement plan. As such, said funds are generally not available to satisfy creditor claims.

The cash value of a whole life insurance policy is also exempt from the bankruptcy estate. As such, the cash value of a whole life insurance policy is not available to satisfy creditor claims.

FOOTNOTES

In addition to information available as described in earlier paragraphs, the footnotes are important for discovering contingent liabilities. Examples are pending lawsuits, guarantees of the debts of others, unfunded pension liabilities, disputes with governmental agencies and other legal disputes. Footnotes also provide a status report on oil and gas reserves, income taxes, compliance with governmental regulations and information on long-term lease obligations.

CREDIT AGENCY REPORTS

D&B Reports

This report is primarily used to obtain background information about a customer. A current D&B report should be obtained on new accounts and on existing accounts that are considered to be risky or trending downward.

D&B, in the past, would deduct all intangibles from the net worth of a company in order to arrive at a "tangible ratable net worth." Companies with large intangible components to their balance sheets would suffer lower ratings due to lower adjusted net worth. D&B now has established three criteria under which, if the intangible asset in question met all three, would result in no deduction from a company's net worth. They are:

1. The asset must be salable at the price stated
2. The asset must contribute profit to the company
3. The asset must constitute a "significant" part of the concern's operations

The resultant increase in D&B ratings from companies with large intangible items on their balance sheet should be noted. One should be mindful of this procedure and, if necessary, adjust the D&B rating downward before determining the overall credit assessment.

BANK REFERENCE INFORMATION

Each customer is requested to provide the name, address and telephone number of their principal commercial bank. Through written or telephone inquiries, the bank with which the customer's principal business is conducted should be contacted. Bank references are useful, however, bank officers tend to report the customer relationship in the most favorable light possible without deliberately misleading the inquirer. Information gathered should include the following six items:

1. *Length of Time As a Customer.*
2. *DDA Balance.* This is the average balance of the customer's demand depository account (DDA) for a given period.
3. *Do you provide credit ratings on your customer?*
4. *NSFs/ODs.* Non-sufficient funds (NSF) mean that funds were not available at the time the check was presented resulting in the check being returned. Overdrafts (ODs) are basically the same as above, however, they are not returned and are covered by the bank.
5. *Line of Credit.* This is an amount the bank determines that the customer may borrow against at any time during the year. For loans outstanding, this is the amount that is outstanding at the time of inquiry against either the line of credit and/or any term loans not related to the line of credit. Ask about the original loan or line of credit and the amount currently owed.
6. *Security.* It is important to determine whether the bank is secured or unsecured on their dealings with the subject customer. Unsecured borrowings represent a higher degree of confidence of the bank in the customer's ability to repay the loan. If secured, obtain a description of the collateral. Also, ask if any personal guarantees have been executed by the company's principals in favor of the bank.

TRADE REFERENCE INFORMATION

Each customer is requested to provide the name, address and phone number of suppliers providing open credit lines. Through written or telephone inquiries, at least three trade references should be contacted which have sales experience near the level of the requested credit line. Trade references may be one of the best sources of credit information, particularly for customers with which there have been no recent experiences.

On the other hand, most customers will furnish you with only good supplier references. Or, the provided suppliers are not appropriate to the amount of credit sought. Good relevant supplier data can be obtained by developing secondary (not furnished by the customer) trade references.

Secondary trade references often provide useful credit histories:

- Obtain a D&B report and look at the pay record section for adequate representation.
- Conduct a UCC-1 search (via a UCC3 or UCC-11 form) with a Secretary of State for secured creditors of the customer. Then, contact a couple of these creditors to identify payment habits of the customer. Compare secured payment patterns to unsecured trade suppliers' payment histories of the customer.

In contacting trade suppliers, ask for the following:

- When was the account established?
- Date of last sale?
- Types of products purchased by the customer?
- What is the high credit limit?
- Is there a balance now owed?
- Is there an amount past due?
- Are there any collection problems?
- Has there been a history of disputes?
- What are the customer payment patterns? Prompt to Slow 30, etc.

In other words, just ask for the facts and don't seek or provide recommendations, opinions or ask for or give information about the customers established line of credit.

Inquire as to the length of time as a customer, the high credit within the last twelve months, credit line assigned, balance owing and past due, terms of sale, payment history, and if there is any security on the line of credit such as letters of credit, corporate guarantees.

FINAL DETERMINATION OF CREDIT LINES

As stated earlier, the final determination of a credit line is not concluded simply through mathematical or analytical processes. The ultimate decision involves judgment. Value judgments must be made by weighing the importance of various factors present in each case. For example, the credit decision may place relatively heavy weight on a slow-payment trade reference with a resulting credit line, which is lower than is justified by the customer's financial statement. Credit judgment ability is formed through exposure to different credit and collection experiences.

Probably the most important key to making good credit decisions, outside of financial statement and reference analysis, is the proper evaluation of the character of the individuals responsible for day-to-day management. The analyst should look for longevity as a barometer of how well the company has survived past storms. Experienced management that has steered a company through 20 or 30 years will be more likely to survive immediate or future economic downturns than will an inexperienced team.

The communication of information from the marketing and field staff is essential to our efforts in avoiding bad debts. You must attempt to verify any negative information about a customer through bank and trade reference sources. As always, any information received concerning a customer's possible credit status should be treated confidentially and not discussed with other companies.

If you want to do a quick review of a company's financial condition and spot trends, use the following "Eye-Ball Analysis" approach.

INTERNAL ANALYSIS (EYE-BALL ANALYSIS)

Are there any intangibles?
1. Deduct intangibles from net worth to find tangible net worth.

Is the business profitable and operated efficiently?
2. Check ratio of net profits on net sales.
3. Check ratio of net profits on tangible net worth.
4. Gross profit average or better than average for the line?

Is the business overtrading?
5. Check net sales to tangible net worth.
6. Check net sales to net working capital.

Is working capital adequate to support operations?
7. Check inventory to net working capital.
8. Check current ratio—Current assets to current debt.
9. Check liquid ratio—Liquid assets to current debt.

Are receivables handled efficiently?
10. Check collection period—(Receivables: annual credit sales) × 365.

Is inventory moving well?
11. Check inventory turnover—Net sales to inventory.

Any stripping of working capital to finance expansion?
12. Check fixed assets to tangible net worth.

How is the business financed? Who owns the business?
13. Check current debt to tangible net worth.

14. Check total debt to tangible net worth.
15. Check ability to pay long-term debt: Net profits + Current year
    depreciation − Current portion of long-term debt.

Can they pay promptly?
16. Check accounts payable turnover: (Accounts payable − Annual
    purchases) × 365.

The following worksheet is a simple but straightforward approach to focusing in on various key financial indicators. Use this in conjunction with the Credit Limit Formula chart on page 24.

CREDIT LIMIT WORKSHEET

Customer_____   Prepared By_____

File Information Available:

    [ ] D&B Report Rating _____   SIC_____   Date_____

Financial Statement:

    [ ] Audited   [ ] Unaudited   Statement Date_____
    [ ] Estimates   [ ] Signed/Unsigned

Factor	Ratio/Score	Quartile	Contribution to Credit Limit
Basic Allowance – 10% of net worth			
1. Pay Habits Paydex _____	H G N F P	_____	_____
2. Years in Business	_____	_____	_____
3. Profit Margin	_____	_____	_____
4. Current Ratio	_____	_____	_____
5. Quick Ratio	_____	_____	_____
6. Total Liab/Net Worth Ratio	_____	_____	_____
7. Quality of Receivables	_____	_____	_____
	PERCENT TOTAL		_____

Net Worth $_____   **Adjusted Net Worth $_____**

Basis for Adjustment   _____
Subtotal $_____
Judgment Factor $_____
Credit Limit Assigned $_____
Percent of Net Worth   _____%

Product Sold:_____

Terms of Sale:_____

Recommended By: _____   Approved By:_____

The following **Credit Limit Formula calculates** a contribution to credit limit based on the various factors identified. This is a basic but effective and quick way to manually push the numbers.

See also the **Credit Limit Worksheet** that accompanies this Credit Formula on the previous page. Transfer the calculated scores from this page to the worksheet.

Description of Factor	Rating	Contribution To Credit Limit
Basic Allowance	D&B Rating must be 5A1-5A2 4A1-4A2 3A1-3A2 2A1-2A2 1A1-1A2 BA1-BA2 BB1-BB2 CB1-CB2 CC1-CC2 DC1-DC2 EE1-EE2 FF1-FF2 GG1-GG2	10 % of Net Worth

1. Pay Habits

Discounts or pays ppt	High	10% of Net Worth
Pays ppt when discount terms available	Good	5% of Net Worth
Pays as agreed	Neutral	0 % of Net Worth
Occasionally late	Fair	minus 2.5% of Net Worth
Considerably late	Poor	minus 5.0% of Net Worth

2. Years in Business

	Under 3 years	0 % of Net Worth
	3 to 10 years	2.5 % of Net Worth
	Over 10 years	5 % of Net Worth

3. Profit Margin
For each 1% of profit margin, add 2% of net worth as contribution to credit limit to a maximum of 10%. Deduct same percentage for loss.

4. Current Ratio

	2:1 or Higher	10% of Net Worth
	1.25:1 up to 2:1	5% of Net Worth
	.75:1 up to 1.25:1	0 % of Net Worth
	.50:1 up to .75:1	minus 5% of Net Worth
	Under .50:1	minus 10% of Net Worth

5. Quick Ratio

	2:1 or Higher	15% of Net Worth
	1:1 up to 2:1	10% of Net Worth
	.80 up to 1:1	5% of Net Worth
	.50 up to .80:1	0 % of Net Worth
Net Selling Terms	.25:1 up to .50:1	minus 5% of Net Worth
	Under .25: 1	minus 10% of Net Worth

6. Debt to Equity

	Under .50 : 1	10% of Net Worth
	.50 : 1 up to 1.50 : 1	5% of Net Worth
	1.50 : 1 up to 3.00 : 1	minus 5% of Net Worth
	3.00 : 1 up to 4.00 : 1	minus 10% of Net Worth
	4.00 : 1 up to 6.00 : 1	minus 15% of Net Worth
	6.00 : 1 up to 9.00 : 1	minus 20% of Net Worth
	Over 9.00 : 1	minus 40% of Net Worth

7. Quality of Receivables

Minimum Standard:	Net Selling Terms + 30 Days	For each 10 days under minimum standard, add 1% of Net Worth

Chapter 4

RATIOS

With ratios it is possible to determine if asset and liability relationships are reasonably aligned. While ratios are not an end in themselves, they should be considered useful information to help determine the final decision with the accompanying information that has been gathered. If used properly, they are useful tools for determining the creditworthiness of an account.[1]

BALANCE SHEET RATIOS

Current Assets

Defined: To qualify for inclusion in the current assets category, an asset must be capable of being converted into cash, sold, or consumed either in one year or in the operating cycle of the company, whichever is longer. Examples include cash, accounts receivable, notes receivable, and inventory.

Current Liabilities

Defined: These are the obligations that are reasonably expected to be liquidated either through the use of current assets or the creation of other current liabilities. Current debt or liability is the total of all liabilities due within one year. Accounts and notes payable to trade suppliers should be at a reasonable level in relation to business volume and normal payment terms.

Particular attention should be paid to the customer's ability to support the cost of any interest bearing short-term debt. Examples include bank overdraft, accounts payable, notes payable, and current maturities of long-term debt.

Tangible Net Worth

This is arrived at by subtracting any intangible assets from the company's equity position. In addition, assets labeled "other" with no explanation, goodwill, or prepaid items should also be subtracted to arrive

---

[1]Roger Hale, *Credit Analysis* (Hoboken, NJ: John Wiley & Sons, 1983), 97.

at tangible net worth. Adjustments made to a company's equity position will be covered in another chapter.

LIQUIDITY RATIOS

Current Ratio

The current ratio is found by dividing Current Assets by Current Liabilities. Creditors tend to stress the current ratio as an indication of short-term solvency and feel that the higher the current ratio the better. However, a high current ratio may indicate that capital is not being utilized productively in the business.

The size of the current ratio should be considered in relation to the seasonal influence at statement date. At the end of a season, inventory should be low and the collection of receivables should cause a sharp reduction in current debt. This is the time of year when a business should show its highest current ratio. This statement holds true if the calendar year coincides with the natural seasonal lull. Furthermore, a step-up or slowdown in seasonal activity will affect the ratio of business that normally reaches a liquidated position at "year-end."

Generally speaking, a current ratio of one to one (1:1) or better is considered satisfactory. A low ratio causes problems with accounts payable, requires other short-term debts (loans) and will lead to insufficient working capital.

Quick Ratio

This is sometimes referred to as the liquid ratio or acid test ratio. It is the sum of cash, marketable securities, and receivables divided by current liabilities. It should provide at least a small margin over current debts. A high liquid ratio can often support a low current ratio. A slow turnover of receivables will worsen the quality of this ratio. The cash amount that makes up this ratio is ideally looked upon to equal one month's expenses of the business. Industry medium is around .20 to 1.00. A low ratio indicates excess funds tied up in inventories, or could indicate cost control problems versus sales and may be pointing to slow paying receivables.

Fixed Assets to Tangible Net Worth

This ratio measures the degree of investments in fixed assets to the equity or ownership interest of the business. When it is higher than average, a low working capital is indicated. A high ratio could mean that the net working capital needed for operations is being diverted to plant and equipment, which would restrict operating funds and leave a company vulnerable to business downturns.

Current Debt to Tangible Net Worth

This ratio measures the relationship between all current debt and the tangible net worth of a company. Ratios greater than 1.0 means the short-term creditors have more at risk in the business than the owners do. Any interruption of cash flow, such as slow receivables or falling prices or sales, may make it impossible for the debtor to meet obligations on schedule.

Total Debt to Tangible Net Worth

This calculation includes funded debt (long-term liabilities) and current debt. It is a good indication of a company's ability to leverage. Successful financial leverage is measured by a company's ability to earn more on the debt funds than the funds cost. If so, then the company realizes favorable financial leverage.

Generally speaking, a high ratio indicates negative leveraging and potential danger to creditors. Anything over a 2:1 debt/equity position is unacceptable. This could possibly indicate excessive long-term debts, an undercapitalized company (low equity), and a heavy use of payables and other current liabilities to finance the business.

Funded Debt to Net Working Capital

This ratio is very important in that it measures long-term obligations to net working capital. When this ratio is high, funded debt is a strain on the company. This strain requires a more frequent turnover of net working capital in order to meet interest charges on the debt.

TURNOVER RATIOS

Turnover ratios have the sales figure as the numerator and generally measure the number of times per period that an asset or resource is used.

Net Sales to Total Assets

This ratio measures the productive use of business assets. Usually only tangible assets for consideration are used. The higher the turnover is, the greater the productivity. A low turnover infers that a portion of the assets is unproductive, while a very high rate may indicate that a company is overtrading. When a company's sales volume seems too great for its financial resources, the question should arise as to whether it is "overtrading." The large amount of inventory needed to meet sales volume increases is usually financed at the expense of trade suppliers.

Net Sales to Inventory

This relationship is a guide to the condition of inventories because it shows the number of times they are turned in the course of a year. Some credit managers use an average inventory figure for this calculation. They add beginning and ending inventories and divide by two. Others use ending inventory only. Regardless of which method is used, it is important to apply it consistently when analyzing the figures of successive years for any company. A low ratio indicates obsolete products, poor inventory management, and low consumer demand. Look at the industry norms for each particular line of business or SIC classification. A SIC number represents a Standard Industrial Classification assigned by the U.S. Government for each company line of business.

DSO Calculations

Days Sales Outstanding (DSO) is a term used for the calculation of receivables turnover, or the collection period. The ratio measures the relationship between net sales for the period and outstanding receivables. It attempts to evaluate the average time required to convert receivables into cash. The ratio can be distorted due to a sales bias, such as seasonal fluctuations. Additionally, it is difficult to compare a company's DSO to an industry's DSO because of variation in company-to-company product mix and terms. It is advised to "just say no" to any request for a DSO calculation.

Having said that, let's at least explore our options and identify the best approaches.

Popular methods have catchy names such as the collection effectiveness index (CEI), best possible DSO, true DSO, percent current, and average days delinquent to name a few. There are approximately 11 popular ways to figure outstanding accounts receivable balances. However, Sales Weighted DSO and Payment Pattern Analysis seem to do the best job of truly removing any sales bias.

Sales weighted DSO provides an index stated in days. The formula for calculating sales weighted DSO is:

Current Balance Outstanding ÷ Current Month's Sales + Balance Outstanding from Last Month ÷ Sales from Last Month + etc. for Other Past Months

Using this method, you are relating the outstanding balance directly to the sale that generated the balance. In doing so, you eliminate any sales pattern from the measurement of collection effectiveness.

Payment Pattern Analysis or "variance analysis" provides you with dollar amounts and sales pattern effects that caused differences to occur from a predetermined benchmark. With this approach, you need to compare the current outstanding accounts receivable balance to a standard. The standard can be a budget, last month's balance, the same month last year, or for some other period. The dollar difference between actual receivables and the selected standard becomes your collection effectiveness variance and sales pattern variance. This method is more complex than sales weighted DSO but does provide information not revealed in the latter. It would be considered time well spent to familiarize yourself with this approach.

PROFITABILITY RATIOS

The profitability of a firm must be evaluated by using a combination of the Income Statement, Statement of Cash Flows and the footnotes. For example, the use of the LIFO inventory method produces lower profits than the FIFO method during periods of increasing prices. The selection of methods for capitalizing oil and gas exploration expenses may significantly affect current profits. Estimation of ongoing profits should exclude gains or losses from capital transactions or discontinued operations reported in the current financial statement. Returns on investment ratios are useful measures of profitability, particularly when a trend of several years can be determined. Trends of profitability in comparison to similar firms in a given industry are very useful as well. Reasons for adverse trends should be determined during the credit evaluation period.

Net Income
The excess revenue over all related expenses and income taxes for a given period is called net income.

Net Income/Sales
This ratio shows how much profit is left from each sales dollar after removing all expenses.

Income from Operations

By definition, this is the excess of revenues over operating expense; it is income from normal and primary operations before adding or subtracting other income and expense items not associated with operations, such as interest income, expense, and extraordinary gains or losses.

- **Interest Coverage Ratio (Before Tax) (Times).** This ratio
  measures the company's ability to meet interest obligations from
  operating income.
  Formula:

$$\frac{\text{Net Profit Before Tax}}{\text{Interest Expense}} = \text{Interest Coverage Ratio (Times)}$$

Example: $\dfrac{\$247}{\$121}$ = 2.0 Times Interest Coverage

Rule of Thumb: Net profits before taxes should normally cover interest expense at least 3.0 times.
Discussion: Lack of sufficient interest coverage causes default on secured debts, and may close the company down.

In summary, financial ratios can be grouped into four areas: Liquidity, Leverage, Activity, and Profitability.

Liquidity ratios evaluate the company's ability to meet current obligations with assets presently available. The current ratio should be at least equal to 1, although industry comparisons should still be done. The quick ratio further reduces the liability coverage by removing inventories from the equation. The thought here is that inventories would take much longer to liquidate and would not generate cash as quickly.

Activity ratios estimate how efficient the company is in collecting receivables, turning inventory, and most importantly, paying its bills. Evaluation of these items will give the analyst an idea about management and if it has the major areas of their business under control.

Leverage ratios provide a measure of how much debt is used to finance the operation. These ratios have become more important with the increase in leveraged buyouts, which will be discussed in a subsequent chapter. A company with a high level of debt is burdened with annual interest payments, which represent a fixed cost to the company. If the economy is in a down cycle and the company's sales begin to decline, the same level of interest is still due. Therefore, in order to meet interest obligations, payments to creditors will slow down.

Profitability ratios measure the margins at both the gross and net income levels. These ratios are best used when comparing statements year-to-year and seeing the trends develop that show which direction the company is headed.

By no means are the above-mentioned ratios the only ratios that can be calculated; however, they are felt to be the most significant and informative for a complete financial analysis.

Once the numbers have been "crunched," the next step is to extract information from the results. Two ways to do this are by comparison to industry averages and comparison of year-to-year statements to determine trends.

One thing to keep in mind concerning financial statements is that they represent a picture for a certain period of time. When receiving financial statements that are more than six months old, consider what changes have taken place during the interim period. Watch out for companies that sell products that are highly seasonal. They will have very high inventory, receivables, and payables during their peak season, while dropping very low in the off-season. The timing of statements will distort the ratio results if they are calculated on an interim period. Look at the interim statements and spot developing trends, but make your true companies analysis by assessing year end results.

The Checklist of Financial Indicators on the next page might come in handy.

Checklist of Financial Indicators   Jerry Dean

Indicator	Calculation	Significance
A. Profitability Ratios		
Gross Profit Margin	Sales less cost of sales divided by sales expressed as a percentage.	Profitability of products and services.
Operating Margin	Operating profit (profit before interest and tax) expressed as a percentage of sales.	Measure of the profitability of the business from its day-to-day activities.
Return on Capital Employed (ROCE)	Operating profit expressed as a percentage of capital employed (capital employed equals fixed assets plus current assets less current liabilities excluding cash and short-term borrowings).	Measure of earning power. How well the business is using its assets to produce an acceptable level of profitability.
B. Activity Ratios		
Asset Turnover	Sales divided by capital employed expressed as a 'number of times'.	Measure of the effectiveness with which assets are being used to generate sales.
Creditor Days	Accounts payable or trade creditors divided by annualised cost of sales.	Length of time taken to pay suppliers.
Debtor Days	Accounts receivable or trade debtors divided by annualised sales times 365 days.	Length of time taken to collect cash from customers. Fundamental measure of the effectiveness of credit control.
Inventory or Stock Turnover Rate	Cost of sales (or sales if the cost of sales figure is not available) divided by average or closing inventories expressed as a 'number of times'. Also calculated as a number of days to give the stock holding period.	Measure of the length of time a unit of stock; raw materials, work in progress and finished goods, stays on the 'shelf' — an indicator of the effectiveness of stock management.

C. Liquidity Ratios

Acid-Test or 'Quick' Ratio	Current assets excluding stocks or inventories divided by current liabilities.	A more rigorous measure than the current ratio for assessing the ability of a business to meet its short-term commitments.
Cash Burn	Cash balances, including those on deposit, divided by cash operating costs (including the cost of sales) times 365 days.	Measure of how long existing cash balances will be able to fund cash expenditure.
Cash Cycle	Stock holding period plus days sales outstanding less the payables period.	Speed with which current assets are converted into cash.
Current Ratio	Current assets divided by current liabilities.	Measure of the ability of a business to meet its short-term commitments.

D. Leverage or Solvency Ratios

Cash Coverage Ratio	Sales less cash operating costs including the cost of sales, (EBITDA) divided by interest or financing costs.	Another measure of the ability of a business to service its financing costs.
Debt-Equity Ratio	Total borrowings including lease obligations less cash balances (current account and on deposit). This is net debt and is divided by the shareholders' interest or equity. Expressed as a percentage.	Measure of the extent to which a business is financed by borrowings rather than by shareholders — using external rather than internal funding sources.
Interest Cover	Operating profit divided by interest or financing charges.	Measure of the ability of a business to service its interest or financing costs.

E. Cash Generation

"Free" Cash Flow	Sales less cash operating costs (including the cost of sales) less/plus the increase/decrease in working capital less capital expenditure and less tax in a financial period.	Measure of the ability of a business to generate cash to meet its financing costs, loan repayment commitments and dividends.

Chapter 5

APPRAISING THE USE OF RATIOS

Ratios have to be used with great care. Because of the way in which they are calculated, they may mislead the uneducated user. For example, a company can improve its current position by substituting long-term debt for short-term debt. This would improve the current ratio, inventory to net working capital, and current debt to tangible net worth. The improved current position would have been gained through the use of long-term debt.

For credit purposes, the financial affairs of an account are usually analyzed by four to eight key ratios, carefully selected to read the current position and profitability of the operation. Of the ratios previously mentioned, selection should be based upon the type of credit being considered and the type of company being analyzed (trading company, LBO, HLC, LLP, LLC).

It would be wise to examine the trend of related ratios in pairs or sets to avoid being misled by the trend of any single one. For example, both the current and quick ratios measure a firm's ability to handle its obligations, particularly current debts, in an orderly manner. Yet, the current ratio might reflect a year-to-year increase while the liquid ratio was actually declining. This could occur through a shifting of current assets into inventory rather than receivables.

Industry Standards or "norms" should be looked at in order to determine the degree of variation of an individual statement from the norm. For example, a normal debt to equity ratio for a construction company would differ from that of a wholesale jobber, yet both would be considered acceptable in their industries. Industry norms can be found in the Robert Morris Associates' reference books or in D&B's publication called *Industry Norms*.

In challenging the traditional use of the current and quick ratios, there are others, including this author, that question their significance. The current and quick ratios have a static character, meaning that they look at the balance sheet at a given point in time. As a result, the current and quick ratios can easily be "window dressed." In order to improve the current ratio and perhaps stay within the established bank covenants, a company could take available cash and pay down current liabilities just to temporarily improve the ratio. This action is not in violation of any established GAAP rule. The long-standing belief is that if a firm's current assets are large relative to the value of current liabilities, there is a high probability that the firm can pay the liabilities as they come due. This probability is reflected in the widespread acceptance of a current ratio of 2:1 as the standard or norm for adequate liquidity. However, financial analysts should view this standard ratio with some skepticism. A high current ratio by itself does not guarantee liquidity. A satisfactory current ratio does not disclose the fact that a portion of the current assets may be tied up in slow-moving inventories and prepaid expenses or slow receivables.

Even the quick ratio should be viewed with skepticism. The widely held rule of thumb for the quick ratio is 1:1. The quick ratio attempts to emphasize values at liquidation rather than at going-concern values thus eliminating differences in operating requirements. The quick ratio makes more sense than the current ratio if the end game is to look at things from a liquidation perspective.

Current and quick ratios are functions of many variables that affect liquidity differently. But the more meaningful question relates to the issue, what is liquidity? Liquidity depends entirely on the relationship between cash inflows and required cash outflows. What is appropriate liquidity for a firm varies widely, and no general standard can possibly be applicable to all firms under all circumstances. Detailed studies of bankrupt and non-bankrupt firms have shown that the average current ratio of the failed firms was above the widely accepted 2:1 standard in all five years preceding the ultimate bankruptcy. Recognition of the relevance of cash flow data to liquidity has led many analysts to question the traditional significance of the current and quick ratios.

Is there a better approach? Yes, there are two additional ratios that should command your attention. They are the Cash Conversion Cycle (CCC) and the Defensive Interval (DI).

CASH CONVERSION CYCLE (CCC)

Analysis of liquidity from a Cash Conversion Cycle perspective is very different than from a current or quick ratio perspective. The CCC approach looks at cash flows occurring over time. As stated earlier, the current and quick ratios have a static character, meaning that they look at the balance sheet at a given point in time.

A large current ratio could mean that a company took on expensive financing to support current assets in excess of current liabilities. Stated another way, net working capital is the difference between current assets and current liabilities. If current assets exceed current liabilities then the firm's current ratio exceeds 1. However, this may be the result of long-term debt and equity capital financing that generates the positive net working capital amount-excess of current asset investment over current liability financing. But long-term debt and equity financing are not costless. Debt bears an interest obligation that must be paid. Equity has an opportunity cost, meaning shareholders expect a fair return on their investment. If the firm can't earn a fair return, then the board of directors should vote to return funds to the shareholders instead of reinvesting them in the company. As a manager, would you rather support assets with free financing or with costly financing? The answer is obvious. The Cash Conversion Cycle provides you with insight into the extent of the problem of using costly financing to support operations. It is a measurement of the number of days a company's operating cycle requires the support of costly financing. Ideally, the CCC number calculated should be small or even negative. The "Operating cycle" = Days sales outstanding in inventories + Days sales outstanding in receivables. However, this concept is deficient as a cash flow measure in that it fails to consider a company's access to free financing for some period of time through accounts payable and accruals. Integrating the time pattern of cash outflows required to satisfy trade payables and accruals is as important for liquidity analysis as evaluating the time pattern of cash flows generated by the conversion of its inventory and accounts receivable investments. In summary, operating cash flow coverage, rather than asset liquidation value embodied in the current and quick ratios is the crucial element in liquidity analysis. It looks at the problem from the perspective of an ongoing entity.

In summary, the current and quick ratios are not able to expose the fact that perhaps a great commitment of resources has been made to less liquid forms of working capital. However, calculation of the firm's CCC reveals this commitment. The current and quick ratios are not able to expose it. After all, operating cash flow coverage is the crucial element in liquidity analysis rather than asset liquidation value presented by the current and quick ratios. A study of a company's Statement of Cash Flows (covered in a subsequent chapter) will support conclusions reached with the CCC approach. The two together help properly assess a company's ability to meet cash obligations.

CCC Formula:

DSO Inventory + DSO Receivables – DSO Spontaneous Financing

Example:
Abridged Balance Sheet

Accounts Receivable	100	Accounts Payable	50
Inventory	200	Accruals	75
Sales: 3000			

How much is the CR?
How much is the CCC?

$$\textbf{Current Ratio} = (100 + 200) \div (50 + 75) = \textbf{2.4}$$
$$\textbf{CCC} = 360 \times \left(\frac{200}{3000} + \frac{100}{3000} - \frac{125}{3000} \right)$$
$$= 24 + 12 - 15 = \textbf{21 days}$$

Current Ratio vs. CCC

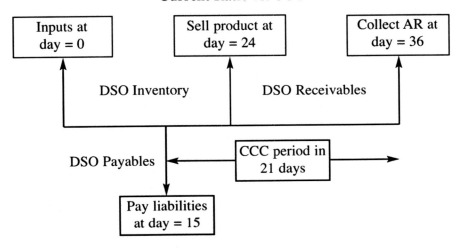

CCC represents the number of days of financing needed to support the operating cycle.

The example below illustrates a CCC trend over the last four years. This view provides the analyst with a quick look at significant changes in all three areas that make up the final conversion cycle number. In this example, the CCC number has improved at the expense of suppliers (DSO Payables). A negative number or anything approaching zero is the best-case scenario with regards to CCC. The company has collected receivables and turned inventory quite well but has elected to slow pay the suppliers, which has dramatically increased cash availability for ongoing daily operating needs. However, it could have been a slow receivable trend that could have provided the insight as to why perhaps the CCC was trending negatively.

Cash Conversion Cycle Breakdown

Company	1999	2000	2001	2002
Days Outstanding in Receivables (DSO)	3.62	5.42	7.78	6.69
Days Outstanding in Inventory (DSO)	7.22	8.49	7.34	9.83
Operating Cycle	10.84	13.90	15.11	16.52
Days Outstanding in Payables and Accruals (DSO)	(20.34)	(26.60)	(25.50)	(22.98)
Cash Conversion Cycle (CCC) (Days)	(09.50)	(12.69)	(10.38)	(06.46)

DEFENSIVE INTERVAL (DI)

The other ratio mentioned was the Defensive Interval (DI). The defensive interval measures the time span during which a firm can operate on present liquid assets without resorting to revenues from future income sources. There will be times when receivables will not come in as expected or sales may decline temporarily or expenses shoot up as a result of increased production requirements. It is in these instances that a company will rely upon its defensive assets without incurring additional liabilities.

What Are Defensive Assets?

Cash is the most defensive asset. Accounts receivable are defensive assets. The receivables serve as a substitute for cash. If management establishes realistic allowance for doubtful accounts, the net amount of accounts receivable should be a good approximation of the future debt paying capacity of these assets. It is true that not all receivables are immediately available to meet disbursements. It is also true that all current liabilities seldom require immediate disbursement.

Prepaid expenses and inventory are not defensive assets. Prepaid expenses will not be converted into cash. In fact, by definition, the company has already paid for these assets. With respect to inventory, sales must be made before it is converted into funds available for the payment of debts. Since the amount of defensive assets is important in the event of a delay or decline in sales receipts, it is clearly inappropriate to include inventory in this group.

A current ratio of 2 simply says that as of the balance sheet date, the firm had $2 of current assets for every $1 of current liabilities outstanding. Wouldn't it be better to know how many days the firm's liquid assets could support the business?

You need to relate the defensive assets to the use for which they are required. This task involves a determination of the amount of present and future operating obligations, which will have to be met with the defensive assets, should the inflow of cash be delayed or reduced. Base the estimate of these obligations on the assumption that the firm will continue its operations as in the past. This assumption is reasonable because the firm's short-term paying ability is being measured, rather than its ability to withstand a long-term cyclical decline in revenues.

Estimating Operating Obligations

There is a relatively easy way to estimate the operating obligations. Follow these four steps:

1. Convert accrual sales on the income statement to cash receipts. Add any decrease in this year's accounts receivable balance to sales, and subtract any increase.
2. Identify the cash flow from operations amount on the Statement of Cash Flows.
3. Subtract the cash flow from operations balance from your cash receipts level.
4. Divide the difference in step three by 360 days. The result is the daily cash expenses figure. It assumes that the firm incurs the expenses at a constant rate. If you have access to quarterly data, you can calculate the daily expenses using the same procedure. However, instead of dividing the amount for cash expenses by 360, divide by 90 days.

Defensive Interval Formula:

DI = Quick Assets ÷ Daily Cash Operating Expenses (as determined above)

Quick Assets:

Cash + Marketable Securities + Receivables

Daily Operating Expenses:

(Cash Sales – Cash Profits) ÷ 360 Days – Cash Sales
= Accrual Sales + Change in A/R – Cash Profits
= CFFO on the Cash Flow Statement

Interpretation of the Defensive Interval: The number calculated indicates how many days the defensive assets can continue to support normal operations despite a complete cessation of revenues. You may attack this concept as being unrealistic since a total stoppage of revenue is unlikely. However, think of the revenue cessation as providing a base measure.

The defensive interval, like the Cash Conversion Cycle, departs from the strictly static analysis of the current and quick ratios. It tries to focus your attention directly on the relationship between liquidity and the need for liquidity. The defensive interval uses the existing level of defensive assets as the source of cash, and not future inflow of cash.

Defensive Interval:

Balance Sheet

Accounts Receivable	100	Accounts Payable	50
Inventory	200	Accruals	75
Sales: 3000		Change A/R	25
CFFO (Cash Flow From Operations): 10			

How much is the CR?
How much is the DI?

Current Ratio = (100 + 200) ÷ (50 + 75) = 2.4

DI = 12.1 Days (100 + 3000 – 25 = 2975 + 10 = 2965 ÷ 360 days)
= Daily Cash Expenses of 8.236 (100 ÷ 8.236 = 12.1)

Quick Assets	100
Accrual Sales	3000
Change in A/R	(25)
Cash Sales	2975
CFFO	10
Cash Expenses	2965
Divide by 360 days	
Daily Cash Expense	8.236
DI	**12.1**

In making a simple comparison based on the example presented above, the current and quick ratios improve while the CCC and defensive intervals deteriorate:

	Current Year	Previous Year
Current Ratio	2.4	2.1
Quick Ratio	0.8	0.7
CCC	21.0	15.0
Defensive Interval	12.1	16.0

Keep in mind that although analysis is a key factor in determining a customer's line of credit, the final credit decision involves value judgments made by weighing the importance of various factors present in each case. Probably the most important key to making good credit decisions, outside of financial statement and trend analysis, is the proper evaluation of the character, reputation, and experience of the company and the individuals responsible for day-to-day management.

Credit judgment is formed through different credit and collection experiences. Through multiple exposures to financially stressed situations, a credit manager gains skills in predicting how a customer will act in various financial situations. It is necessary to react quickly to negative signs and to reduce or eliminate exposure before the customer suffers a complete financial collapse.

Chapter 6

CASH FLOW ANALYSIS

Definition: The amount of cash generated or consumed by an activity over a certain period of time.

Profit is generally looked upon as the best way to measure a company's success. However, this approach does not assess the quality of these earnings. Managing cash is more important than adequate profits. Earning a good profit does not necessarily ensure adequate cash flow to take care of operations. Cash flow analysis smooths the comparison of companies with different accounting methods and provides a check on the quality of earnings. A company can make the mistake of waiting too long to turn profits into cash, which reduces the true value of the profits. If management is to be successful running a business, they must understand the difference between profits and cash flows and how accounting profits (revenue minus total costs) differ from economic profits (revenue minus total costs which include implicit costs such as interest that could be earned and the cost of capital used to finance the business). Credit analysts responsible for writing and monitoring debt covenants are particularly concerned with these assessments.

Cash flow analysis is of significant value when reviewing an account for the following type of sale:

- Short-term: Net 2 to Net 10 days.
- Sale is of operational importance to your company, but on financials the buyer appears to be in a downward trend.
- Long-time account with your company, which in the current industry climate is suffering losses.
- Accounts, which, through normal credit evaluation, are marginal. That is, they appear on paper to be not terribly bad or good.

In light of all the financial and operational developments in the industry, the old attitude of "let's just cut them off" or "LC or nothing" is fading somewhat. Almost all companies have had a difficult year or two. The traditional evaluation did not always answer the question of cutting off an old friend or making a new one. Some very large companies have had earnings and economic deterioration due to mergers, acquisitions and price swings. What else should you or could you look at on the financial statement? The answer is cash flow. You might be able to make a positive decision and save a customer for your company, enhance profitability and/or maintain a customer's relationship. Keep in mind that cash flow analysis is only a short-term evaluation. One cash manager says it is not valid for more than 60 to 90 days.

One extremely important factor is to look at borrowing lines and debt structure. Obviously, if large debt payments fall due in the quarter, or even the year you are considering, you need to find out from the buyer if this debt is being amortized, rolled over, actually paid out, totally refinanced or otherwise, as it could dramatically influence their cash flow.

If they have short-term borrowing lines available and they have large balances outstanding, find out why. If they have large balances outstanding, it could mean a serious or potentially serious cash flow problem. If the line is there, but with little or no borrowings, this is another positive sign that cash flows are good.

If credit has been extended based mainly on a very positive cash flow position, then you should insist on receiving quarterly reports that continue to reflect this positive condition. In effect, you need to follow up to ensure positive cash flows are being maintained.

It is helpful to make your customer aware you are issuing a line of credit or spot credit based in part on a very positive cash flow. Then you can feel free to ask the hard questions and insist on those quarterly reports. Also, if you see trends going the wrong way, you can pull the line and easily explain to your customer why this was necessary. You certainly give the appearance you are trying to work with your customer. You leave a good taste in their mouth and leave the door open for reinstating the line should cash trends improve.

A positive cash flow generally means a company is covering their operational expenses, debt and interest payments and taxes, and still has a good amount of cash left over which has been generated by their basic operations. The Statement of Cash Flows classifies cash flow according to business activities: operations, financing, and investments. A word of caution when it comes to interpreting cash flow from operations that shows an operating loss. Gains and losses are income statement concepts that reflect accrual rather than cash-flow accounting. The negative cash from operations number on the Statement of Cash Flows does not reflect a loss, but rather it indicates that XYZ Company paid for more inventory than it sold and the cash associated with all the sales has not yet been collected. If XYZ continues to report negative cash from operations, it will need additional financing. In the long run, firms must generate positive cash flow from operations.

An important question is this: Is their basic core business generating positive cash flows, or are they having to subsidize cash flows from outside sources such as stock offerings, short- or long-term debt, sale of assets, etc.?

An erroneous definition for cash flow is Net Income plus Depreciation and Amortization and other non-cash expenses. A non-cash expense does not generate cash flow.

SOURCES AND USES OF FUNDS

You are encouraged to conduct an in-depth analysis to fully understand the benefits associated with cash flow analysis by building a composite picture of where cash is coming from and how cash is being used. A cash flow analysis method begins with the sources and uses of funds. This will help to understand where funds are coming from and how they are used. It must be identified whether these changes are "sources" or "uses" of "funds." The rules for identifying sources and uses in each balance sheet account from one year to the next are:

	Sources	Uses
Assets	Decreases	Increases
Liabilities	Increases	Decreases
Equity	Increases	Decreases

Rules for calculating changes in balance sheet accounts:

- Treat an increase in an asset as a use (outflow) of cash and a decrease as a source (inflow) of cash
- Treat an increase in a liability or equity account as a source (inflow) of cash and a decrease as a use (outflow) of cash
- Treat revenues as sources (inflows) of cash and expenses as uses (outflows) of cash

Example: (see Figure 6-1)

Figure 6-1: Balance Sheet Analysis of Sources/Uses

	Jan 1	Dec 31	Source	Use
Cash	10	15		5
Short-Term Investment	15	10	5	
Accounts Receivable	205	190	15	
Inventory	230	240		10
Fixed Assets (Gross)	200	220		20
Accumulated Depreciation	60	70	10	
Land	40	40		
Accounts Payable	200	210	10	
Accruals	70	65		5
Short-Term Debt	130	170	40	
Bonds	100	50		50
Common Stock	100	100		
Retained Earnings	40	50	10	
Total Sources and Uses			**90**	**90**

DEVELOPING A STATEMENT OF CASH FLOWS

Preparation of the Statement of Cash Flows requires the following information:

1. The balance sheet for the current period
2. The balance sheet for the prior period
3. Income statement for the current period
4. Supplemental information from the balance sheet accounts

Steps in developing the Statement of Cash Flows:

1. Compute the changes in the cash and cash equivalent accounts from the prior period to the end of the current period, which represents the net increase (decrease) in cash.
2. Compute the net change in each balance sheet account, except for cash and cash equivalent accounts. The explanation of why the cash and cash equivalent accounts changed is in the balance sheet accounts excluding the cash and cash equivalent accounts.
3. Determine the cash flows, the non-cash investing and financing activities, and the effect of exchange rate changes, using the net

change in the balance sheet accounts, the income statement for the current period, and the supplemental information. Separate the cash flows into cash flows from operating activities, cash flow from investing activities, and cash flows from financing activities.
4. Prepare the Statement of Cash Flows.

For example:

Step #1: Compute the change in cash and cash equivalents
Step #2: Compute the net change in each balance sheet account other than the cash account:

Assets:

Accounts receivable decrease	$ 500	Operating
Inventories increase	2,000	Operating
Land increase	15,000	Investing
Equipment increase	2,000	Investing
Accumulated depreciation increase	7,000	Operating
(contra-asset—a change would be		
similar to a change in liabilities)		

Liabilities:

Accounts payable decrease	2,000	Operating
Taxes payable increase	200	Operating
Bonds payable increase	5,000	Financing

Stockholder's Equity:

Common stock increase	3,000	Financing
Retained earnings increase	200	**

**This is a combination of operating, financing, and investing activities.

Step #3: Separate the cash flows into cash flows from operating, investing, and financing activities. Non-cash investing and/or financing activities should be shown in a separate schedule with the Statement of Cash Flows.

Having completed this exercise, rearrange "sources" from largest to smallest and do the same for each "use." Then analyze/interpret whether the company's cash flow position has improved or worsened since the previous balance sheet.

Questions to be asked:

- What are the primary cash flow sources?
- Are they from operations or refinancing?
- Is the cash being reinvested back into the business?

Total "sources" must equal total "uses" of resources. The changes in the balance sheet from one period to the next in order to identify the sources and uses of resources must be analyzed. Unfortunately, this does not provide the complete picture of the major resource flows. These also need to be considered:

- Change in retained earnings
- Accounting entries that do not require cash
- Change in net fixed assets

Financial ratios that relate to the Statement of Cash Flows have evolved over time as we added to the traditional ratios, relating an income statement item to a balance sheet item. Furthermore, the Statement of Cash Flows did not become a required statement until 1987. So, it took a while for analysts to become familiar with the statement.

Ratios have now been developed that relate directly to the cash flow statement. Some of these ratios are as follows:

- Operating Cash Flow ÷ Current Maturities of Long-Term Debt and Current Notes Payable.
- Operating Cash Flow ÷ Total Debt
- Operating Cash Flow per Share
- Operating Cash Flow ÷ Cash Dividends
- Operating Cash Flow ÷ Interest Expense
- Operating Cash Flow ÷ Total Current Liabilities

$$\frac{\text{Operating Cash Flow}}{\text{Current Maturities of Long-Term Debt and Current Notes Payable}}$$

This ratio indicates a firm's ability to meet current debt maturities. The higher the ratio is, the better the firm's ability to meet their current debt maturities. The higher this ratio is, the better the firm's liquidity.

$$\frac{\text{Operating Cash Flow}}{\text{Total Debt}}$$

This operating cash flow/total debt ratio indicates a firm's ability to cover total debt with their annual cash flow. The higher the ratio, the better the firm's ability to carry their total debt. This is a very important ratio from a debt standpoint. It's similar to the income view of debt, except that operating cash flow is the focus instead of an income figure.

$$\frac{\text{Operating Cash Flow} - \text{Preferred Dividends}}{\text{Common Shares Outstanding}}$$

In the short run, the operating cash flow per share is a better indication of a firm's ability to make capital expenditure decisions and pay dividends than is earnings per share (EPS). It's not to be used as a substitute for EPS in terms of a firm's profitability assessment. However, it is a complimentary ratio that relates to the ratios pertaining to investor activity.

- **Cash flow from operations (CFFO) divided by interest expense**
  The higher the ratio, the better the debtor's ability to service debt
- **CFFO divided by total current liabilities**
  Results provide a measure of a debtor's ability to service short-term credit obligations

In summary, ratio analysis provides a useful financial technique for measuring the financial condition of a company and its creditworthiness for the extension of open credit. The types of ratio analysis tests, which can be prepared, do not, however, evaluate a company's cash flow and its ability to service its debts over the next few years. The bottom line in credit decisions may more frequently come down to measuring prospective and existing customers' net cash flow. That's why the technique of assessing a company's sources and uses of funds is so important and should be practiced when the situation at hand falls into one of the categories mentioned earlier.

STATEMENT OF CASH FLOWS

ROA, ROE, financial leverage, sustainable growth will be covered in another chapter to follow. Although that analysis is important for understanding a company's financial condition, creative accounting to hype revenues or defer expenses could plague it. That's what could happen when dealing with accrual accounting. The effect of accrual accounting will either increase current profits or sometimes hide them for a later period. It is important to understand the effect of various accounting practices on cash flow. You do this with an understanding of the cash flow statement.

An Overview of the Cash Flow Statement

Cash flow statements come in two varieties: direct and indirect. More than 99 percent of all companies use the indirect approach. Both approaches balance to the same cash number and both approaches contain three sections: operating, investing, and financing activities.

The Operating Activities section shows the effect of converting the income statement from an accrual accounting basis to a cash accounting basis. You can think of the resulting number for this section as representing cash profits—instead of accrual accounting profits.

The next section in the Statement of Cash Flows is labeled Investing Activities. It summarizes cash investments or sales from the period in property, plant and equipment, securities of other companies, and acquisitions. The last section summarizes the Financing Activities: debt raised or repaid, equity issued or retired, and dividends paid.[2]

With one or two exceptions, the sum of the results for the operating, investing and financing activities equals the change in the company's cash balance for the year. Thus, the importance of the cash flow statement is that you see where money came from and where it went. Understanding the cash flow statement is critical to understanding the difference between cash accounting and accrual accounting. Once you understand the difference, you will understand the company's quality of earnings.

As stated earlier, you construct a cash flow statement by taking changes in the balance sheet from one period to the next. Increases in assets are treated as "uses" of resources. Classify decreases in assets as "sources" of resources. You change the rule when looking at changes in liability and equity accounts. Increases are now "sources" and decreases become "uses."

Cash Flow from Operating Activities

The indirect cash flow statement (*see* Figure 6-2) begins with net income, the number shown on the company's income statement. However, the next three lines differ from how a normal presentation of the cash flow statement looks in an annual report. The rationale for not following the format approved by the Financial Accounting Standards Board (FASB) is as follows. The intent of the "cash flow from operations" section is to capture cash operating profit. The FASB approach fails to derive operating

---

[2]Harvard Business School, *Understanding the Statement of Cash Flows* (December 1992).

profit because it allows interest expense and interest income to be part of operating activities. Think about this for a moment. Is interest expense an operating expense or a financing expense? Interest expense is the cost of using debt funds to finance the business. Interest expense and debt financing have nothing to do with sales, cost of goods sold, and SG&A. If a company used all equity financing instead of some debt and some equity, it would still incur the same levels of revenues, cost of goods sold, and SG&A. In other words, operations wouldn't be affected. Thus, you should adjust upward the net income number by pulling out the interest expense. Because net income is an after-tax number, so must the interest expense adjustment be an after-tax amount.

A similar argument holds for interest income. Any interest income shown on the income statement has no effect on sales, cost of sales, and SG&A and should be pulled out of the net income number on an after-tax basis. Simply stated, interest income is not an operating income amount. It arises from investing excess cash in marketable securities. You can think of excess cash as negative financing. Management could use the excess cash, if it so decided, to pay down interest-bearing debt financing instead of investing the funds in marketable securities.

By pulling interest expense and interest income out of operations, you don't exclude them from the analysis. You include them in the financing activities section, which we will cover shortly.

The third adjustment to convert net income from the accrual accounting reported number to an accrual accounting operating profit number looks at non-operating expenses and revenues. Items included in this category are restructuring charges, extraordinary gains or losses, and any other non-ongoing item that would be identified in the income statement.

The impact of the above three adjustments is to adjust the company's cumulative net income. The adjusted amount is labeled "net operating profit after taxes." It is still an accrual accounting number but represents operating profits.

Recommended adjustments to cash flow from operations section:

- Interest expense (a financing expense)
  - Pull out and adjust net income upward
- Interest income (from investing excess cash)
  - Pull out
- Non-operating expenses and revenues (such as restructuring charges, extraordinary gains or losses and other non-ongoing items)

Figure 6-2: Indirect Statement of Cash Flows

($000)	2000	2001	2002	2003
Net income				
After-tax interest expense				
After-tax interest income				
After-tax non-operating costs				
Net operating profit after taxes				
Depreciation & amortization				
Change in receivables				
Change in inventories				
Change in other current assets				
Change in payables & accruals				
Change in LT deferred taxes				
Change in other LT liabilities				
Cash flow from operations				
Net purchases of fixed assets				
Change in other LT assets				
Cash flow from investing				
Free cash flows				
Change in ST interest bearing debt				
Change in long-term debt				
After-tax interest expense				
After-tax interest income				
Preferred dividends paid				
Common dividends paid				
Preferred stock issued/retired				
Common stock issued/retired				
Cash flow from financing				
Cash flow from nonop. activities				
Net change in cash				
Beginning cash balance				
Ending cash balance				

The end result equals the adjusted net operating profit number still at accrual accounting basis. So, now you calculate the cash flow from operation (CFFO), add back depreciation and amortization, because they are non-cash expenses. Then add changes in AR, inventory, other current assets, payables, deferred taxes, etc. to the adjusted net operating profit number.

After making all the adjustments, you now have your first glimpse at the company's quality of earnings from the perspective of the cash flow statement. The difference between cash profits and accrual operating profits could be large.

If the difference is large, you need to ask what has caused the difference. The conclusion to draw with any large difference in the two numbers is that even though the company might be showing improved accrual-based accounting profits each period, it has been at the expense of cash flow. Because balance sheets balance and sources of funds must equal uses, the company cash-consuming performance sometimes means it must fund cash elsewhere to cover the deficit in cash flow from operations.

Cash Flow from Investing Activities

This part of the cash flow statement identifies the investments management has made in non-working capital type assets, primarily in property and plant, and equipment. If you compare the depreciation amounts incurred each year (shown in the operating activities section) against the capital expenditures, you will find out if the company is spending more on capital investments than it is incurring through depreciation. On the surface, it is positive to see more spent than what has depreciated. It means that management is investing more resources into the business than have been consumed through wear and tear on these assets. In other words, the company is growing in size and, hopefully, becoming more dominant in its markets.

A potential negative implication associated with all these capital expenditures is that when you couple these cash outflows for investment activities with the cash outflows from operating activities, the net cash outflows in the business become even larger. This result is labeled "free cash flows" on the worksheet (Figure 6-2). Does a consistent negative free cash flow each year mean the company is growing too quickly? You won't know that until looking at the company's sustainable versus actual growth rate to be covered later.

Cash Flow from Financing Activities

This section of the cash flow statement indicates how the company has supported the business from a financing perspective. An important point to take away with you is that from an accrual accounting perspective, it is possible that accrual accounting net income exceeds any dividend paid. Thus, you would probably conclude that a company could afford to pay dividends. However, when viewed from a cash flow perspective, a different conclusion can emerge. You may come to the conclusion on occasion that management needed to borrow funds or issue equity to make the dividend payments.

A Potential Frustration Point

If you compare the cash flow statement worksheet to the company's Statement of Cash Flows, you will sometimes notice very different numbers. If the company in question were a very simple and small company, the cash flows statement worksheet (Figure 6-2) and the company's statement would probably agree—or at least have only minor differences. As stated earlier, you can think of items included in the cash flows statement as consisting of changes in balance sheet accounts, net income, and depreciation and amortization. What happens if a company buys another company? Well, it buys receivables, inventories, and other assets and liabilities. And it may pay for goodwill. On the FASB required presentation of the Statement of Cash Flows, these items are captured in investing activities under acquisitions of a company. However, on the balance sheet, receivables, inventories, and so forth that it bought are shown in the appropriate accounts. Purchased receivables are part of the receivable balance. Purchased inventory becomes a part of the inventory account. The other purchased assets and liabilities are handled in a similar fashion. This worksheet takes the change in the accounts and places the amounts in their "proper" cash flow categories. Receivables, inventories, prepaid expenses, payables, and accruals become part of operating activities. Property, plant and equipment, and goodwill become part of investing activities. As a result, the model allocates these differently purchased assets and liabilities to their appropriate operating and investing categories in the cash flow statement. The interesting part is that FASB will require the allocation of assets as described above to be done this way next year. So, assets and liabilities incurred in an acquisition are "correctly" treated according to FASB but with a lag. It isn't until the year following the acquisition that FASB treats receivable, inventories and payables as operating items. The worksheet (Figure 6-2) would suggest that it be done this way in the first place.

In summary, the cash flow statement captures departures of accrual accounting from cash accounting. Other than identifying the various sources and uses of resources; it also converts reported income statement profits to a cash basis. The difference between accrual income and cash income provides you with insight into the company's quality of earnings. For example, if management decides to enhance sales by extending payment terms, accrual based sales and income will increase and show the company as growing. However, until the credit sales are collected, there are no sales or profits on a cash basis. The higher accounting sales and profits are reversed in the Statement of Cash Flows, as if they never occurred in the first place.

What you should understand from the Statement of Cash Flows is that important differences exist between accrual and cash accounting approaches. By recognizing these differences, you should have a better understanding of the company's quality of earnings and its ability to sustain growth.

Direct Statement of Cash Flows

Why study the direct SCFs if few companies use them? The primary reason to study Direct Statements of Cash Flow (Figure 6-3) is to help you better grasp the meaning of the line item "cash from operations." The indirect method derives cash from operations indirectly—it is reconciliation from income to cash from operations. Thus, understanding the meaning of cash from operations is readily apparent from the direct method. A second reason to study the direct method is some users believe that it is more informative than the indirect method. Some practitioners, analysts and regulators have argued that the indirect format is so confusing that it fails to meet what they consider to be the Statement of Cash Flows' primary objective—to explain why cash changed. FASB also expressed a preference for the direct method in SFAS95, but discouraged its use by requiring that it had to be accompanied by the indirect method.

WHAT SHOULD THE ANALYST DO?

Analyst Should Scrutinize the Statement and:

- Look at difference between accrued operating profits and cash profits and ask what has actually caused the difference.
  - Does the firm show accrued based accounting profits but at expense of cash flow?
- Do one-time events contribute to the difference?
- Are the changes in receivables, inventories, and payables normal?

Figure 6-3: Direct Statement of Cash Flows

($000)	2000	2001	2002
Revenue	___	___	___
Change in receivables	___	___	___
Cash receipts	___	___	___
Cost of sales	___	___	___
Change in inventories	___	___	___
Change in payables & accruals	___	___	___
Cash cost of sales	___	___	___
Cash gross margin	___	___	___
Cash gross margin %	___	___	___
Gross margin	___	___	___
Gross margin %	___	___	___

- How strong is internal cash flow generation?
- CFFO minus Cash outflow from investments = Free cash flow.
  - Does FCF exist?
  - Is this a long-term trend?
- Can the company meet short-term obligations from operating cash flows?
- Was internal cash used to finance growth?
- Were dividends paid from FCF or was external financing used?
- What type of external financing does the company rely on?
  - Equity.
  - Short-term debt.
  - Long-term debt.
- Is there a mismatch of funds? Are LT assets funded by ST liabilities?
- If so, there is an increase in interest rate risk.

Questions Raised by the SFC

1. How strong is internal cash flow generation?
2. Is cash flow from operations positive, why? If negative, why?
3. Is the company growing? Too quickly?
4. Can the company meet short-term obligations from operating cash flow?
5. How much is invested in growth?

6. Are these investments consistent with the business strategy?
7. Was internal cash used to finance growth?
8. Does free cash flow exist? Is this a long-term trend?
9. Were dividends paid from free cash flow? Or was external financing used?

WHAT HAVE WE LEARNED?

- The Statement of Cash Flows:
  - Cash flow statement captures departures of accrual accounting from cash accounting.
  - Identifies the various sources and uses of cash.
  - Converts reported income statement profits to cash basis. *Notes:* accrual incomes increases if sales are enhanced by extending payment terms, however, the higher accounting sales and profits are reversed in the Statement of Cash Flows. Until credit sales are collected, there are no sales or profits on a cash basis.
  - Provides an insight into the firm's quality of earnings and its ability to sustain growth.
- The difference between accrual income and cash income provides you with insight into the firm's quality of earnings and its ability to sustain growth.
- Important differences exist between accrual and cash accounting approaches.

Chapter 7

PROFITABILITY ANALYSIS USING THE EXTENDED DuPONT MODEL

We previously looked at the traditional liquidity analysis approach used to evaluate a company's financial condition. We have also added to this discussion the importance of understanding cash flow and how to conduct a cash flow analysis. Let us now turn our attention to an area frequently overlooked, which is profitability analysis.

As with any art, financial analysis is subject to fad and fashion. A ratio is adopted, rises in repute, declines and is replaced. One measure of profit currently enjoying favor is that of earnings before interest, taxes, depreciation and amortization (EBITDA). It is argued that this measure strips out all the incidentals to highlight the real profitability of a business, and is not biased by capital structure, tax systems or depreciation policies.

The holy grail of financial analysis is the discovery of a single foolproof measure of company performance. EBITDA can be useful as part of a detailed analysis of a company but there are flaws in its claimed perfection. EBITDA ignores the cost of fixed assets employed in a business, yet surely these are as much an operating cost as anything else. As a measure of profitability, it is a long way from the bottom line of the income statement, and so ignores not only depreciation but also interest and tax. A company delivering an after-tax loss from a huge investment in fixed assets financed by equally substantial borrowings could look quite healthy on an EBITDA basis.

One of the best tools that breaks down the various profit components related to a firm's ROE is the DuPont Model. A little history about the DuPont Model is appropriate before beginning our discussion on what may be the best way to assess a firm's profitability. Management at the EI DuPont de Nemours and Company developed this approach to analysis profitability. The main purpose for using this approach is to bring analysts' awareness level up a few notches and get them to recognize that the ROE number can be influenced by several financial decisions. This DuPont model clearly spells out the relationships between various components and

Figure 7-1: Using DuPont Model to Uncover Asset Turnover Slowdown

	Return on Assets	Net Profit = Margin	Total Asset × Turnover
Firm A			
Year 1	10%	= 4.0%	× 2.5
Year 2	8%	= 4.0%	× 2.0
Firm B			
Year 1	10%	= 4.0%	× 2.5
Year 2	8%	= 3.2%	× 2.5

highlights both the positive and negative factors leading up to the final ROE number.

The owners of a business want to improve ROE, and the DuPont model shows how this can happen. Increasing ROE can be attributed to price changes, decreasing expenses, improving asset turnover or using more leverage. The Extended DuPont model clearly shows how this takes place. This approach involves critical thinking on the part of the financial analyst.

The extended DuPont Model (Exhibit 1) provides a good starting point for analyzing a firm's financial condition because it highlights three important factors: (1) expense control, (2) asset utilization, and (3) debt utilization. The total asset turnover measures asset utilization, which may lead to minimizing the investment in various types of assets. At the same time, a company's treasury staff can analyze the effects of alternative financing strategies on the equity multiplier which is a combination of the effect of interest expense and risk brought on by using debt as the company uses leverage to increase the rate of return on equity.[3]

It is best to look at net profit margin and total asset turnover together because of the influence they have on return on assets. When these ratios are reviewed together, it is called the DuPont Return on Assets (ROA). Analyzing these two ratios allow for improved analysis of changes in the return on assets percentage. EI DuPont de Nemours and Company developed this method of separation into two parts. The end result is the DuPont ROA which is calculated as follows:

ROA = Net Income before Minority Share of Earnings and Nonrecurring Items ÷ Average Total Assets. This number is equal to Net

---

[3]Charles A. Gibson, *Financial Statement Analysis* (Mason, OH: South-Western College Publishing, 1998), 389.

Income Before Minority Share of Earnings and Nonrecurring Items ÷ Net Sales (net profit margin) × Net Sales ÷ Average Total Assets (total asset turnover). In Figure 7-1, two firms could have identical return on asset turnover and the DuPont analysis could uncover how one firm is experiencing a slowdown in asset turnover. Firm A is generating fewer sales for the assets invested. Perhaps Firm B has a good asset turnover but suffers from the reduction in net profit margin. It is generating less profit per dollar of sales.

ROE Decomposition

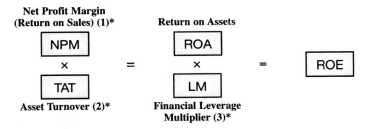

*3 Critical Dimensions

The Return on Equity (ROE) measures income earned on invested capital. Using the DuPont Method to combine a series of ratios to assess Return on Investment (ROI) in a system of interrelationships can provide several forms of equations, one of which deals with ROI.

$$\text{ROE} = \frac{\text{Net Sales}}{\text{Total Assets}} \times \frac{\text{Total Assets}}{\text{Stockholders' Equity}} \times \frac{\text{Net Income} - \text{Preferred Dividends}}{\text{Net sales}}$$

Again, the benefit of the DuPont Method is that it can be used to consider simultaneously several responses to a single question. For example, the question "How can return on investment be increased?" might be answered in several ways—such as by increasing asset turnover through increased sales, or by increasing net income through cost-cutting policies, or by a combination of changes.

The return on common equity (ROE) measures the return to the common shareholder.

$$\text{ROE} = \frac{\text{Net Income before Nonrecurring Items} - \text{Preferred Dividends}}{\text{Average Common Equity}}$$

Exhibit 1: Extended DuPont Model

	2000
Operating Return	
Sales	100.00%
– Cost of Sales	(98.61%)
= Gross Profit Margin	1.39%
– Selling, General & Administrative	(1.03%)
– Depreciation	(0.02%)
– Other Operating Expenses	0.00%
= Operating Return on Sales	0.34%
x Efficiency in Managing Assets	
Cash & Mkt. Sec. / Sales	0.00
+ Receivables / Sales	0.06
+ Inventory / Sales	0.02
+ Other Current Assets / Sales	0.00
- Accounts Payable & Accruals / Sales	(0.05)
= Net Current Assets / Sales	0.03
Net Fixed Assets / Sales	0.00
+ Other Long-Term Assets / Sales	0.00
= Total Assets / Sales	0.04
1 divided by Total Assets / Sales	
= Asset Turnover Ratio	28.33
= Return on Assets Before Taxes	9.54%
x Financial Leverage	
1	1.00
– Interest Expense / Operating Earnings	(0.48)
= After Interest Expense Multiplier	0.52
Current Debt / Common Equity	3.30
+ Long-Term Debt / Common Equity	0.01
+ Other LT Liabilities / Common Equity	0.07
+ Preferred Stock / Common Equity	0.00
= (Debt + Pf. Stock) / Common Equity	3.37
+ 1	1.00
= Financial Leverage Multiplier	4.37
Joint Int. & Fin. Leverage Multiplier	2.27
= ROE Before Considering the Tax Effect	21.64%
x Income Tax Effect	
1	1.00
– Income Tax / Pretax Income	(0.05)
= After Income Tax Multiplier	0.95
= Return on Equity (excl. special items)	20.57%
+ Non-op. Income Effect (Incl. Int. Income)	7.37%
– Pref. Dividends / Com. Equity	0.00%
= Return On Common Equity (ROE)	27.94%
Com. Earnings Retention % (RR)	100.00%
Sustainable Growth Rate	20.57%
Actual Growth in Sales	9.90%
Actual Growth in Assets	15.16%
Actual Growth in Debt	16.14%
Actual Growth in Equity	5.72%

The DuPont Model can be set up on a spreadsheet as indicated in Exhibit 1. This model captures operating revenue results (ROS), efficiency in managing assets (ROA) and ROE. It also indicates whether the concept of financial leverage is favorable or unfavorable (i.e., the joint interest and financial multiplier).

For example, we can see from the numbers presented that the Operating Return on Sales (EBITA) is at .34 percent, which indicates small margins are being made and, therefore, leaves little room for mistakes.

Interest Expense ÷ Operating Earnings is at (0.48) which indicates that for every dollar of EBITA, the company pays .48 in interest. Debt financing is eating up almost 50 percent of the operating profits.

(Debt + Pf. Stock) ÷ Common Equity is at 3.37, which translates to mean that for every dollar of Equity, the company has $3.37 in debt.

Total Assets ÷ Sales is at 0.04 which means that for every dollar of sales, the company has .4 invested in assets. We can look here to see if the company is leaning on trade creditors to support accounts receivable.

Another read from this set of figures is Sustainable Growth, which is discussed in Chapter 8. In this example, we see that the company can grow at a faster pace than it is currently doing.

In summary, we see a company where interest expense could be getting out of hand with small profit margins to cover fixed expenses. However, favorable leverage does exist as indicated by the joint interest and financial leverage multiplier. To get at this leverage multiplier number, multiply the after interest expense multiplier by the financial leverage multiplier to get the joint interest and financial leverage multiplier. A result of 1 means financial leverage is neither favorable nor unfavorable. A result in excess of 1 means favorable and anything less than 1 means unfavorable leverage exists. In this example, the use of debt financing is not having an unfavorable impact on equity as was previously thought. The joint impact of determining how much of each $1 of EBIT is left after the company incurs interest expense along with knowing how many dollars of assets are supported by each dollar of equity will determine if the financial leverage is favorable.

ANALYSIS OF RETURN ON SALES

To begin your analysis of profitability, start with common-sized income statements that capture the operating components. By this, I mean that your analysis focuses solely on operating activities and excludes all financing factors such as interest expense or interest income, extraordinary

Figure 7-2: Common Size Income Statement Analysis

	12/31/00	12/31/01	12/31/02
Sales	100.00%	100.00%	100.00%
– Cost of Goods Sold	(66.21)	(69.18)	(65.90)
= Gross Profit (GP)	33.79%	30.82%	34.10%
– Selling, General Administrative	(14.48)	(12.51)	(14.50)
– Depreciation Expenses	(6.44)	(7.04)	(9.44)
– Other Operating Expenses	(7.15)	(6.03)	(8.15)
= Operating Return on Sales	5.72%	4.97%	2.01%

events, restructuring charges and so on. The reason for such a narrow focus is that you want to gain an understanding of the profitability of operations—the revenues and costs involved with the core business of the company. Ask questions like the following:

- Are margins changing?
  - Why?
  - What were the underlying causes?
- Is the company managing its overhead and administrative costs well?
  - What are the activities driving these costs?
  - Are the activities necessary?

The worksheet in Figure 7-2 provides the common-sized income statement information by pegging each year's sales at 100 percent and taking each of the remaining items on the income statement as a percentage of sales. For instance, gross profits may have increased over the years and the common-sized income statement could show this improvement as a result of lower cost of sales. You should ask, what has caused the improvement? Higher selling prices? Lower cost prices? Change in product mix from lower margin product in favor of higher margin products? Change in the classification of expenses for accounting reasons? Or is this improvement a combination of all the factors identified. Verbiage in the Management Discussion and Analysis section of a 10-K report will perhaps uncover the reasons for this change.

SG&A increases? Why? Are management salaries increasing faster than growth in sales. Bottom line is to see the operating return on sales increasing (EBIT ÷ Sales). If a small return has been realized, there is not a lot of room for mistakes.

Figure 7-3: Management of Assets Analysis

	12/31/00	12/31/01	12/31/02
Cash & Marketable Sec./Sales	0.01	0.00	0.02
+ Receivables/Sales	0.15	0.14	0.19
+ Inventory/Sales	0.23	0.25	0.28
+ Other Current Assets/Sales	0.03	0.02	0.02
– Accts Payables & Accrual Sales	(0.11)	(0.11)	(0.12)
= Net Current Assets/Sales	0.31	0.31	0.39
+ Net Fixed Assets/Sales	0.05	0.03	0.05
+ Other Long-Term Assets/Sales	0.13	0.04	0.08
= Total Assets/Sales	0.49	0.38	0.52
1 ÷ Total Assets/Sales			
= Asset Turnover Ratio	2.05	2.65	1.91

EFFICIENCY IN MANAGING ASSETS

The Management of Asset Analysis worksheet (Figure 7-3) is an analysis to examine the management of assets. Usually this analysis is done using turnover ratios—that is, divide sales by asset items. However, it makes more sense to turn the calculation over and divide the asset items by sales. The result is that various calculations are additive so you can see the contribution of management of a particular asset relative to the management of total assets. When you analyze numbers in this section, you want to keep the following issues in mind:

- How well is the company managing its credit policies?
- How well do they manage their inventory?
- What is the underlying business reason for the change in inventory ratios?
- Is there a mismatch between demand forecasts and actual sales?
- Do they have a good policy of acquisitions and divestitures?
- What is the estimated age of the assets?

Before-Tax Return on Assets Ratio

You now have enough information to analyze a company's before-tax return on assets ratio, ROA. You calculate ROA by multiplying the operating return-on-sales ratio by asset turnover. This number tells you that for every dollar invested in assets, the company either gained or lost a compounded dollar amount. For instance, if a loss is indicated with the operating return on sales figure (2.76%) or ($2.76) becomes a ($3.57) loss on invested assets if the assets were turning over 1.29 times a year. The math would be (2.76) × 1.29 = (3.57). In this example, the company would be better off to turnover the assets less than once a year. Doing so would have resulted in a smaller loss on assets.

The next issue you need to address is how to evaluate whether the results for return on asset are good enough. As an absolute minimum benchmark, ask this question: Does the ROA ratio exceed the yield on a 20- or 30-year treasury bond? If not, then management needs to re-deploy the assets more efficiently in the future. Failure to do so will result in destroyed market value of the company and will probably cause financial distress problems, which may even result in bankruptcy.

There is a better measure to use to evaluate the return-on-asset performance, but it requires additional modeling and analysis beyond the scope of this exercise. It is called the Weighted Average Cost of Capital (WACC). If you are familiar with it, you might want to calculate the firm's WACC on a before-tax basis and compare it to the ROA numbers. If WACC exceeds ROA, the firm's management needs to improve performance through higher return on sales, increased asset turnover, or both.

In summary, you have broken down the problem into parts. Start with understanding the profitability of sales through the use of common-sized income statements. Next, look at how efficiently assets are managed by relating the various asset items to sales. Last, tie the two analyses together into a return-on-asset measure that tells you how well management has deployed the assets. At this point, it is important to ascertain whether the company is earning a fair return on its net asset investment.

Now, you want to tie the ROA performance number with financial leverage to calculate before-tax ROE numbers (*see* p. 59, ROE Decomposition).

What Is Financial Leverage?

Financial leverage occurs whenever a firm finances with interest-bearing debt. The objective of analyzing a company's financial leverage is to ascertain whether management is able to earn more on the debt funds than the funds cost. If so, then the company realizes favorable financial leverage. If not, then it earns unfavorable financial leverage. If a company does not have any interest bearing debt financing, then it does not have any financial risk and cannot realize financial leverage. In this situation, the only risk the firm faces is business or operating risk. This type of risk arises from the mix of fixed and variable costs in the business, how competitive the market happens to be for the same product, the availability of material, the rapidity of technology changes, and the like.

If we analyze how interest expense impacts the income statement and then examine the balance sheet to see how much debt financing is used per $1 of equity financing—or equivalently, how many dollars of assets does $1 of equity support, you can then merge these two calculations and get an understanding whether the leverage is favorable or not.

Interest Expense Multiplier

The objective in analyzing interest expense is to see how much of every $1 of earnings before interest and taxes (commonly called EBIT) is left after paying interest on debt financing. You can think of the problem in a mathematical sense as (EBIT − Interest Expense) ÷ EBIT or as $1 − (Interest Expense ÷ EBIT). These are equivalent statements.

Just analyzing this piece of financial leverage component fails to tell you whether management was able to realize favorable leverage or not. You won't know the answer to this issue until after analyzing the balance sheet debt to equity relationship.

Balance Sheet Financing Multiplier

This part of the analysis looks at each of the debt components relative to the company's equity financing. Liabilities for accounts payable and accruals are excluded because they are subtracted from current assets to derive a net current asset number. You can see that this section summarizes the balance sheet debt to equity relationships. The interpretation of each debt component is relative to $1 of equity financing.

An explanation is required for the $1 opposite the label "+ 1" (*see* Exhibit 1, p. 60). You are familiar with a debt-to-equity ratio but probably don't use an assets-to-equity ratio in your analysis. Well, you will now when you follow this approach. The relationship between the debt to equity ratio and the asset to equity ratio is direct. Recall the balance sheet formula: assets = debt + equity. Think of preferred stock as a form of debt. If you divide both sides of this equation by equity, the result is Assets ÷ Equity = (Debt ÷ Equity) + (Equity ÷ Equity). This result is what is shown on the line labeled (Debt + Preferred Stock) ÷ Common Equity is nothing more than Debt ÷ Equity—it must be because Assets = Debt + Equity. The line labeled "+ 1" represents Equity ÷ Equity, which of course equals 1. The next line "financial leverage multiplier" is Asset ÷ Equity. So, what is the interpretation of the line labeled "Financial Leverage Multiplier"? It is simply this, $1 of equity financing supports "x" dollars (financial leverage multiplier number) of asset investment. Is this leverage good or bad?

Favorable or Unfavorable Financial Leverage?

To answer the question, you need to multiply the income statement leverage component by the balance sheet leverage component. In other words, multiply the after interest expense multiplier by the financial leverage multiplier to get the "joint interest and financial leverage multiplier."

You interpret whether favorable or unfavorable leverage exists by comparing the results for the joint interest and financial leverage multiplier to the number 1. A result of 1 means financial leverage is neutral—neither favorable nor unfavorable leverage exists. A result in excess of 1 means favorable leverage exists. A result of less than 1 means an unfavorable leverage exists. Let's say that we calculate a (5.85) joint interest and financial leverage multiplier.

What is the impact on profitability of the financial leverage? Well, it causes the before-tax return on assets number of (3.57) mentioned in our earlier example to become (20.86) percent return on equity before taxes. The loss on assets (3.57) "Return on Assets before Taxes" was multiplied by 5.85 times (the joint multiplier) to derive the loss on equity "ROE before Considering the Tax Effect." The primary reason for this occurrence stems from the fact that for every $1 of EBIT, there was only a small amount left after incurring interest expense.

What is the appropriate benchmark to compare against return on equity? As a rough benchmark, estimate the company's cost of debt and add another 500 basis points. This approach is one of several methods used by investment bankers on Wall Street. It will at least give you a ballpark estimate. You can get an idea of the cost of debt from the 10-K report. If it states that debt raised costs 10.75%, the cost of equity is around 16 percent. Now look to see if the company earned in excess of this 16 percent.

To summarize, you need to break the problem into parts. In order to understand the significance of financial leverage, start by determining how much of each $1 of EBIT is left after the company incurs interest expense. Next, determine how many dollars of assets are supported by each dollar of equity. The joint impact of these two effects determines whether financial leverage is favorable or not. A result greater than 1 means debt financing provides favorable leverage less than 1 means unfavorable leverage, and 1 means neutral leverage.

Let us now gain an understanding of how income taxes affect the return on equity ratio and how a company's profitability performance and dividend policy affect its sustainable growth rate.

Profitability and Tax Effects

Because income taxes are a cost of doing business, you need to adjust the before-tax return on equity numbers to after-tax numbers. Interpret the row labeled "1" as meaning $1 of earnings before income taxes. The next row, labeled "income tax / pretax income," represents the effective amount of income taxes that a company incurs on the $1 of before tax earnings.

Let's say that the after-income tax multiplier turns out to be $.69. This means that $1 of before-tax income became $.69 after taxes were considered and, therefore, you had a "– Income tax/pretax income of $.31 cents" ($1 – $.31 = $.69). By multiplying the before-tax return on equity ratio by the "after income tax multiplier," you derive the company's after-tax return on equity performance before considering any non-operating effects.

Non-Operating Effects on Profitability

In an effort to gain as much insight as possible into a company's performance, this model separates non-operating effects from normal activities. Included in the non-operating section are items like restructuring charges, accounting charges, and extraordinary gains or losses.

The DuPont Model allows you to assess the impact of non-operating income and expense items on a company's return on equity ratio each year. A non-operating adjustment will increase the loss on the equity return ratio and allow you to see the full impact it has had on the overall ROE number. More importantly, you begin to look for reasons to explain the difference identified between the ROE number that excludes non-operating data and that the one that is an all-inclusive after-tax return on equity.

Sustainable Growth

The next phase of this worksheet (*see* Exhibit 1) pertains to a company's sustainable growth rate. The financial definition of sustainable growth is the rate of growth in sales, assets, debt, and equity that can be sustained indefinitely without management altering the debt to equity relationship, the return on equity performance or the dividend payout rate.

Several years ago, a study conducted by a professor at the Harvard Business School concluded that management's ability to manage growth of the company is an important factor of differentiating value-enhancing companies from companies that destroy shareholder values. You will find that understanding a firm's sustainable growth rate provides a peek into whether the firm is likely to encounter financial distress in the future. Firms that file bankruptcy do so, with minor exceptions, because they grow too quickly. Their profits and cash flow fail to follow their strong sales growth. The analysis of sustainable growth will tie directly to analysis of cash flows in the company, which can be found, on another worksheet.

Sustainable growth can be defined in different ways. The most prevalent approach is to multiply the return on equity ratio by the firm's profit retention rate. The retention rate is 1 − (Dividends paid ÷ Net income), stated as a percentage number. Excluded are the non-operating effects. After all, by definition, the non-operating effects should not be ongoing. Thus, sustainable growth is return on equity (excluding special items) multiplied by the retention ratio. You need to compare the sustainable growth rate number to actual growth performance to draw conclusions about growth. Notice on the worksheet that annual growth rates are shown for sales, assets, debt, and equity. Use the first two items, sales and assets, to assess growth. Use the next two items, debt and equity, to see how management decided to finance growth that is either higher or lower than the sustainable growth rate.

So long as the sustainable growth rate is bracketed by actual growth rates for sales and assets, you assume that the company can sustain its actual growth rate without encountering financial difficulties. If the sustainable rate is less than both the actual growth rates for sales and assets, you conclude that without access to new capital, the company will probably face financial difficulties in the near future. If capital suppliers dry up, the company must slow its actual growth, increase its sustainable growth, or a combination of these two approaches. If sustainable growth exceeds both actual growths in sales and assets over two or three consecutive years, then maybe management is missing opportunities in the firm's markets to capture more sales, profits and cash flows. The firm is possibly losing market share to competitors. If this situation is not corrected, the firm may become the target of a takeover or merger. Look for the primary source of financing to be debt increases in order to support the higher than sustainable growth rate if the assets number doesn't decline accordingly.

By continuing with this breakdown of the problem process into several parts, you should have a good understanding of the financial performance of a company and its likelihood of sustaining growth into the future without financial problems arising. Whatever your conclusions about the company's profitability, they are transferable to your analysis of growth.

The reason is that sustainable growth analysis is nothing more than the extension of analyzing the company's return on equity performance.

What Is an Acceptable ROE & ROA?

Rule of thumb for ROE:

- Cost of capital + 500 basis points
- C of C = 10.75% + 5% = 16% minimum ROE

Rule of thumb for ROA:

- Does ROA ratio exceed the yield on a 20- or 30-year treasury bond?

TAT Decomposition

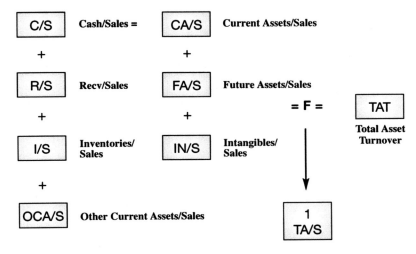

NPM Decomposition

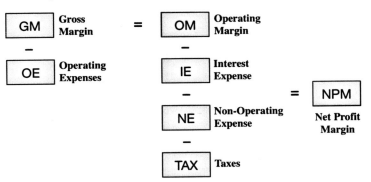

Financial Leverage Multiplier Decomposition

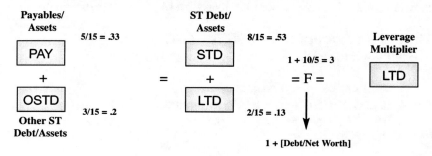

ROE Decomposition

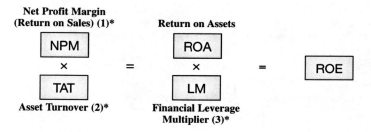

*3 Critical Dimensions

Chapter 8

FINANCIAL PLANNING
AND SUSTAINABLE GROWTH

We can learn several things from business failures—that there are many ways to mismanage a business. One of the main reasons for business failure was that they grew too fast and ran out of cash to pay the bills.

The central problem for fast-growing companies is that sales, and the assets to support the sales, have been growing at a faster rate than the reinvested profit after taxes, which is a significant part of the growth capital. A good ratio calculation that measures this pace is the long-term sustainable growth rate formula. The LTSGR is equal to the firm's average return on equity (ROE). The ROE is equal to profit after tax divided by shareholder's equity. Sustainable growth analysis is nothing more than the extension of analyzing the firm's return on equity performance.

Two key assumptions made are that the company will maintain a constant ratio of sales to assets called "asset turnover" and the company will maintain a constant ratio of debt to equity. Having constant sales to asset turnover ratio assumes that as sales grow, the assets to support sales will grow at the same rate.

LTSGR FORMULA

- *Definition:* Growth the firm can sustain in perpetuity without issuing new equity while maintaining current financial policies
- It is based on "sources" = "uses" concept

Example:

	LY	TY		LY	TY
Assets	200	330	Sales	400	700
Debt	40	80	Cost	300	550
Equity	160	250	Profit	100	150
Sales Growth = 75%			Dividends	40	60
Asset Growth = 65%			Retained	60	90

71

$$\text{Growth} = \frac{\text{Retention Ratio} \times \text{ROE}}{1 - (\text{Retention Ratio} \times \text{ROE})}$$

$1 - p$ = Retention ratio; p is dividend payout

= .60 × .625 / (1 − .60 × .625)	60%
= .60 × .60 / (1 − .60 × .60)	56.3%

(ROE − Return on Equity)

For a firm in sustainable growth equilibrium, where it does not issue new equity (any equity growth is the result of retaining profits), the ongoing annual growth in sales is equal to the growth in assets, debt, earnings, and equity. However, if sales expand at a rate faster than the sustainable growth rate, something in the company's financial objectives has to give which is usually a weakening of the company's financial position.

A growth index can be constructed by subtracting sustainable growth from actual growth. An index of zero means that actual growth is in equilibrium with sustainable growth. When the index is positive, the firm is growing faster than it can sustain under current financial policies. A negative index indicates that the firm can support higher sales growth. When actual growth exceeds sustainable growth, the company is an absorber of cash. It is a generator of cash when the reverse situation exists.

If actual sales growth is at any rate other than the sustainable growth rate, then either sales, retentions, D/E, reduction in payout ratio, change in selling prices, cut in operating costs, increase in leverage, selling new equity, or selling marginal businesses must change.

Chapter 9

PREDICTING A COMPANY'S SUSTAINABLE GROWTH

In this chapter, you will be provided with a model that predicts a company's acceptable level of growth. As you know, companies often establish goals for sales and earnings growth. These established goals might end up improving or adding pressure to a company's financial condition. As discussed, Sustainable Growth Analysis identifies a sustainable growth rate. Growth that exceeds this rate will add financial pressure. By using the identified sustainable growth rate, we should be able to calculate how fast a given company's sales, earnings or any other item in its financial statements should grow and, furthermore, what it must do if the decision is made to exceed the identified SG rate. Keep in mind that a company's "SG" rate can be achieved by improving operating or financial performance.[4]

Let's begin our analysis by looking at the following abbreviated Financial Statement:

	2001	2002
Sales	$90,269	$100,000
Costs and Taxes	83,950	93,000
Net Income	$6,319	$7,000
Net Income	$6,319	$7,000
Dividends	2,844	3,150
Additions to Retained Earnings	$3,475	3,850
Total Assets	$56,418	$62,500
Debt	$20,704	$22,936
Owner's Equity	35,714	39,564
Total Assets	$56,418	$62,500

---

[4]Dr. Gary W. Emery, "Sustainable Growth for Credit Analysis," *Business Credit* (Feb. 2000), 35.

You can learn a lot about a company's growth potential and its alternatives for increasing its growth by using the DuPont analysis to study the components of ROE. This form of financial ratio analysis decomposes return on equity into three ratios that measure three key areas of financial performance. The formula for DuPont analysis is as follows:

$$\frac{\text{Total Assets (2001)}}{\text{Owners Equity (2001)}} \times \frac{\text{Sales (2002)}}{\text{Total Assets (2001)}} \times \frac{\text{Net Income (2002)}}{\text{Sales (2002)}} = \text{ROE}$$

The product of these three ratios equals return on equity (ROE) because total assets cancels from the numerator of the first ratio and the denominator of the second while sales cancel from the numerator of the second ratio and the denominator of the third, leaving net income divided by owner's equity.

From left to right, the three ratios in the formula for DuPont analysis are the Leverage ratio (LEV), the Total Asset Turnover ratio (TAT), and the Profit Margin (PM). The results from our abbreviated financial statement above are:

$$\text{LEV} = \frac{\text{Total Assets (2001)}}{\text{Owners Equity (2001)}} = \frac{\$56,418}{\$35,714} = 1.5797$$

$$\text{TAT} = \frac{\text{Sales (2002)}}{\text{Total Assets (2001)}} = \frac{\$100,000}{\$56,418} = 1.7725$$

$$\text{PM} = \frac{\text{Net Income (2002)}}{\text{Sales (2002)}} = \frac{\$7,000}{\$100,000} = 0.0700$$

Multiplying the values of these ratios gives you an ROE of 1.5797 × 1.7725 × 0.0700 = 0.1960. The interpretation of these numbers is that for each dollar the owners invested they acquired $1.5797 of assets (using debt for the additional $0.5797), from each dollar of assets they generated $1,7725 of sales, and from each dollar of sales they obtained $0.07 of profit, providing a return on the owners' original investment of 19.60 percent.

Now that we have the DuPont formula ratios, we can use them to project financial statements for the year 2003 and this will demonstrate that ROE is a comprehensive constraint on growth.

STEPS IN PROJECTING FINANCIAL STATEMENTS

The **first step** is to calculate the Total Asset Turnover ratio to determine how many dollars of sales the company will generate in 2003 using the total assets available at the beginning of the year.

- Sales (2003) = TAT × Total Assets (2002) = 1.7725 × $62,500 = $110,781

The **second step** is to use the company's Profit Margin to determine how many dollars of net income they will obtain from these sales.

- Net Income (2002) = PM × Sales (2003) = 0.07 × $110,781 = $7,755

The **third step** is to use the Retention ratio (RET) to compute the amount of net income that it will retain in the company.

- Addition to Owner's Equity (2003) = RET × Net Income (2003) = 0.55 × $7,755 = $4,265

This addition to retained earnings increases equity from $39,564 to $43,829 of equity.

But how did we come up with the RET ratio? The formula is:

$$RET = \frac{\text{Net Income for (2002)} - \text{Dividends for 2002}}{\text{Net Income for 2002}}$$

$$= \frac{\$7,000 - \$3,150}{\$7,000}$$

$$= \mathbf{0.5500}$$

The **final step** is to use the company's Leverage ratio to determine how many dollars of assets the company will support with $43,829 of equity.

- Total Assets (2003) = LEV × Owner's Equity (2003) = 1.5797 × $43,829 = $69,237

The company's total debt equals its total assets minus the owners' equity: $69,237 − $43,829 = $25,408. The resulting projected financial statements are noted below:

	2001	2002
Sales	$100,000	$110,781
Costs and Taxes	93,000	103,026
Net Income	$7,000	$7,755
Net Income	$7,000	$7,755
Dividends	3,150	3,490
Addition to Retained Earnings	$3,850	4,265
Total Assets	$62,500	$69,237
Debt	$22,936	$25,408
Owners' Equity	39,564	43,829
Total Assets	$62,500	$69,237

You can verify that ROE is a comprehensive growth constraint by computing the rate of growth in each line of the income statement, statement of retained earnings and balance sheet. You'll find that sales, net income and every item in these financial statements, grew at an annual rate of 10.78 percent, which is the company's sustainable growth rate. This company cannot grow its sales, earnings, or any other item in its financial statements by more than 10.78 percent *unless* it increases its sustainable growth rate by improving its operating or financial performance.

What alternatives exist for increasing the Sustainable Growth Rate? Well, we can clearly see a company's alternatives for increasing its sustainable growth rate by using the DuPont formula in the formula for ROE.

$$= \frac{\text{Total Assets (2001)}}{\text{Owners Equity (2001)}} \times \frac{\text{Sales (2002)}}{\text{Total Assets (2001)}} \times \frac{\text{Net Income (2002)}}{\text{Sales (2002)}}$$

$$= \text{LEV} \times \text{TAT} \times \text{PM} \times \text{RET}$$

Written this way, the formula says that a company can increase its sustainable growth rate by:

- using more borrowed money to increase its leverage ratio,
- using assets more intensively to increase its total asset turnover ratio,
- reducing costs to increase its profit margin, or
- investing more of the owner's money in the business to increase its retention ratio.

Increasing the values of these ratios or some combination of them is the only alternative for increasing the sustainable growth rate.

Using the numbers presented above and making the assumption that this company wants to set a targeted growth rate of 15 percent higher than the sustainable growth rate of 10.78, what must be done? The company must increase its LEV, TAT, PM, RET, or a combination thereof. A look at four possible policy changes that enable this company to achieve this target growth rate are summarized below:

Policy	LEV	TAT	PM/RET	G
Current Policy	1.5797 0.1078	1.7725	0.0700	0.5500
Increase Leverage	2.1981 0.1500	1.7725	0.0700	0.5500
Increase TAT	1.5797 0.1500	2.4664	0.0700	0.5500
Increase PM	1.5797 0.1500	1.7725	0.0974	0.5500
Increase Retention	1.5797 0.1500	1.7725	0.0700	0.7653

A company can increase its sustainable growth rate by using its assets more intensively or by reducing its costs. These improvements are viable alternatives if the company's operations are below capacity or not cost effective. Some companies are in this situation and can improve operations to increase their sustainable growth rates while others are not. Consequently, there is no general tendency for companies to use an improvement in operations to increase their growth rates.

A company can also increase its sustainable growth rate by using more borrowed money or by investing more of the owner's money in the business. There are two ways to increase the owners' investment: the company can reduce its dividends to increase retained earnings or issue additional common stock. Always look for a company's growth and its increased use of debt to see if it tracks closely together. This would indicate the owners' preference to use borrowed money to finance growth because they don't want to increase their own investment in the company.[5]

In summary, the above has hopefully demonstrated that companies must change their operating or financing policies to achieve growth targets that exceed their sustainable growth rates.

---

[5]Terry S. Maness, *Short-Term Financial Management* (Eagan, MN: West Pub. Co, 2000), 488.

Chapter 10

DERIVATIVES RISK ANALYSIS

INTRODUCTION

In general, companies can use derivatives for two distinct purposes, hedging and speculating. Companies try to protect a position or reduce exposure to price movements by using derivatives to hedge. Speculation is the word used to describe a position taken when there is nothing to protect and a company tries to profit from market movement. As a result of continued company trends, credit departments need to identify the role they must play in order to protect the company's assets.

Derivatives are financial instruments (contracts) that do not represent ownership rights in any asset but, rather, derive their value from the value of some other underlying commodity or other asset. When used prudently, derivatives are efficient and effective tools for isolating financial risk and "hedging" to reduce exposure to risk.

Derivative contracts transfer risk, especially price risk, to those who are able and willing to bear it. How they transfer risk is complicated and frequently misinterpreted. Derivatives have also been associated with some spectacular financial failures and with dubious financial reporting.

There are five general types of risk that are faced by all businesses: **market risk** (unexpected changes in interest rates, exchange rates, stock prices, or commodity prices), **credit/default risk** (broken contracts, bankruptcy), **operational risk** (equipment failure, fraud, off-spec cargoes, shipping delays), **liquidity risk** (inability to buy or sell commodities at quoted prices), and **political risk** (new regulations, expropriation). Businesses operating in the petroleum, natural gas, and electricity industries are particularly susceptible to market risk—or more specifically, **price risk**—as a consequence of the extreme volatility of energy commodity prices. Electricity prices, in particular, are substantially more volatile than other commodity prices.

Price volatility is caused by shifts in the supply and demand for a commodity. Natural gas and wholesale electricity prices are particularly volatile, for several reasons. Demand shifts quickly in response to weather conditions, and "surge production" is limited and expensive. In addition, electricity and natural gas often cannot be moved to areas where there are unexpected increases in demand, and cheap local storage is limited, especially for electricity.

Derivatives allow investors to transfer risk to others who could profit from taking the risk. The person transferring risk achieves price certainty but loses the opportunity for making additional profits when prices move opposite his/her fears. Likewise, the person taking on the risk will lose if the counterparty's fears are realized. Except for transaction costs, the winner's gains are equal to the loser's losses. Like insurance, derivatives protect against some adverse events. The cost of the insurance is either forgone profit or cash losses. Because of their flexibility in dealing with price risk, derivatives have become an increasingly popular way to isolate cash earnings from price fluctuations.

The most commonly used derivative contracts are forward contracts, futures contracts, options, and swaps. A **forward contract** is an agreement between two parties to buy (sell) a specified quality and quantity of a good at an agreed date in the future at a fixed price or at a price determined by formula at the time of delivery to the location specified in the contract. For example, a natural gas producer may agree to deliver a billion cubic feet of gas to a petrochemical plant at Henry Hub, Louisiana, during the first week of July 2005 at a price of $3.20 per thousand cubic feet. Forward contracts between independent generators and large industrial customers are used extensively in the electricity industry.

Forward contracts have problems that can be serious at times. First, buyers and sellers (counterparties) have to find each other and settle on a price. Finding suitable counterparties can be difficult. Discovering the market price for a delivery at a specific place far into the future is also daunting. For example, after the collapse of the California power market in the summer of 2000, the California Independent System Operator (ISO) had to discover the price for electricity delivered in the future through lengthy, expensive negotiation, because there was no market price for future electricity deliveries. Second, when the agreed-upon price is far different from the market price, one of the parties may default ("non-perform"). As companies that signed contracts with California for future deliveries of electricity at more than $100 a megawatt found, when current prices dropped into the range of $20 to $40 a megawatt, enforcing a "too favorable" contract is expensive and often futile. Third, one or the other party's circumstances might change. The only way for a party to back out of a forward contract is to renegotiate it and face penalties.

WHERE DOES RISK LIE—FORWARDS

When looking at cash trading or the forward market, financial managers in the oil industry tend to focus on the underlying value on the transaction:

- How many barrels
- At what price

The principal concern is over payment and performance, and one of the primary credit decisions is whether to grant open credit, the size of the open credit lines (if any), or whether bank letters of credit will be required.

Marking forward trades to market is not typical, except in periods of extreme price movements. Exposure arising from the difference between the agreed trade price and current market price is not closely monitored.

That's not to say that we shouldn't be doing this. Recommendations as to how this should be handled will be addressed under the topic "Suggested Principles for the Assessment of Derivatives."

Futures contracts solve the above-mentioned problems but introduce some of their own. Like a forward contract, a futures contract obligates each party to buy or sell a specific amount of a commodity at a specified price. Unlike a forward contract, buyers and sellers of futures contracts deal with an exchange, not with each other. For example, a producer wanting to sell crude oil in December 2006 can sell a futures contract for 1,000 barrels of West Texas Intermediate (WTI) to the New York Mercantile Exchange (NYMEX), and a refinery can buy a December 2006 oil future from the exchange. The December futures price is the one that creates offers to sell to equal bids to buy—i.e., the demand for futures equals the supply. The December futures price is public, as is the volume of trade. If the buyer of a December futures finds later that he does not need the oil, he can get out of the contract by selling a December oil future at the prevailing price. Since he has both bought and sold a December oil future, he has met his obligations to the exchange by netting them out.

Figure 10-1 on the next page illustrates how futures contracts can be used both to fix a price in advance and to guarantee performance. Suppose in January a refiner can make a sure profit by acquiring 10,000 barrels of WTI crude oil in December at the current December futures price of $28 per barrel. One way he could guarantee the December price would be to "buy" 10 WTI December contracts. The refiner pays nothing for the futures contracts but has to make a good-faith deposit ("initial margin") with his broker. NYMEX requires an initial margin per contract. During

Figure 10-1: Example of an Oil Futures Contract

Date	Prices per Barrel WTI Spot	December Future	Contract Activity	Cash In (Out)
January	$26	$28	Refiner "buys" 10 contracts for 1,000 barrels each and pays the initial margin.	($22,000)
May	$20	$26	Mark to market: $(26 - 28) \times 10{,}000$	($20,000)
September	$20	$29	Mark to market: $(29 - 26) \times 10{,}000$	$30,000
October	$27	$35	Mark to market: $(35 - 29) \times 10{,}000$	$60,000
November (end)	$35	$35	Refiner either: (a) buys oil, or (b) "sells" the contracts. Initial margin is refunded.	($350,000) $22,000

Source: Energy Information Administration.

the year, the December futures price will change in response to new information about the demand and supply of crude oil.

In the example, the December price remains constant until May, when it falls to $26 per barrel. At that point the exchange pays those who sold December futures contracts and collects from those who bought them. The money comes from the margin accounts of the refiner and other buyers. The broker then issues a "margin call," requiring the refiner to restore his margin account by adding $20,000 to it.

This "marking to market" is done every day and may be done several times during a single day. Brokers close out parties unable to pay (not able to make their margin calls) by selling their clients' futures contracts. Usually, the initial margin is enough to cover a defaulting party's losses. If not, the broker covers the loss. If the broker cannot, the exchange does. Following settlement after the first change in the December futures price, the process is started anew, but with the current price of the December future used as the basis for calculating gains and losses.

In September, the December futures price increases to $29 per barrel, the refiner's contract is marked to market, and he/she receives $30,000 from the exchange. In October, the price increases again to $35 per barrel, and the refiner receives an additional $60,000. By the end of November, the WTI spot price and the December futures price are necessarily the same, for the reasons given below. The refiner can either demand delivery and buy the oil at the spot price or "sell" his/her contract. In either event his/her initial margin is refunded, sometimes with interest. If he/she buys oil he/she pays $35 per barrel or $350,000, but his trading profit is $70,000 ($30,000 + $60,000 − $20,000). Effectively, he/she ends up paying $28 per barrel [($350,000 − $70,000) ÷ 10,000], which is precisely the January price for December futures. If he/she "sells" his/her contract he/she keeps the trading profit of $70,000.

Several features of futures are worth emphasizing. First, a party who elects to hold the contract until maturity is guaranteed the price he/she paid when it was initially bought. The buyer of the futures contract can always demand delivery; the seller can always insist on delivering. As a result, at maturity the December futures price for WTI and the spot market price will be the same. If the WTI price were lower, people would sell futures contracts and deliver oil for a guaranteed profit. If the WTI price were higher, people would buy futures and demand delivery, again for a guaranteed profit. Only when the December futures price and the December spot price are the same is the opportunity for a sure profit eliminated.

Second, a party can sell oil futures even though he/she has no access to oil. Likewise a party can buy oil even though he/she has no use for it. **Speculators** routinely buy and sell futures contracts in anticipation of price changes. Instead of delivering or accepting oil, they close out their positions before the contracts mature. Speculators perform the useful function of taking on the price risk that producers and refiners do not wish to bear.

Third, futures allow a party to make a commitment to buy or sell large amounts of oil (or other commodities) for a very small initial commitment, the initial margin. An investment of $22,000 is enough to commit a party to buy (sell) $280,000 of oil when the futures price is $28 per barrel. Consequently, traders can make large profits or suffer huge losses from small changes in the futures price. This leverage has been the source of spectacular failures in the past.

Futures contracts are not by themselves useful for all those who want to manage price risk. Futures contracts are available for only a few commodities and a few delivery locations. Nor are they available for deliveries a decade or more into the future. There is a robust business conducted outside exchanges, in the over-the-counter (OTC) market, in selling contracts to supplement futures contracts and better meet the needs of individual companies.

An **option** is a contract that gives the buyer of the contract the right to buy (a call option) or sell (a put option) at a specified price (the "strike price") over a specified period of time. **American options** allow the buyer to exercise his/her right either to buy or sell at any time until the option expires. **European options** can be exercised only at maturity. Whether the option is sold on an exchange or on the OTC market, the buyer pays for it up front. For example, the option to buy a thousand cubic feet of natural gas at a price of $3.60 in December may cost $0.73. If the price in December exceeds $3.60, the buyer can exercise the option and buy the gas for $3.60. More commonly, the option writer pays the buyer the difference between the market price and the strike price. If the natural gas price is less than $3.60, the buyer lets the option expire and loses $0.73. Options are used successfully to put floors and ceilings on prices; however, they tend to be expensive.

Swaps (also called contracts for differences) are the most recent innovation in finance. Swaps were created in part to give price certainty at a cost that is lower than the cost of options. A swap contract is an agreement between two parties to exchange a series of cash flows generated by underlying assets. No physical commodity is actually transferred between the buyer and seller. The contracts are entered into between the two counterparties, or principals, outside any centralized trading facility or exchange and are therefore characterized as OTC derivatives.

Because swaps do not involve the actual transfer of any assets or principal amounts, a base must be established in order to determine the amounts that will periodically be swapped. This principal base is known as the "**notional amount**" of the contract. For example, one person might want to "swap" the variable earnings on a million-dollar stock portfolio for the fixed interest earned on a treasury bond of the same market value. The notional amount of this swap is $1 million. Swapping avoids the expense of selling the portfolio and buying the bond. It also permits the investor to retain any capital gains that his portfolio might realize.

The following illustration (Exhibit 2) is an example of a standard crude oil swap. In the example, a refiner and an oil producer agree to enter into a 10-year crude oil swap with a monthly exchange of payments. The refiner (Party A) agrees to pay the producer (Party B) a fixed price of $25 per barrel, and the producer agrees to pay the refiner the settlement price of a futures contract for NYMEX light, sweet crude oil on the final day of trading for the contract. The notional amount of the contract is 10,000 barrels. Under this contract the payments are netted, so that the party owing the larger payment for the month makes a net payment to the party

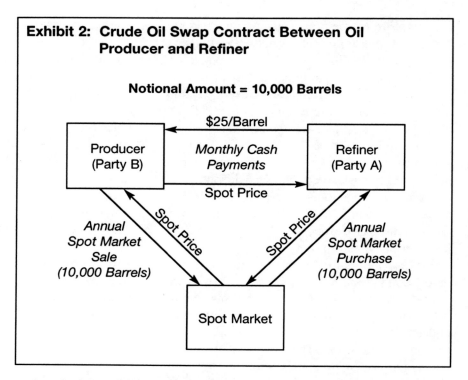

Exhibit 2: Crude Oil Swap Contract Between Oil Producer and Refiner

owing the lesser amount. If the NYMEX settlement price on the final day of trading is $23 per barrel, Party A will make a payment of $2 per barrel times 10,000, or $20,000, to Party B. If the NYMEX price is $28 per barrel, Party B will make a payment of $30,000 to Party A. The 10-year swap effectively creates a package of 120 cash-settled forward contracts, one maturing each month for 10 years.

So long as both parties in the example are able to buy and sell crude oil at the variable NYMEX settlement price, the swap guarantees a fixed price of $25 per barrel, because the producer and the refiner can combine their financial swap with physical sales and purchases in the spot market in quantities that match the nominal contract size. All that remains after the purchases and sales shown in the inner loop cancel each other out are the fixed payment of money to the producer and the refiner's purchase of crude oil. The producer never actually delivers crude oil to the refiner, nor does the refiner directly buy crude oil from the producer. All their physical purchases and sales are in the spot market, at the NYMEX price. Exhibit 3 shows the acquisition costs with and without a swap contract.

Many of the benefits associated with swap contracts are similar to those associated with futures or options contracts. That is to say, they allow

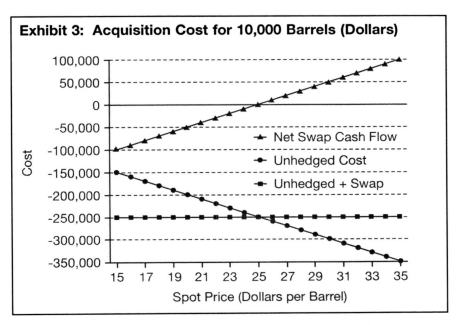

Exhibit 3: Acquisition Cost for 10,000 Barrels (Dollars)

users to manage price exposure risk without having to take possession of the commodity. They differ from exchange-traded futures and options in that, because they are individually negotiated instruments, users can customize them to suit their risk management activities to a greater degree than is easily accomplished with more standardized futures contracts or exchange-traded options. So, for instance, in the example above the floating price reference for crude oil might be switched from the NYMEX contract, which calls for delivery at Cushing, Oklahoma, to an Alaskan North Slope oil price for delivery at Long Beach, California. Such a swap contract might be more useful for a refiner located in the Los Angeles area.

Although swaps can be highly customized, the counterparties are exposed to higher credit risk because the contracts generally are not guaranteed by a clearinghouse as are exchange-traded derivatives. In addition, customized swaps generally are less liquid instruments, usually requiring parties to renegotiate terms before prematurely terminating or offsetting a contract.

WHERE DOES RISK LIE—SWAPS

Simple swaps can be viewed as equivalent to a series of forward trades. The credit risk is similar to forward trades, but each settlement point of the swap must be evaluated.

In order to measure credit exposure, you need a forward price curve for the product involved in the swap. The curve will show forward prices for the entire term of the swap. This information can be obtained from traders, planning departments, outside data services, or futures markets.

Swaps are settled in cash, based on the price difference between the fixed price and floating price established in the swap. Payments are netted, so credit risk is generally a small fraction of the "nominal" or "notional" swap amount.

There is no physical delivery involved in swaps but exposure should be measured and applied against any existing credit line or established security amount. More on this assessment and application will follow.

SWAPS TERMINOLOGY

In the cash market the terms "buyer" and "seller" are well understood, but the swaps market generally uses terms borrowed from the financial markets.

Cash Market	Swaps Market
Buyer	Fixed Price Payer
Seller	Floating Price Payer

To confuse matters further, the fixed price payer can be referred to as the "buyer" of a swap, and the floating price payer as the "seller" of a swap.

When the market price of a product such as oil is higher than the swap price, the buyer (fixed payer) has credit exposure.

When the market price is lower than the swap price, the seller (floating payer) has credit exposure.

In some cases, each party may have credit exposure at different points along the price curve. The actual exposure is the net of the exposures at each settlement point. Please refer to Exhibits 2 and 3.

MARKING SWAPS TO MARKET

There are two basic components of swap credit risk—actual risk and potential risk. Actual risk is determined by calculating the market value of a swap, or marking to market. Potential risk attempts to measure how actual risk may change during the life of the swap. This will be covered below.

The process of marking swaps to market takes several steps (*see* Exhibit 4).

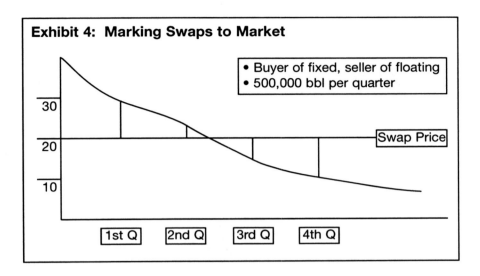

Exhibit 4: Marking Swaps to Market

- Buyer of fixed, seller of floating
- 500,000 bbl per quarter

1. Determine market price curve for the product covered by the swap.
2. For each settlement point, compare the market price to the established fixed price in the swap.
3. If the market price is higher than the fixed price, the buyer, or fixed payer, has credit exposure. If the market price is lower than the fixed price the seller, or floating payer, has credit exposure.
4. Discount future exposures at an appropriate interest rate to obtain a net present value.
5. Add up net present values to obtain the market value of the swap.

Credit risk is equal to the market value of the swap, as you are at risk for the future payments under the swap. To determine credit exposure for a counterparty, you must add up the exposure on all outstanding swaps.

Marking swaps to market—Issues to consider:

- Price curve may be difficult to determine on a long-term basis or for products with no liquid futures contract.
- Does your credit system handle swaps?
  - Marking to market on a regular basis
  - Monitoring counterparty exposure
  - Doing sensitivity analysis
- If you can't value swaps on a regular basis, can you obtain quotes from outside sources or internally from trading or risk management areas?

Exhibit 5: Derivatives Risk Tracking Report

*(Crude Oil and Heating Oil at 1,000 Barrels per Contract)
*(Natural Gas at 10,000 MMBTU's per Contract)
Dollars in thousands

Corporate Credit Services

Open positions and market prices as of 00/00/0000

counterparty	Commodity	Open Contracts	Mark to Market	Credit Limit*	Stress Test** High	Stress Test** Low	Worst Case Stress Remaining Credit Limit
counterparty XYZ	Natural Gas	44	(90)	8,000	(5,044)	5,001	2,956
counterparty XYZ	Natural Gas	6	(12)	15,000	56	56	15,000
counterparty XYZ	Natural Gas	1	(56)	2,000	(56)	(56)	1,944
counterparty XYZ	Natural Gas	6	220	20,000	(663)	780	19,337
counterparty XYZ	Natural Gas	12	(132)	50,000	(132)	(132)	49,868
counterparty XYZ	Natural Gas	163	1,215	50,000	8,818	(6,388)	43,612
counterparty XYZ	Natural Gas	17	(594)	0	(1,036)	(151)	(1,036)
counterparty XYZ	Natural Gas	155	(458)	50,000	346	(1,263)	48,737
counterparty XYZ	Natural Gas	3	24	2,000	24	24	2,000
counterparty XYZ	Natural Gas	10	4	10,000	(144)	151	9,856
counterparty XYZ	Natural Gas	8	274	1,000	(316)	864	684
counterparty XYZ	Natural Gas	2	75	5,000	129	20	5,000
counterparty XYZ	Natural Gas	67	1,880	16,000	(1,341)	5,103	14,659
counterparty XYZ	Natural Gas	6	(157)	4,000	(27)	(287)	3,713
counterparty XYZ	Natural Gas	29	(255)	150,000	2,408	(2,918)	147,082
counterparty XYZ	Natural Gas	6	(19)	100,000	(19)	(19)	99,981
counterparty XYZ	Natural Gas	46	625	30,000	7,562	(6,312)	23,688
counterparty XYZ	Natural Gas	1	15	10,000	15	15	10,000
counterparty XYZ	Natural Gas	10	626	15,000	91	1,161	15,000
counterparty XYZ	Natural Gas	3	322	10,000	175	470	10,000
counterparty XYZ	Natural Gas	154	(639)	30,000	3,023	(4,300)	5,700
counterparty XYZ	Natural Gas	30	614	30,000	4,712	(3,484)	26,517
counterparty XYZ	Natural Gas	14	50	10,000	(1,167)	1,268	8,833
counterparty XYZ	Natural Gas	1	16	10,000	(100)	133	9,900
counterparty XYZ	Natural Gas	29	(417)	5,000	(439)	(395)	4,561
counterparty XYZ	Natural Gas	1	15	30,000	15	15	30,000
counterparty XYZ	Natural Gas	1	7	4,000	7	7	4,000
counterparty XYZ	Natural Gas	24	242	50,000	94	389	50,000
counterparty XYZ	Natural Gas	1	21	5,000	21	21	5,000
counterparty XYZ	Natural Gas	13	1,082	7,000	1,082	1,082	7,000
counterparty XYZ	Natural Gas	(14)	921	50,000	6,275	246	50,000
counterparty XYZ	Natural Gas	55	(720)	50,000	(3,467)	2,033	46,533
counterparty XYZ	Crude Oil	(500)	(556)	100,000	944	(2,056)	97,712
counterparty XYZ	Natural Gas	4	(131)	(49)	311		
counterparty XYZ	Light Oil Products	77	47		(184)	278	
counterparty XYZ	Light Oil Products	(228)	288	50,000	973	(395)	49,605
counterparty XYZ	Natural Gas	26	(147)	30,000	78	(372)	27,482
	Crude Oil	(300)	(642)		258	(1,542)	
	Light Oil Products	457	767		(604)	2,138	

Mark to Market positions with positive values represent a receivable to you, while negative values represent liabilities.

*Customers with a zero credit limit must be secured with a Bank Letter of Credit.

**Price environment sensitivity utilizes a plus or minus $.50/mmbtu higher natural gas and plus or minus $3.00/bbl higher crude oil prices than current market prices.

EVALUATING POTENTIAL SWAPS RISK

Many swaps transactions have little or no actual credit risk at inception. However, it is important to evaluate potential credit exposure, which may develop during the life of the swap. Potential exposure depends entirely on your assumptions for future price movements.

HOW IS POTENTIAL RISK QUANTIFIED?

- Create a "worst case" price scenario for the underlying price curve.
- Mark the swap to market under the new price scenario. Keep in mind the following guidelines:
  - You need to look at price movements in either direction.
  - Evaluate the entire counterparty portfolio.
  - Price movements in the short-term price curve are always more extreme than the long-term price curve.
  - If you are not reasonable in your "worst case" assumptions you may limit trading by being too conservative.

CONTROLLING SWAPS CREDIT RISK

As with any extension of credit, each counterparty must be evaluated individually for capital, financial performance, etc. There are several ways to control swaps credit exposure:

- Trading limits
- Margin/Collateral
- Documentation triggers
- Transaction flexibility

SETTING TRADING LIMITS

Swaps trading limits must be set and monitored differently than cash trading limits. Things to be considered with this evaluation are as follows:

- Nominal Value or Notional Value limits measure the full underlying value of the swap (Quantity × Fixed Price). This measure is not very accurate, but will give you a basis for measuring potential credit risk.
- Mark-to-Market (MTM) Exposure limits measuring the actual credit risk at a given point in time.

- "Worst Case" Exposure measures the potential risk which would result if the market moved significantly in either direction.
- Maximum Term of swaps transactions should be established for each counterparty. As the term increases, the probability increases of (1) a larger price move, or (2) financial deterioration of the counterparty.
- An alternative limit methodology involves a risk formula, which is typically used by banks to manage currency, and interest rate swaps risk. The formula accounts for:
  - Terms of swap
  - Notional amount
  - Underlying product risk

This is obviously a more sophisticated credit approach, but should be considered if you become active in trading swaps. The utilization of stress test formulas that incorporate factors such as Periodicity, Volatility, and Standard Deviations to predict Value at Risk should be properly assessed.

See the Derivatives Risk Tracking Report spreadsheet (Exhibit 5), which attempts to summarize the various risk positions from MTM to "Worst Case" against a given counterparty credit limit.

MARGIN/COLLATERAL

The use of margin or collateral is an effective way of controlling swaps and options risk, but has not been widely accepted in the industry. Margin or collateral is paid to the party that has credit exposure. A predetermined credit limit is set, and no margin is paid until credit exposure exceeds that limit by an agreed upon dollar amount. Additional margin is paid (or returned) as the credit exposure changes over time.

Margin/Collateral Issues

- What is the initial margin threshold where payments begin?
- What form does margin/collateral take:
  - Cash
  - Securities
  - Letters of Credit
- What party is responsible for the calculations?
- Can your credit system and operations staff deal with monitoring margin and making required payments? Paying and collecting dollars between companies and accurately monitoring exposures could be an administrative challenge.

STANDARD CREDIT TERMS

Financial Transactions Under a Master Agreement

The standard ISDA will have either an adequate assurance clause or a material adverse change clause. These clauses are in addition to the Credit Support Annex which gives firm collateral rights (with the threshold going to zero in the event that a party triggers an Event of Default or Termination Event. Changes to the Adequate Assurance Clause and the Material Adverse Change clause are approved by credit analysts, but are only seen by the credit manager in special circumstances. No ISDAs are done without a CSA unless express authority is given by a credit manager.

> ***Adequate Assurance.*** If a party (the "Demanding Party") has reasonable good faith belief, that, due to a change in the financial condition or other event of the other party (the "Failing Party"), or the other party's Credit Support Provider, the ability of the other party or its Credit Support Provider to perform its obligations to the Demanding Party under this Agreement or any Credit Support Document is materially impaired (the "Good Faith Belief"), then the Demanding Party may demand Adequate Assurance of performance of those obligations. The Failing Party shall provide said Adequate Assurance within two (2) business days after receipt by the Failing Party of a written demand from the Demanding Party for such assurance, which demand shall describe the specific information on which the Good Faith Belief is based. "Adequate Assurance" shall be in a form acceptable to Demanding Party acting in its own discretion and in any case Adequate Assurance in the form of Eligible Credit Support (as defined in the Credit Support Annex, if applicable) shall be deemed acceptable. The Demanding Party may hold the Adequate Assurance only so long as the Demanding Party continues to have the Good Faith Belief. Any Adequate Assurance in the form of Eligible Credit Support shall be held in addition to any requirements to post Eligible Credit Support under the Credit Support Annex, if applicable. The failure of the Failing Party to provide Adequate Assurance within two (2) business days after receipt of demand therefore shall be considered an Additional Termination Event with the Failing Party as the sole Affected Party.

> ***Material Adverse Change.*** The occurrence of a Material Adverse Change (as hereinafter defined) with respect to a Party ("X") (which will be the Affected Party). "Material Adverse Change" means: a reduction in Credit Rating of X by either Standard and Poor's Ratings

Group (a division of The McGraw-Hill Companies, Inc.), or its successor (S&P) to below "BBB-"; or Moody's Investors Service, Inc., or its successor ("Moody's") to below "Baa3"; or the Credit Ratings of the relevant entity are withdrawn by both of S&P and Moody's. For the avoidance of doubt, it will not be a Material Adverse Change if X is no longer rated by one of S&P or Moody's and the remaining agency issuing a Credit Rating rates the relevant entity BBB- or higher (if it is S&P) or Baa3 or higher (if it is Moody's). If X has a Credit Support Provider, Material Adverse Change shall be determined instead, solely with respect to such Credit Support Provider, and the Credit Rating or lack thereof of X shall not constitute a Material Adverse Change. A Material Adverse Change shall be treated as an Illegality for all purposes of this Agreement.

Another check that must be performed prior to engaging in derivatives activity with a given counterparty is to confirm that the entity is eligible to engage in such activity. The following verbiage illustrates this point as established by the U.S. Commodity Futures Modernization Act.

CERTIFICATE OF ELIGIBILITY AS AN ELIGIBLE COMMERCIAL ENTITY UNDER THE U.S. COMMODITY FUTURES MODERNIZATION ACT

1. _____ ("Energy Derivatives Counterparty") hereby certifies that it is and will continue to be an **"eligible commercial entity"** as defined in Section 1a of the U.S. Commodity Exchange Act (as amended) unless and until Energy Derivatives Counterparty notifies Demanding Party otherwise in writing. The definition of the term "eligible commercial entity" is attached. Demanding Party cannot provide legal advice to its counterparties, and Energy Derivatives Counterparty should direct any questions respecting its categorization to its legal counsel.

The term "eligible commercial entity" means it has (with respect to an agreement, contract, or transaction in a commodity):

- a demonstrable ability, directly or through separate contractual arrangements, to make or take delivery of the underlying commodity;
- at least total assets that equal or exceed the required amount;

- other various rules which you should be familiar with before engaging with a given counterparty.

Documentation Credit Issues—Typical Clauses

- Netting and bankruptcy language should be included which gives you the right to net and offset all swaps with a counterparty in case of default or bankruptcy. This language will avoid "cherry picking" risk.
- Merger and Ownership language will trigger a default if the counterparty (1) sells off a substantial part of its assets, or (2) merges with another entity, which does not assume its obligations.
- Default based on specific credit ratings or minimum capital levels are often used to monitor credit risk. However, these can work against you too.
- Material Adverse Change (MAC) clauses are blanket clauses that allow you to declare a default if there is a material change in the counterparty's business of financial standing. Many companies avoid MAC clauses because they are vague and open to interpretation.
- Cross-Default clauses allow you to declare a default if the counterparty defaults on other obligations to you and/or their parties.
- In the case of a default, the non-defaulting party has the right to close out open trades and compute a net settlement, which is due immediately.

SWAPS FLEXIBILITY

There are a few ways that deals can be structured to help reduce credit risk, or at least give you more flexibility in managing credit risk.

- Frequency of settlements will have an impact on credit risk management. The more frequently you settle during the swap life, the greater your ability to gradually reduce credit risk.
- If you can reset the fixed price level during the life of the swap, it allows credit risk to be brought back to a reasonable level. Price reset agreements are not typical.
- Swaps involving liquid energy products (WTI, Brent, or Gulf Coast product for example) allow for more accurate risk management due to price availability and numerous market participants. Less liquid

products limit your ability to monitor risk, as do highly customized deals.
- The more actively traded products offer the best opportunities to close out a position in case of default.

KEYS TO SWAPS CREDIT

- *Understand the Products*. Learn about swaps and how they are used in your company. Build relationships with your traders and risk managers to tap into their knowledge.
- *Systems*. Build or buy systems to value swaps and monitor counterparty credit risk. This is generally a difficult process.
- *Establish Swaps Guidelines*. Determine credit requirements for swaps counterparties, and internal guidelines for size, term, etc. Work to apply these consistently.
- *Integrate Trading and Credit*. Learn what the traders want to do, and try to accommodate their needs within the credit guidelines. Educate traders on credit requirements for swaps. Communicate!
- *Careful Documentation*. Do not ignore this critical area, and do not assume legal personnel will address all credit concerns.
- *Know Your Counterparty*. Do they hedge or speculate? What is their industry trading reputation?

BASIS RISK

As we know, very few hedged transactions result in a "perfect" hedge. The movement between cash and futures prices is rarely perfectly parallel. Basis is the term used for the difference in cash and futures prices. Changes in the basis refer to the relative price movements of cash versus futures prices. The price of the actual commodity is often referred to as the "cash price" or simply the "cash." More exactly, basis is cash price minus the futures price, and not the other way around. The basis narrows if cash prices rise more or they fall less than futures prices. The basis widens if cash prices rise more or fall less than futures prices.

How is basis risk measured? There are three possible ways:

1. *Historic vs. Current*. The simplest method of basis risk measurement is to determine the range of the basis over time using historical price data, and compare the current basis with its historical range.

2. *Standard Deviation*. Dispersion around the mean of the basis should be calculated. This is a standard statistical measure of overall variability. The higher the standard deviation relative to the value of the cash and futures prices, the higher the dispersion and the greater the basis risk.

3. *Correlation Coefficient*. Determines the degree of correlation between two price data series. This measures the degree to which two prices tend to move together, or correlate. A high percentage correlation indicates a stable basis.

When analyzing basis risk statistics, it is important to remember that the time period of the data and various delivery locations will have an enormous impact on results. Seasonal factors, significant political events and other important factors that can affect supply/demand fundamentals (major oil spills, refinery shut-downs, pipeline breaks, etc.) will affect basis relationships.

In summary, potential risk must be measured and monitored. We qualify the type of basis risk (location, quality, calendar), then measure the risk with several measurement methods, manage the risk with a hedge, and monitor the risk daily.

As stated, there are three types of basis risk:

1. *Location Risk*. When the physical market is a different location than that specified by the futures contract.

2. *Quality Risk*. When the physical commodity is a different grade or quality than that specified by the futures contract. Also known as intermarket risk.

3. *Calendar Risk*. The price of the nearby futures contract and the underlying physical market change over time. How do the seasonal patterns differ?

As an extremely flexible delivery option, the exchange for physical (EFP) provides a mechanism for managing basis risk. EFPs can be affected by trading parties (one must be a long hedger, the other a short hedger) as long as there is a concurrent physical transaction between the parties.

EFPs allow delivery to take place in a different location than that specified by the futures contract. In addition, the EFP delivery may alter the quality specification.

In an EFP, traders effectively swap their futures positions, resulting in futures hedge liquidation for both parties, and the transfer of the physical commodity takes place according to their own terms.

It is important that we measure the reduction of risk achieved by hedging. The formula for calculating hedge efficiency is:

$$HE = \frac{var\ (hedge)}{var\ (exposure)}$$

Var (hedge) represents the variance of the value of the hedge position. The var (exposure) term represents the variance of the value of the unhedged exposure series.

+1.0 = Perfect Hedge: 100% of risk is eliminated
+0.5 = Poor Hedge: 50% of risk is eliminated
0.0 = Useless Hedge: No risk at all is eliminated
−0.5 = worse than useless Hedge: Hedge is riskier

RISK CATEGORIES AND DEFINITIONS

Basis Risk. The risk that arises when a hedge and the instrument being hedged is imperfectly matched; since their prices may not move in tandem there is a possibility of losses arising.

Credit Risk. The risk that a counterparty to a transaction will not live up to its financial obligations. Derivative credit risk is different from loan credit risk because the amount at risk is dynamic and reflects changing prices and volatility of the underlying asset.

Market Risk. The risks brought about by changes in market conditions. Major components of market risks are price, volatility, time decay, and basis (correlation) risk.

Operational Risk. The risk of unexpected losses arising from deficiencies in management information, support control systems.

Price Risk. The exposure resulting from a change in the price of an underlying asset or instrument.

Systemic Risk. The risk associated with segments of the financial system breaking down due to its inability to cope with large quantities of market, credit, or settlement risks.

Value-at-Risk. A measure of the aggregate market risk facing a company. It is the amount of money a company could lose or make due to price changes in the underlying markets. Since companies are more worried about potential losses rather than gains, VAR has become synonymous with the maximum losses over a certain time period and for a selected level of confidence.

Volatility. A measure of the price fluctuation of an asset. Volatility is measured in terms of standard deviations, and the norm is to express the volatility of an asset as a one or two standard deviation price change, in percent, over a one-year period. So if an asset had a volatility of 15 percent, that meant that the asset's price would be expected to fluctuate within a range 15 percent higher or lower than the forward price. The higher the volatility, the higher the expected price range and the more expensive the option (since the chances of the option becoming profitable are higher).

SUGGESTED PRINCIPLES FOR THE ASSESSMENT OF DERIVATIVES

Credit Risk

When it comes to assessing a customer's Derivatives Credit Risk, your evaluation should include two separate elements, Payment Risk and Performance Risk. Other than these two, there are other inherent risks such as market liquidity risk, sovereign risk, document risk; but payment and performance are the two primary risks.

Payment Risk

This describes the risk of payment not being made after product has been delivered and passed legal title, or a swap has been priced out. This can arise from two basic causes:

(i) The payment instrument put in place (e.g., letter of credit) proves to be unenforceable.

(ii) An open credit counterparty "chooses" not to make payment or can't make payment in accordance with the terms of sale.

Item (i) is a matter of having the appropriate operational controls to ensure that appropriate payment documentation is in place prior to contract delivery.

Item (ii) is the risk that we traditionally evaluate and define as "credit risk." A qualitative and quantitative evaluation of the counterparties' financial status is conducted in advance of the transaction. This determines the amount of "open credit" (if any) we are willing to advance such as the monetary value of the cargo or instrument (e.g., a swap) against which we will transfer legal title without further protection. (Note, in the case of state or quasi-state owned companies, there is an element of "sovereign risk" and this evaluation should encompass broader aspects of ability or willingness to meet financial obligations on payment commitments). This risk can be mitigated by the provision of certain contractual protections—Master Trade Agreements (MTA) or Net-Out Agreements and other security enhancements (credit derivatives, call options, credit insurance).

Performance Risk

This describes the risk that a counterparty will non-perform on a contract before title passes on a physical cargo or the contract prices out in the case of a swap. Beyond that point the risk transfers from being performance risk to payment risk per our definition. There are two elements to this exposure on any given contract:

1. The MTM (Mark-to-Market) exposure on the open deal at current prices.
2. A statistical calculation as to how far out of the money (for the counterparty) this contract might reasonably be expected to move between now and physical delivery (or pricing out of a swap) occurring. Clearly, the longer the contract has before delivery, the greater this risk is.

In theory, one should weigh performance risk on a graded scale, the presumption being that a counterparty is increasingly likely to non-perform against a contract as the MTM goes against them on an open contract. One could further debate whether a counterparty is likely to default just because an open MTM is well out of the money—would they not wait until the last moment in the hope of a recovery from their perspective? In practice, one should be content with setting absolute limits to the performance risk one is prepared to tolerate. When weighing the performance risk of a counterparty on a "graded scale," the weaker the counterparty, the greater the chance that the company is likely to default.

For exchange-traded business this risk is very largely eliminated because of the obligation on all counterparties to post daily margins. (Elimination of risk comes from the Exchange itself who stands behind the deal and allows only so many contracts per company and sets very high financial standards. Margin calls serve as a barometer but true risk mitigation exists in knowing that the Exchange is there backing each deal). This facility does not formally exist in OTC paper or physical business. Instead, we must seek to devise performance risk limits, expressed in dollar terms that capture both the volume and forward duration of open contracts with any given counterparty.

Strictly speaking, performance risk exists on all contracts. A complex matrix would allow the same theories to be applied to floating price contracts whereby you calculate the current MTM exposure (if any), plus the theoretical change in any basis risk. Thus, a forward purchase of Urals, to be priced off Platt's Urals assessment on B/L date would constitute a lower risk than one loading at the same future date but priced at a fixed differential to dated Brent. In the interests of a speedy and practical application, at this stage we propose to only evaluate performance risk on forward fixed price contracts.

From the VAR (Value at Risk) database we can readily calculate the expected change in MTM price of any forward fixed price contract between now and the contract undergoing delivery or pricing. Using the absolute price of Brent as an example, the average volatility over the past year can be calculated as measured by time to contract maturity.

Presuming we have an MTA in place with a counterparty, we can legally offset contracts and limit our performance risk to the MTM difference in the offsetting contracts. However, this offers no protection in the event that no offset exists, i.e., we have a net long or short position with the counterparty. In this case we have the following trading options to cap or limit our ongoing performance risk.

A. A ban on future business does nothing to cap risk on the existing positions, it just ensures that we do not increase our volumetric exposure.

B. Only agree to future business that generates offsets, but refuse anything that increases our net exposure.

C. Demand a margin payment from the counterparty, either as a term of the original contract negotiation or as a condition for conducting further business.

Points A, B, and C above are most commonly used to mitigate risk, but other forms do exist such as credit derivatives or buying call options. They can be expensive alternatives, however.

QUESTIONS WE SHOULD ASK OURSELVES IN ORDER TO MITIGATE CREDIT RISK

1. The question we should ask is how much performance risk are you prepared to tolerate with each counterparty?
2. Will we be able to limit performance risk prescriptively with some counterparties, i.e., with margin-type provisions?
3. Even if we conduct no new business with a counterparty and market prices don't change, our performance risk can increase over

time. For example, we are long one June Crude Oil Cargo and short one July; in May these positions offset to net zero under an MTA, but after the June cargo delivers we show a net open exposure. Can we set prescriptive limits for performance risk that accurately capture this aspect of changing exposure, or must we accept the need to respond by adjusting our trading patterns over time, for example, by generating new offsets as earlier ones expire?

Derivatives Credit Risk Management

Credit risk is the risk that a loss will be incurred if a counterparty defaults on a derivatives contract. The loss due to a default is the cost of replacing the contract, less any recovery.

The derivatives credit role should be defined within each company. This definition should consist of the following:

- explicit definition of what constitutes derivatives credit risk;
- monitor the defined risk with the development of a consolidated tracking report; and
- ensure that all trading parties stay in compliance with the established and published levels of counterparty credit.

Derivatives credit risk can be explicitly defined by referencing five separate areas that require daily monitoring. The previous Excel spreadsheet (Exhibit 5) represents a consolidated tracking report approach to identifying this risk and also total risk exposure based on future market volatility. The five risk areas for tracking and their definitions are as follows:

1. *Mark-to-Market*. Calculated change between the contract price and current market price.
2. *Value-at-Risk*. The possible loss related to uncertain movements in various market risk factors.
3. *Counterparty Risk*. The possible loss incurred if the counterparty is unable to honor its engagements.
4. *Brokerage/Bank Risk*. The possible loss of money and representation if financial difficulties were to cause a closing.
5. *Equity Risk*. A firm is required to make daily deposits and margin calls. These dollars reside in the respective broker accounts. In the event of a firm's failure, the company's money would be tied up in bankruptcy court for an indefinite period of time.

Figure 10-2: Petroleum and Natural Gas Price Risks and Risk Management Strategies

Participants	Price Risks	Risk Management Strategies and Derivative Instruments Employed
Oil Producers	Low crude oil price	Sell crude oil future, buy put option
Petroleum Refiners	High crude oil price	Buy crude oil future or call option
	Low product price	Sell product future or swap contract, but put option
	Thin profit margin	Buy crack spread[a]
Storage Operators	High purchase price or low sale price	Buy or sell futures
Large Consumers • Local Distribution Companies (Natural Gas)	Unstable prices, wholesale prices higher than retail	Buy future or call option, buy basis contract[b]
• Power Plants (Natural Gas)	Thin profit margin	Buy spark spread[c]
• Airlines and Shippers	High fuel price	Buy swap contract

[a] Essentially, buy crude oil future and simultaneously sell product future.
[b] A basis contract fixes the transportation cost between Henry Hub and a local market.
[c] Buy natural gas future and sell electricity future.

Source: Energy Information Administration

The credit department should factor the identified exposure against any existing credit line for a given counterparty, brokerage firm, or financial institution. If the established credit line is exceeded as a result of this additional exposure, then consideration should be given to raising the credit line or requesting security or a wire payment that lowers the overall paper and physical exposure; or obtain a written waiver from the appropriate marketing authority to cover the overage amount.

Derivatives credit risk management should be viewed as a proactive process, where at each step, the company must ask whether the expenditure of resources adds adequate qualitative and quantitative benefits to the company.

OIL AND NATURAL GAS MARKETS: A GROWING ROLE FOR DERIVATIVES

Diversification and insurance are the major tools for managing exploration risk and protecting firms from property loss and liability. Firms manage volume risk (not having adequate supplies) by maintaining inventories or acquiring productive assets. Derivatives are particularly appropriate for managing the price risk that arises as a result of highly volatile prices in the petroleum and natural gas industries. The typical price risks faced by market participants and the standard derivative contracts used to manage those risks are shown in the table on the previous page.

The Internet is responsible for the latest innovation in energy trading. In November 1999, Enron Online was launched to facilitate physical and financial trading. Enron Online was a principal-based exchange in which all trades were done with Enron as the counterparty. As a consequence, Enron's perceived creditworthiness was crucial to its ability to operate Enron Online. After the launch of Enron Online, several other online exchanges quickly followed, including Intercontinental-Exchange (ICE), which was backed by major producers and financial services companies, and TradeSpark, which was backed by major electric utilities, traders, and gas pipeline companies. Both ICE and TradeSpark provide electronic trading platforms offering registered users anonymity for posting prices and executing trades. Unlike Enron Online, they do not take trading positions. ICE offers swaps on crude oils other than Brent and West Texas Intermediate and on refined products in numerous locations, to complement the futures contracts trading of NYMEX and the International Petroleum Exchange (IPE).

CONDENSED SUMMARY SHEET OF OPTIONS, FUTURES AND SWAPS

Exhibit 6, which follows, was designed as a simple tool to assist in understanding some of the essential points when looking at Options, Futures and Swaps. This should add some clarity to a rather complex array of transactions.

Terminology

Forward Contract: A contract between a buyer and seller, whereby the buyer is obligated to take delivery and the seller is obligated to provide delivery of a fixed amount of commodity at a predetermined fixed price on a specified future date. Payment in full is due at the time of, or following, delivery. This differs from a futures contract where settlement is made daily, resulting in partial payment over the life of the contract.

Futures: Must be traded on an exchange (NYMEX, IPE) and valued and margined daily.

Futures Contract: An exchange traded contract between a buyer and a seller and the clearinghouse of a futures exchange, whereby the buyer is obligated to take delivery and the seller is obligated to provide future delivery of a fixed amount of a commodity at a predetermined price at a specific location. Futures contracts are most often liquidated prior to the delivery date and are generally used as a financial risk management and investment tool rather than for supply purposes. These contracts are traded exclusively on regulated exchanges and are settled daily based on their current value in the marketplace.

In-the-money: Buyer will want to exercise or liquidate to gain profit.

In-the-money, at-the-money, out-of-the-money: The strike price, or exercise price, of an option determines whether that contract is in-the-money, at-the-money, or out-of-the-money. If the strike price of a call option is less than the current market price of the underlying security, the call is said to be in-the-money because the holder of this call has the right to buy the stock at a price which is less than the price he would have to pay to buy the stock in the stock market. Likewise, if a put option has a strike price that is greater than the current market price of the underlying security, it is also said to be in-the-money because the holder of this put has the right to sell the stock at a price which is greater than the price he would receive selling the stock in the stock market. The converse of in-the-money is, not surprisingly, out-of-the-money. If the strike price equals the current market price, the option is said to be at-the-money.

The amount by which an option, call, or put, is in-the-money at any given moment is called its intrinsic value. Thus, by definition, an at-the-money or out-of-the-money option has no intrinsic value; the time value is the total option premium. This does not mean, however, these options can be obtained at no cost. Any amount by which an option's total premium exceeds intrinsic value is called the time value portion of the premium. It is the time value portion of an option's premium that is affected by fluctuations in volatility, interest rates, dividend amounts, and the passage of time. There are other factors that give options value and therefore affect the premium at which they are traded. Together, all of these factors determine time value.

OTC: Over-the-counter market.

Out-of-the-money: No exchange of money. Option worthless—seller keeps premium.

Swap: The obligation to pay or receive cash based on a physical commodity at a later date. A swap is an agreement to exchange different cash flows (i.e., fixed for floating price, involves exchanging variable commodity price payments for a fixed commodity price).

Exhibit 6: Analyzing Energy Transaction Risk

	Credit Risk				Market Risk			
	XYZ Buys		XYZ Sells		XYZ Buys		XYZ Sells	
	Put	Call	Put	Call	Put	Call	Put	Call
NYMEX	No	NYMEX is the counterparty and guarantees performance.	No credit risk as NYMEX guarantees payment of premium. NYMEX margins the option seller everyday.		No market risk. Premium paid up front by buyer. NYMEX guarantees performance, and pays when option is exercised or liquidated, regardless of in/at/out-of-money status.		Unlimited market risk as price goes in-the-money. Buyer (through NYMEX clearinghouse) exercises option and receives payment from seller. NYMEX guarantees performance, but buyer exercises option.	
OTC	Credit risk is unlimited and based on creditworthiness of counterparty and their ability to pay when option is in-the-money and exercised. Credit exposure is evident as the replacement cost may be higher should the counter-party fail to pay as required.		Credit risk until premium received. Standard payment term is three (3) days from execution of contract. When option is exercised, and physically settled, credit risk is unlimited and based on creditworthiness of counterparty and their ability to pay.		No market risk. counterparty assumes all market risk. Buyer pays premium up front and is paid when option is in-the-money and exercised. However, if the option is tied to physical and buyer exercises the option, buyer assumes the risk of having to replace physical barrels on the spot market is the counterparty defaults. This will be referred to as performance risk.		When seller sells an option, they are, in turn, acting as a company establishing the base line value of the option. Seller assumes the market risk when the option is in-the-money and exercised. seller might cover this risk by buying a counter back-to-back hedge in the market. This has unlimited market risk to seller when the counterparty exercises option as the option goes in-the-money.	

Table title row: Options

	Futures		Swaps	
	Credit Risk	**Market Risk**	**Credit Risk**	**Market Risk**
NYMEX	No credit risk, when buyer enters into a futures contract on NYMEX. The NYMEX guarantees payment. NYMEX is protected by clearing mechanisms and margins.	Unlimited market risk as the price deviates from your position on the futures (e.g., Buy fix/Sell index or Sell fix/Buy index).	NA	NA
OTC	NA	NA	Credit risk is unlimited and based on creditworthiness of counterparty. Negligible if cleared through NYMEX Clearport.	Market risk is unlimited and defined as the amount price deviates from your position on the Swap (e.g., Buy fix/Sell index or Sell fix/Buy index).

Chapter 11

EVALUATING HLCs, LBOs, LLCs AND SUBCHAPTER "S" CORPORATIONS

THE VARIOUS FORMS OF BUSINESS ENTITIES

In a commercial context there are numerous forms of business entities under which a potential customer can operate and carry on business. The form of business entity can be an important element in your analysis of the overall risk of nonpayment with respect to credit sales. Each entity shares some common attributes and has some unique characteristics. Credit professionals should keep in mind that state law generally controls each form of business entity. Therefore, some variation among different jurisdictions may exist. Because there has been a slow evolution in the types of business entities operating today, one should always be diligent when encountering a new form of business entity so as to maximize the likelihood that payment will be made on a complete and timely basis.

Corporations

A "corporation" is an artificial person or legal entity created by or under the authority of the laws of a state or nation. A corporation can be either privately or publicly held.

A "close" corporation is one whose shares are held by either a single or small group of shareholders. Typically, there are no public investors and the shareholders are directly involved in the management of the company.

A "public" corporation is one whose securities are registered under the securities laws of the applicable jurisdiction. Typically, a public corporation has public investors or shareholders who are not actively involved in the management of the company. The shareholders of a corporation elect a board of directors whose job is to oversee the officers of a company in the management of the business on a day-to-day basis.

A "C" corporation is the most common form of a corporation. The corporate entity is treated as a separate taxable unit. Therefore, profits earned by the corporation are taxed at the corporate level. Thereafter, if the profits are distributed to the shareholders in the form of "dividends," such dividends are again taxable to the shareholders individually as income.

An "S" corporation is often found in smaller corporations. This combines the limited liability of a corporation with the taxable benefits of a partnership. Under the Internal Revenue Tax Code, certain profits and losses are not taxed at the corporate level, but are rather passed through the corporation to the shareholder. This avoids the imposition of a "double tax" often found in a C corporation.

Limited Liability Companies

An LLC is a legal entity created by or under the authority of the laws of a state. An LLC, when properly structured, provides limited liability protection to its owners, often referred to as "members," and provides similar tax advantages to that of an S corporation. The benefit of an LLC to its owners is that the members, like shareholders of a corporation, have limited liability, while at the same time they enjoy the same tax benefits as that of a partnership (e.g., the profits and losses are passed through the LLC to the individual members). The benefit to a seller is that, if structured properly, all of the LLC's cash flow should be available to satisfy creditor claims with all tax liabilities being the responsibility of the member rather than the LLC. When dealing with an LLC, be aware that new companies which expect losses during the early years often choose the LLC designation because of the tax benefits. As a result, make sure that the LLC was properly structured to begin with so that it enjoys the expected tax benefits without cash flow interruption that will allow it to take care of ongoing business requirements and short-term payment obligations. Therefore, a credit professional may wish, where possible, to obtain an opinion from an outside accountant or similar professional to ensure that the LLC has been correctly structured.

General Partnership

A general partnership is formed when two or more competent persons agree (whether orally or in writing) to place their money, efforts, labor, and skill in lawful commerce or business with the understanding that there shall be proportional sharing of the profits and losses between them. General partnerships are generally a pass-through entity and are therefore not independently subject to taxation. All taxes are due and payable by the individual members of the partnership directly. In addition, each partner is jointly and severally liable for all of the debts and obligations of the partnership.

Limited Partnership

A limited partnership is a partnership consisting of one or more general partners and one or more limited partners. In a limited partnership, the general partners are jointly and severally liable for the obligations of the partnership while the limited partners are only responsible for the debts or liabilities of the partnership up to the amount of the capital, which such limited partner contributed to the partnership.

Sole Proprietorship

A sole proprietorship generally consists of a single individual operating in a business context without the use of a corporation, partnership, or similar type of entity. The owner is directly responsible for all the liabilities of the sole proprietorship.

Trust

A trust is a contractual or fiduciary relationship created for the receipt of property to be administered by a trustee for another person's benefit. During the formation of a trust, beneficiaries must be designated and a trustee specifically appointed. A trust is most often governed by a trust agreement.

What are the benefits and dangers of selling on credit to entities operating in other than an individual capacity? As noted above, generally only sole proprietorships and general partnerships automatically make all of the owners of the business entity liable for the debts of that entity. In most circumstances, when dealing with a corporation, limited liability company or trust, you can only look to such entity for repayment of the debt, absent (1) some other agreement such as a guarantee or (2) a court determines to "pierce the corporate veil" and hold shareholders or members liable for such entity's debts, or (3) there has been a distribution in violation of the law. Only the general partners of a limited partnership will have direct liability for the obligations of such business entity. As mentioned above, the limited partners of the a limited partnership will only have liability up to the amount of their contributed capital, although limited partners may be liable as general partners if they participate in the management of the partnership business.

EVALUATING THE VARIOUS FORMS OF BUSINESS ENTITIES

Being able to differentiate between the safe and the risky HLCs (highly leveraged companies), LBOs (leveraged buyouts), LLCs (Limited

Liability Companies), and Subchapter S Corporations has become a major challenge and responsibility.

Highly Leveraged Companies (HLCs)

The key to assessing the financial health of an HLC is its operating cash flow. It is vital that the credit manager, therefore, monitor the cash flow of the highly leveraged customers. A highly leveraged customer can be identified as such if its debt-to-worth ratio exceeds 3-to-1.

Financial Analysis

The Statement of Cash Flows allows the reader to see how the company receives and disburses funds. This statement is an important gauge of operating performance. Many HLCs fail because they are unable to pay their various debt obligations as they come due.

Since many HLCs have exhausted their access to borrowed funds, cash generated from operations is closely linked to their financial survival. And because many HLCs have calculated their debt-service capacity closely, even a relatively small glitch or market downturn, in operating performance can signal serious trouble.

HLCs rely heavily on their operating margins to generate funds to pay interest and retire debt on schedule. Insufficient cash flow may force companies to sell assets and/or subsidiaries to generate funds to avoid default. A cash flow shortage may force layoffs and cause late payments to suppliers.

The most critical ratio to look at when selling to HLCs is the interest coverage ratio. All HLCs depend, for their financial survival, on their ability to pay their bank interest expenses promptly. The formula for calculating interest coverage is:

$$\frac{\text{Operating Cash Flow}}{\text{Interest Expense Paid}}$$

A ratio above 3:1 is desirable. If the ratio falls below 3, a default could result from liquidity problems, that is, not having cash readily available when needed. Interest coverage approaching 1:1 constitutes an emergency problem. Generally speaking, bankruptcies have occurred where the firm's interest coverage ratio was below 1:1. Other LBOs with low interest coverage ratios have avoided bankruptcy by the discounted sale of a profitable subsidiary.

In summary, the Statement of Cash Flows becomes invaluable when gauging the company's borrowing needs to see what ability the company has to pay the bank's interest and principal. Cash Flow and Debt Service should be tracked quarterly to measure progress. A good steady flow of current and accurate information from the company is critical for this measurement.

Leveraged Buyouts (LBOs)

LBOs generally can be defined as the change in ownership of a company, primarily for cash, which is financed by debt that is secured by targeted assets, with little equity put up by the investors. The debt is to be managed and retired with the sale of assets and future cash flow.

In a typical LBO, a group of investors, aided by an investment firm specializing in this field, buys out the company's shareholders by leveraging or borrowing heavily against the target company's assets. The purchase price is financed in large part by layers of loans from banks, insurance companies, pension funds and the junk bond markets. These lenders are rewarded with interest rates that usually float well above prime. In addition, they obtain senior security interests in virtually all of the assets of the business as collateral for their loan.

In addition to the investment banker, attorneys and accountants earn huge fees for negotiating and closing the transactions. Everyone seems to be a winner except for the unsecured creditor.

The unsecured creditor becomes the risk taker that was originally borne by the former shareholders. The asset-based lenders holding security interest are at a complete advantage.

Eight key areas thought to be critical in the credit extension process to an LBO have been identified.

1. Financial Information

A new LBO company must provide a Pro Forma Financial Statement as of the date the company changed ownership. Based upon the purchase price of the LBO involved, you will note that the balance sheet will be revalued to fair value for financial reporting purposes. Basically what we have is a write-up of assets to the actual purchase price. This intangible asset will be reflected as Goodwill on the balance sheet and will reflect the excess of the transaction price over the Net Fair Value of the assets of the company. The LBO company should also be able to provide a cash flow projection, one should look at the cash versus non-cash expenses being reflected. Depreciation and amortization of fixed assets and intangibles are non-cash expenses on the income statement. While they have a direct effect on the bottom-line profit of the company, they will not affect cash flow in any way. The intangibles such as excess of Cost Over Book Value and Goodwill should be deducted from equity to determine the company's true Tangible Net Worth. This number is actually negative in most LBOs.

2. Banking Relationship

It is imperative to establish a direct relationship with the LBO company's senior lenders and subordinated debt lenders. If available, a copy of the loan agreement should be obtained from the lender for review. This loan agreement will state very clearly the covenants of the loan, its term, the default provision, interest rate charged, and whether it is fixed or floating at a specified level above prime. The loan agreement will specify the collateral held, which most likely will include absolutely every asset of the company. A quarterly or semi-annual review with the customer's lender would allow you to have access to current information as to whether the customer is in default of any loan covenants.

3. Trade References

Verbal trade references with the customer's major suppliers will keep us advised of any new industry information and allow us to determine if all suppliers are being paid in a timely manner.

These references must be kept current because the supplier is the lifeblood of an LBO company. When a major supplier pulls out, it does not take long for this information to circulate through the industry and others will follow quickly. This can rapidly shut down any operation.

4. Cash Flow

This is the single most important element of an LBO or an HLC. In looking at the cash flow of an LBO, find out how management intends to improve the cash flow of the original business, as it will need to improve in order to service the heavy burden of debt now assumed. Any company that undergoes LBO status must make swift changes to enhance the cash flow of the new company. These changes will depend upon management. Therefore, management should be asked the following questions:

- How will expenses be controlled or reduced?
- How will the assets be utilized to maximize cash flow?
- What level of cash flow is needed for debt coverage and yet have sufficient working capital for continuing operations?

Unlike publicly held corporations that have sufficient cash, LBO companies cannot afford any deviation or errors that will cause reductions in cash.

Most LBO companies will reflect massive negative net worth figures and will show substantial bottom line losses each year. However, one must focus directly on cash flow from continuing operations and totally discount any expenses for amortization that are non-cash charges.

5. Communication
A direct contact with such individuals as the Vice President of Finance is important to develop a professional relationship. This improves the communication ties and creates a better partnership between the companies. This level of communication is necessary to obtain all the information required. A visit to the customer's headquarters to meet the counterparts and observe their operations is also very important.

6. Changes in Structure
With most LBOs selling at seven to eight times the earnings before interest and taxes, there will be tremendous pressure on management to enhance the earnings of the company to service the new debt. This can usually lead to several changes in the company structure. This information should be obtained in communicating with LBO management so that the events can be monitored to see if they are completed.

7. Credit Terms
Most suppliers in the industry utilize the shortest possible term when dealing with an LBO customer. The short terms are very important when attempting to keep the overall exposure at a minimum. Also, there are benefits of shortened terms when considering the possibility of bankruptcy preference treatment.

8. Economic Conditions
Most of the debt tied to the LBOs business carries floating rates, adjustable with fluctuations in the prime rate. A recession, followed by increased interest rates could severely squeeze profit margins.

What is it that makes leverage buyouts so attractive? The fact that it puts ownership back in the hands of managers is a most positive development. Since the management owns a percent of the new firm, the new owners will find ways to cut the fat. Public companies with strong cash flows and strong name brand recognition will continue to be candidates for an LBO.

Here is a summary of items to be considered in evaluating LBOs:

A. <u>Financial Information</u>
  1. Pro Forma Statement:
     Fair Market Value/A write-up of assets
  2. Cash Flow Projections—Over one year
  3. Deduct the Goodwill or Cost Over Book Value from NW to
     arrive at Tangible Net Worth
B. <u>Bank</u>
  1. Banks will not provide a copy of the loan agreement but would
     be nice to have knowledge of the customer's loan covenants, etc.
  2. Develop a relationship with the banker.
C. <u>Trade References</u>
  1. The supplier is the life-blood of an LBO company. Keep in
     touch with them.
D. <u>Cash Flow from Operations</u>
  1. Is the most important issue.
  2. Must have better cash flow than before the LBO in order to
     service its debt.
  3. What will it take in cash flow to service the debt?
E. <u>Communication</u>
  1. Direct contact and personal relationship.
F. <u>Structure Change</u>
  1. Because of the leverage this is needed.
  2. Need to *enhance* earnings.
  3. Set the game plan for the future.
G. <u>Credit Terms</u>
  1. Short terms so your cash flow analysis can be accurate.
H. <u>Interest Rates</u>
  1. Most LBOs are tied to fluctuating rates that go up and down
     with the prime rate.
  2. Watch for these interest rate swings for they may squeeze profit
     margins.

In Summary

Perform the necessary due diligence when evaluating the new credit
risk. Continue on a quarterly basis to monitor the success of an LBO. A
positive cash flow over the short credit term is a safe credit risk.

Not all LBOs are formed for the same reason. Try to assess this
immediately. Is management's personal money being put on the line? This
would ensure prudent investment and expense decisions. Some LBOs are
takeover candidates from day one depending on how they are structured.

LIMITED LIABILITY COMPANY ANALYSIS—LLCs

Subchapter S Corporations are often organized for smaller entities. With the advent of LLC legislation now existing in all 50 states, all entities regardless of size, can now enjoy the dual advantages of limited liability and partnership tax classification that were previously reserved for Subchapter S Corporations.

LLCs are organized into two types. They can be centralized, "manager management," or decentralized, "member managed." Most states reportedly look at decentralized management as the default rule and don't require any one type of structure. In the member managed LLC, the members are responsible for running the company. Unless otherwise provided in an operating agreement, each member has authority to bind the LLC to a counterparty. Like corporations, LLCs are separate entities, independent and separate from their owners. However, LLC members can lose the liability protection offered in four different ways: (1) defective formation of the LLC, (2) member misconduct, (3) abuse of the LLC form, and (4) failure to abide by statutes that address capital related requirements, which arises in "piercing the corporate veil" cases.

Our discussion and risk analysis will focus on the defective formation mentioned above. It is important to note that new companies who are expecting losses during the early years often choose LLCs. As a result, one should make sure that the LLC was properly structured to begin with so that they enjoy the expected tax benefits without cash flow interruption which will allow them to take care of ongoing business requirements and short-term payment obligations.

One way to ensure that proper structuring has taken place is to obtain an opinion from an outside accounting firm. In addition, one might consider obtaining a subordination agreement from the LLC members that would restrict profit distributions until their outstanding account is current.

A note of caution, most state LLC approved legislation was passed prior to the enactment of the American Bar Association (ABA) uniform state law in 1995. As a result, variations among state LLC legislation does exist. Knowing this should require specific state statute familiarization prior to granting unsecured credit.

As with the Subchapter S Corporation, liability protection and favorable tax treatment accounts for much of the entity's appeal. Double taxation incurred by C Corporations, first at the corporate level and then at the individual stockholder level, is avoided with this business classification. All income, credits and deductions flow directly to the members of the LLC.

The bankruptcy laws do not specifically mention LLCs. Your best bet is to look at how partnerships are treated under the Tax Code in order to get a sense of how LLCs will be treated.

In conclusion, LLCs are very appealing from a tax and flexibility standpoint for a wide variety of business structures both large and small. It is therefore essential that you familiarize yourself with the LLC legal concept, its structure, and the particular state statutes. This thorough analysis will provide the risk manager insight as to what steps should be taken to secure one's interest when doing business with an LLC.

SUBCHAPTER S CORPORATION ANALYSIS

Under a Subchapter S Corporation, which carries the limited liability of a standard or C Corporation, all income flows to the shareholders. Because the money is considered a "distribution" rather than a salary, the unreasonable compensation rules do not apply. Owners can take unlimited sums of Subchapter S Corporation distributions. Additionally, they are not taxed at the corporate level, which causes a lower aggregate tax than with standard corporations.

Capital

The net income of a Subchapter S Corporation is divided into two general classes: that distributed among stockholders, and that retained in the business and not distributed to the stockholders. The distributed income from the corporation is taxed to the stockholders based on the amount of the distribution each receives.

Undistributed income is taxed to the stockholders based on the percentage of ownership. Undistributed income from prior years earnings, for which the owners have previously paid personal income tax, can be distributed in later years to the stockholders without any tax liability.

A review of the capital section of the balance sheet will allow one to determine the amount of the available undistributed income.

Since Subchapter S Corporations usually pay out profits each year, the net worth remains the same but cash funds are depleted. These funds are used by the stockholders to pay their personal income taxes on distributed and undistributed earnings. In some cases, however, the stockholders will pay personal income taxes on distributed earnings and return the remaining cash to the business as stockholders loans. Then, stockholders loans will grow and the debt-to-worth ratio will deteriorate.

Liability

A Subchapter S Corporation is a corporation in all respects, except for the treatment stockholders are given for the federal income taxes. They are exempt from all federal income taxes. As a result, they are treated more like a partnership in that the earnings are considered ordinary income to the stockholders.

Additionally, any losses sustained by the Subchapter S Corporation can pass to the stockholders as business deductions from their personal income tax in proportion to their percentage of ownership.

From the credit review point of view, shareholders of a Subchapter S Corporation are protected against corporate creditors. If their loans to the corporation become excessively high, we should obtain a subordination or an assignment of the stockholders loans payable. Personal guarantees from the stockholders should also be considered. The best alternative or course of action to follow would be for the shareholders to reinvest the profits.

Chapter 12

INTERNATIONAL CREDIT RISK

The international market offers increasing opportunities for all companies to expand business activities abroad. This can be in terms of increasing the sale or purchases of either manufactured goods or basic commodities. In some respect, the international market can be an unfamiliar, frustrating, and risky environment. These difficulties can be minimized, however, by taking the time to understand the special requirements of international trade, especially documentation, and by developing an understanding of the common payment arrangements used in facilitating international trade.

An international transaction contains the same basic elements as a comparable domestic transaction. For example, if the transaction is the sale of a commodity to a customer in the United Kingdom, the buyer and seller must first reach agreement on the following points: type and quantity of merchandise, price, shipping arrangements, sales terms, and method of payment. In dealing with a foreign buyer, it is particularly important to have a clear and detailed understanding regarding the terms and conditions governing the sale with specific attention given to the method and timing of payment.

The choice of payment method with respect to international trade is based on the same factors that govern sales and payment terms in the domestic market. While the seller would like to obtain his money as quickly as possible, he must realize that the buyer would prefer to delay payment until the goods have been delivered, inspected, and in some cases, resold. In negotiating the payment arrangements, you must take into account competition in the relevant market, price of the commodity, buyer's creditworthiness, usual industry terms, and the total amount of the transaction and overall exposure. In addition to these factors, you must also consider local exchange and import restrictions as well as the general political and economic climate in the country concerned. This is generally referred to as Sovereign or Country risk.

COUNTRY RISK

One of the greatest limiting factors regarding the growth of international trade is the availability of credit. When credit is associated with the obligation of a sovereign government, country risk should be examined. Country risk is defined as the probability that a loss could be incurred due to events that are under the control of the government. Country risk, therefore, is a function of political, social, and economic circumstances.[6]

The attitudes and policies of its government directly influence the economy and business climate of any nation. The degree of promotion or regulation often makes the difference between dynamic activity and economic stagnation. The political orientation of the government also affects its economic policy and the degree to which it regulates internal commerce and external trade. An individual nation, therefore, can exercise considerable control over business operations.

Country risk can include the risk of expropriation of assets without compensation. Other examples of country/political risk include radical ideological shifts, rioting and terrorism against personnel or property, and military coups.

Country risk can best be assessed by examining the history of a country. Factors such as government stability and social conditions influence political risk. In addition, external factors such as ideological orientation and participation in international organizations may be examined to assess the potential for such risk.

The following table presents a list of several factors to consider when analyzing country risk:

1. Political Risk Assessment
   A. Political System: Structure and Evolution
   B. Stability of Leadership
   C. Cooperation with International Bodies
   D. Geopolitical Importance to Western Bloc Countries
2. Social Risk Assessment
   A. Disparity of Income: Per Capita Income
   B. Unemployment Levels
   C. Environmental/Governmental Regulation
   D. Social Order

---

[6]L. Fargo Wells and Karin B. Dulat, *Exporting from Start to Finance* (New York: McGraw-Hill, 1996), 413.

    E. Population Growth Rate
    F. Infrastructure/Transportation Problems
3. Economic Risk Assessment
    A. Balance of Payments Flexibility
    B. Inflation Rate/Interest Rates
    C. Natural Resources/Degree of Product Diversification
    D. Growth Rate in Output of Goods and Services
    E. Ability to Service Debt Burden
    F. Ability to Attract Investment
    G. Current Taxation Levels: Flexibility in Future Taxation Levels

The above factors represent a good starting point for country risk analysis. Information can also be obtained from the following sources:

1. D&B International Risk and Payment Review—Published monthly with risk factor narrative and country risk indicator rating
2. D&B Exporters Encyclopedia
3. Chase Manhattan Bank World Guide for Exporters
4. FCIB-NACM
5. Standard and Poor's
6. Major Money Center Banks
7. Rundt's Country Reports
8. World Trade Data Reports (WTDR) prepared by U.S. commercial officers abroad in answer to requests for information about a certain firm in a specific country. These reports contain information on the firm's business activities, it's standing in the local business community, its general financial reputation, and its overall reliability and suitability as a trade contract.
9. Teikoku Databank America, Inc.
10. Owens OnLine, Inc.
11. Graydon America—A U.S. subsidiary of the European firm

The prime tools for credit decisions and information on overseas customers are identical to those for domestic transactions. Accounting is a universal language, although rules for content and preparation of a specific account are far from universal. Credit evaluation and extension is not. This is not to say that foreign financial statements are of no value, just that there is a need to be aware of practices in those countries in which you do a lot of business or have major investments. Their practices are not always according to what your accountant understands to be generally accepted accounting principles (GAAP).

INSURING CREDIT RISK

Ex-Im Bank is likely to be your best source for receivable insurance, which it created because of the difficulty all but the largest exporters were having in obtaining this kind of insurance.[7]

The alternative to insuring foreign accounts receivable with Ex-Im Bank is through the private sector insurance market. This market has been limited, especially in this country, but in the last few years there has been marked improvement. For most firms, the best approach is to contact one of about 18 insurance brokers specializing in foreign country and commercial credit risk insurance. Four of them are very large and have headquarters in New York and multiple branch offices. They are: Intercredit Agency, a division of Frank B. Hall; Alexander & Alexander; Johnson & Higgins; and Marsh & McClennan Credit International Associates (CIA), division of Republic Hogg Robinson. A fifth firm is Sedgwich James, based in London but also having offices in New York.

---

[7]Risk Management 2000, *Effective Strategies for the Global Corp* (TMA Journal 2000).

Chapter 13

BANK ANALYSIS

Bank evaluation requires consideration of both profitability and financial condition. Looking at profitability alone can be misleading, for if high profits are made by risk-taking, the bank may be vulnerable to adverse developments. Several measures can be used to judge the quality of earnings and financial strength. Such measures are most useful when trends are looked at over a period of time and when compared with data on other banks of similar size.

The following guidelines may be used in evaluating the financial condition of a bank, which has or is supposed to issue a letter of credit for collateral. These guidelines will be used to quantify whether or not a financial institution represents an acceptable credit risk. The risk evaluation centers on the bank capital structure and asset quality. Seven measures will be used in the evaluation. Four of the measures relate to the capital adequacy or asset quality of the institution; two of the measures tie into the bank's rating by Sheshunoff, and a final measure involves an aggregate letter of credit exposure as it relates to the bank's capital.

Capital adequacy is a relative measure indicating the capacity of the capital base to absorb losses in loans and in other assets and to provide an underlying equity base for depositors. A weak capital position implies that a bank might not be able to sustain its past lending policies and that, in times of strong economic expansion, it might be at a competitive disadvantage.

The banks will receive a score of 0, 5 or 10 for each measure. The score received depends on how the bank compares to the guidelines assigned to each measure. Each measure will be weighed and a composite rating for each bank will be made. The following is a list of the measures to be used in our evaluation and measures' respective weighting:

Measurement	Weighting
1. Primary Capital/Total Assets (Primary Capital defined as stockholders' equity plus reserve for loan losses)	15%
2. Non-Performing Loans/Primary Capital (Non-Performing Loans are those on which income is no longer being accrued and for which repayment has been rescheduled.)	15%
3. Non-Performing Loans/Gross Loans	15%
4. $100M Time Deposits/Total Assets	10%
5. Sheshunoff Rating: Grade	15%
6. Sheshunoff Rating: Numerical	15%
7. Total Letters of Credit Exposure/Primary Capital	15%

A bank must have a score of 5.5 or better to be considered acceptable.

This monitoring and evaluation process will be instituted on all new banks prior to accepting their letter of credit (LC) and periodically on all existing banks that have met your criteria in the past. If they fall below the acceptable score the customer would be requested to obtain an LC from an acceptable financial institution upon its maturity. (See Exhibit 8 for the

---

Exhibit 7: Bank Analysis Format

	Ratio Level	(1) Score	Weighting	Net Score
1. Primary Capital Ratio	_____	_____ *	_____ =	_____
2. Non-Performing Loans/ Primary Capital	_____	_____ *	_____ =	_____
3. Non-Performing Loans/ Gross Loans	_____	_____ *	_____ =	_____
4. $100M Time Deposits/ Total Assets	_____	_____ *	_____ =	_____
5. Sheshunoff: Grade	_____	_____ *	_____ =	_____
6. Sheshunoff: Numerical	_____	_____ *	_____ =	_____
7. LC Exposure	_____	_____ *	_____ =	_____
			Total Score	_____

*(1) Score is determined based on where ratio falls in range of acceptability.

ratio weighting percentage and Exhibit 7 (previous page) for the worksheet to be used along with your analysis.)

Exhibit 8: Ratio Weighting Percentage

Measurement	Level	Acceptable Scoring
1) *Primary Capital/Total Assets	7%	< 7.0% = 0 7.0 to 9.0% = 5 > 9.0% = 10
2) **Non-Performing Loans/Primary Capital	40%	> 60% = 0 40% to 60% = 5 < 40% = 10
3) Non-Performing Loans/Gross Loans	7.5%	> 7.5% = 0 4% to 7.5% = 5 < 4% = 10
4) $100M Time Deposits/Total Assets	35%	> 35% = 0 20% to 35% = 5 < 20% = 10
5) Sheshunoff Rating: Grade	C+	C, NR = 0 C+, B = 5 B+, A, A+ = 10
6) Sheshunoff Rating: Numerical	50	< 50 = 0 50 to 74 = 5 75 to 99 = 10
7) Letter of Credit Exposure/Primary	7.5%	> 7.5% = 0 5% to 7.5% = 5 < 5% = 10

*Primary Capital: Total equity capital plus the loan loss reserve.
**Non-Performing Loan: All loans no longer accruing interest and those which are still accruing but payments are 90 days past due.

Chapter 14

SECURITY INSTRUMENTS

Having completed a financial review, the customer may not qualify for an open line of credit. This may be due to one or more of the following reasons:

1. Lack of information due to time restraint to make the sale or customer's unwillingness to provide adequate information
2. Financial information presented is not sufficient for the amount under consideration
3. Overall poor financial condition

There are various forms of security instruments to protect or reduce exposures. Two of the most frequently used and widely accepted instruments are bank Letters of Credit (LCs) and Guarantees.

WHAT IS AN LC?

Traditionally, an LC is a commitment by a bank to pay a third party upon presentation of certain documents. Under Section 105 of the Uniform Commercial Code, an LC is defined as an "engagement by a bank or other person made at the request of a customer and of a kind within the scope of this Article (Article 5) that the issuer will honor drafts or other demands for payment upon compliance with the conditions specified in the credit."[8]

In offering a word of caution, they are undeniably useful, but like any other protective device, they must be used judiciously. Studies over the years show discrepancy rates for letters of credit as high as 50 percent, which means that one out of every two LCs loses its original protection. This is so because bankers are relieved from their payment responsibility under the LC when the beneficiary does not correctly present documents. Some LC clauses can actually be considered built-in discrepancies that could cause the unwary exporter long delays in receiving money that is due and

---

[8]George A. Christie, Ph.D., *Credit Executive Handbook* (Columbia, MD: Credit Research Foundation, 1986), 109.

owning after title has passed. Therefore, it behooves the credit or financial manager to scrutinize each LC received to make sure stated requirements can be met or else be prepared to face possible serious consequences.

TYPES OF LCs

There are two types of LCs, commonly referred to as Documentary and Standby.

It is understood that documentary LCs are the vehicle for a customer's payment. Upon presentation of documents that are deemed to be "in compliance" with the LC requirements, the issuing bank will make payment to the seller on the buyer's behalf.

As the name would imply, standby LCs are standing by in the event that the Buyer does not or cannot pay the Seller directly. If the buyer fails to pay as agreed, the seller has the right to present the stipulated documents for the bank to pay.

Standby Letter of Credit

Of the two, the most commonly utilized form of a letter of credit is the Irrevocable Standby LC. You should not accept a revocable LC. Irrevocable LCs cannot be altered or canceled without the mutual consent of all parties. In order to modify the terms of the credit, the buyer (applicant) must give instructions to the issuing bank regarding the proposed change. The issuing bank in turn notifies the beneficiary of the changes by means of an amendment. All parties to the LC must agree to the amendment. If you do not agree with the amendment, inform the bank in writing immediately. A Standby Letter of Credit can be more specifically defined as a binding agreement by an issuing bank, acting at the request and on the instruction of a customer (the buyer), to make payment to a third party (the seller), in the event the buyer does not make payment to the seller. Standby letters of credit should require only a copy of a commercial invoice and a statement from an officer in your company, which is the seller, stating that "payment has not been received and is due under invoice payment terms."

Standby Letter of Credit Language Guidelines

1. All letters of credit must be irrevocable.
2. All dollar amounts should be preceded by the word "approximate." This allows drawings up to 10 percent greater than the face amount of the letter of credit.

3. Drafts against letter of credit must require that it be accompanied by only the following:
   a. Copy of commercial invoice(s) that should not contain any specifications such as reference to unit price, quantity, product descriptions, delivery month, and delivery facility.
   b. Statement signed by a purported, authorized representative of your company, stating that "payment has not been received and is due under invoice(s) payment terms."
   c. Do not accept requirement that supplier provide a delivery document.
   d. Partial drawings are acceptable and drawings may be made for sales prior to and during the term of this credit. This language is required to protect against drawings denied due to under shipment greater than 10 percent.
   e. State that Stale Documents are acceptable and make an exception to Article 47, ICC Publication No. 500.

The above requirements keep the letter of credit "clean" and easy to draw upon in the event that it becomes necessary. If delivery documents are insisted upon by the applicant, then amend letter "b" above to read: "In lieu of item number (the document number requiring delivery receipts) above, a statement signed by a purported officer... etc."

NOTE: *See* Exhibit 9 on page 133 for a sample Standby Letter of Credit format.

Documentary Letter of Credit

An Irrevocable Documentary Letter of Credit can be defined as a binding agreement by an issuing bank, acting at the request and on the instructions of a customer (the buyer), to make payment to a third party (the seller), based upon presentation by the seller of shipping documents in accordance with the terms and conditions of the Letter of Credit.

The seller presents the required documents directly to the bank for either sight or deferred payment, whereas, under a standby LC, documents are presented to the buyer, and only in the event of nonpayment by the buyer is the bank requested to make payment.

A documentary LC also differs from a standby LC in that it only provides for payment against specific shipping documents relating to a single shipment. Typically, the documents required are a commercial invoice, original bills of lading and certificates of quantity, quality and origin. In the event that the bills of lading and certificates are not available at the time payment is due, the documentary LC must allow for payment against a commercial invoice and a Letter of Indemnity.

The ICC Banking Commission has formulated a set of rules, which govern letters of credit. These rules apply to documentary and, where applicable, standby LCs. They are known as the Uniform Customs and Practice for Documentary Credits, 1994, ICC Publication Number 500. You may obtain a copy by writing to ICC Publishing, Inc. 156 Fifth Avenue, New York, New York 10010 or by calling 212-206-1150. I would encourage you to get familiar with this set of governing rules.

Documentary Letter of Credit Beneficiary Checklist

1. Beneficiary name and address are correct and appear as such on the customer's invoice.
2. The face amount of the LC has the word "approximate" or +/– 10 percent added.
3. The identified points of shipment and destination are as agreed.
4. The document requirements listed in the Letter of Credit can be obtained in the format required.
5. The currency of the credit is as agreed, and changes under the Letter of Credit are as agreed.
6. The type of credit, its terms and conditions are in conformity with the sales contract.
7. The description of the merchandise or commodity and any unit price or price basis (F.O.B., C&F, etc.) is in accordance with the sales contract.
8. The amount of credit is sufficient to cover all costs permitted in the sales contract.
9. There are no unacceptable conditions that could cause a discrepancy (i.e., unusual certifications, obscure phrases, etc.)
10. The shipping date, the expiration dates and the period of time allowed after shipment for presentation of documents to the bank, are sufficient to cover your needs.

Checklist for Documentary Items under Letters of Credit

Letter of Credit at Time of Receipt by Beneficiary
1. Do credit terms agree with the terms of the contract?
2. Can credit terms be met?
3. Is shipping schedule (date lift range) as stipulated in the credit?

Documents at Time of Presentation

1. Ensure that the credit is not overdrawn (dollar amount or quantity of product shipped).
2. Is presentation being made in time (before expiry and other time limits indicated in the credit—or within 21 days after date of shipping documents?
3. Are all documents accounted for, do they relate to each other and are they consistent?
4. Do all documents show letter of credit number or other identification, if required by the letter of credit?

Commercial Invoices

1. Does the commercial invoice conform with:
   a. Credit terms?
   b. Total dollar amount?
   c. Unit prices and computations?
   d. Description of crude oil and terms; i.e., FOB, etc.?
2. Is the commercial invoice made out in the name of the applicant for the LC?
3. Is the commercial invoice properly signed if stipulated by the credit?
4. If partial shipments are prohibited, is all merchandise shipped or if partial shipments are permitted, is the merchandise invoiced in proportion with the shipment?

Bills of Lading

1. Are bills of lading in negotiable form?
2. Are all negotiable copies being presented to the bank and are they properly endorsed?
3. Do bills of lading indicate that merchandise was loaded on board and within the time frame specified by the credit?
4. Are the bills of lading made out as prescribed by the credit (names and addresses of beneficiary, applicant, etc.?
5. Does carrier or agent initial all corrections?

Other Shipping Documents (Certificates of Quantity, Quality and Origin)

1. Are names and addresses as per commercial invoice and per letter of credit? Is country of origin, if required, as per commercial invoice and per letter of credit?

2. Are they issued by the proper party and signed, and do they show a description of the crude oil relative to the commercial invoice and credit?
3. Are they in exact compliance with letter of credit and dated reasonably current?
4. Ensure that the proper number of bills of lading and appropriate certificates are forwarded to the bank in accordance with the credit.

Letters of Indemnity (LOI)

A Letter of Indemnity (LOI) is a document used primarily in transactions involving cargo-sized shipments of product. The LOI can be generally defined as a promise by the seller of a cargo to provide required shipping documents (bills of lading, inspection reports, etc.) to the cargo buyer at a later date. The LOI is issued in lieu of shipping documents that for some reason are not available at the time that payment is due. In requesting that the buyer make payment based upon the LOI, the seller agrees to hold the buyer harmless in the event that the shipping documents do not later become available and damages arise due to the lack of these documents.

In the event that you are buying a shipment and the supplier is not worthy of open credit, think about getting the LOI countersigned by a bank or parent company you find acceptable. Don't take on any unnecessary risks.

LC Terms

All terms agreed to between the parties must be clearly stated in the LC, including:

- Amount of the credit
- Last day on which a drawing can be made
- Documents that must be presented at time of drawing
- Terms and conditions that must be reflected by the documents
- Manner of payment under the credit, including location of bank where presentment and payment are to occur
- Makes reference to being in conformance with either Article 5 of the UCC or the UCP

Advantages of Using LCs

- It enables your company to complete a sale that they would not have been able to due to risk of financial loss.

- Will generally ensure payment for goods supplied in the event that your buyer files for bankruptcy. You can even draw down on the LC without first obtaining relief from the automatic stay in the buyer's bankruptcy case as long as the LC was issued and in effect more than 90 days prior to the bankruptcy filing and before the invoice(s) became past due.
- Allows you to avoid a preference lawsuit in the event your buyer files for bankruptcy assuming the amount of the LC is greater than the payment you received from the buyer because, as a result of the LC, you are secured up to the amount of the LC. Preference law states that if you, the creditor, received a payment from the debtor within the 90 days prior to the bankruptcy filing on account of a past-due debt (which allows you to obtain more money than you would receive in a Chapter 7 case) the full amount of the payment made can be challenged as a preferential payment. If the preference challenge is successful, your company will have to refund the full amount of the payment to the debtor.

Automatic Reduction Clause

This is a clause inserted in the LC that reduces the value of the LC by any payments made to the beneficiary through the issuing bank on behalf of the buyer in the normal course of business or even in antecedent debt. The bankruptcy courts deem any type of payment which reduces the value of the LC as a "draw down" against the LC and therefore outside the preference rule. As a result, it would be wise to allow your customers to use the reduction clause.

Confirmations

A bank confirmation is an agreement between the issuing bank and a second bank whereby the second bank, (the confirming bank), agrees to be held liable under the terms of the LC. In essence, you draw against the confirming bank for payment and they, in turn, will draw against the issuing bank. There is a bank fee associated with the confirmation and the confirming bank must be willing to take on the risk of the LC from the issuing bank.

Confirmations are used to protect against sovereign risk. Having a foreign bank issue an LC that is confirmed by a U.S. domiciled bank is one way to avoid this type of risk.

Advisements

The issuing bank will send a telex LC to the bank you have designated as your advising bank. The advising bank will test the telex to ensure validity and that it did originate from the issuing bank. Also, the authorized individual with authority to issue the LC on behalf of the issuing bank is validated as well. The advising bank is not responsible in any way to make payment under the LC. A bank fee is assessed for all advisements.

Discrepancies

Be certain that you will be able to comply with all of the listed requirements for payment under the LC. If not, ask for an amendment and do so before shipment has been made to your customer. Banks have advised that approximately 85 percent of all LC drawings have discrepancies. Any discrepancy will delay or perhaps invalidate a perfectly good claim. Just remember that LC requirements are very strict and must be complied with in order to obtain payment. Suggest that you set up an approval process that matches invoice to issued LC and that credit as well as marketing review for acceptance as per the terms and conditions of the contract. Remember to keep the LC simple. See Exhibit 9 for an example.

GUARANTEES

Introduction

By definition, a Guarantee is an undertaking on the part of one or more person(s) (the guarantor(s)) that is collateral to the obligation of another person (the debtor or obligor), and which binds the guarantor to performance of the obligation in the event of a default by the debtor or obligor.

Corporate Guarantees

Corporate Guarantees are sought in a variety of circumstances. For example, if you have financial information on the parent company, but your sales are to a subsidiary company, which will not supply financial information or the financial information that you have does not support the requested line, then a corporate guarantee would be appropriate.

A resolution of the Board of Directors must be obtained with a signed corporate guarantee to ensure that the person signing the guarantee has the authority to do so. The resolution should bear the same date as the guarantee or a later date.

Exhibit 9: Standby Letter of Credit Format

Letter of Credit Number: _____   Date: _____

Beneficiary Name
Address

Attention: _____

We hereby open our Irrevocable Letter of Credit in your favor available to you by drafts drawn on _____ Bank for any sum or sums.

Checklist

- Be sure to reference which state law governs
- It is advisable to have an aggregate value listed although acceptable if unlimited
- It is advisable to have an expiration date listed although acceptable if not expiring
- It is strongly recommended that each company check their local laws (state) and ask that your legal department review the state laws applicable to the guarantee. In addition, it may be appropriate to obtain an in-house or outside counsel opinion as to the enforceability of the guarantee under the applicable state law

Personal Guarantees

When a corporation is involved, thought should be given to obtaining a guarantee from one or more principal stockholders who may also be officers or directors of the company. Should it be necessary to obtain a personal guarantee in order to approve the requested credit line, a personal financial statement should be obtained and evaluated prior to the acceptance of said guarantee. A credit line may, therefore, be established based on a review of the company's financial statement plus the merit given to any personal statement that might be available.

Credit should never be granted solely based on obtaining a personal guarantee. It should be used in assisting to support a line of credit.

Be aware there may be risk in dealing with the following:

- Taking a guarantee from a "non-interested" party, i.e., a spouse without interest in the business. Try to get declaration from the guarantor as to their interest or benefit from providing the guarantee.

- *Homestead States* (as many are, such as Texas, Oklahoma, Ohio, etc.): State laws limit the value of your personal guarantee due to homestead laws. Certain assets you may see on a personal financial statement may not be available to you when you exercise your guarantee.
- *Community Property States* (which many are, including Texas, Oklahoma, California, etc.): Again, you may be relying on assets that will not be available to you under state community property laws.

In exercising a guarantee, the following are not attachable: 401Ks; IRAs; retirement accounts; and single premium annuities or life insurance policies, especially if a minor, spouse or both are listed as beneficiaries.

Personal Guarantee Signature Verification

Personal guarantees are not required to be notarized, but you should make every effort to get this accomplished anyway. Signature verification is very important. Falsifying a signature on a guarantee is fraud.

What if a guarantor dies? The guarantor's death would cancel the "offer" of a guarantee. You then have three options:

1. Persuade the heirs to assume the guarantee or issue a new guarantee
2. Revoke their credit line
3. File a claim with the deceased estate

As long as the guarantee agreements benefiting/protecting your company are unconditional guarantees of payment, you have an executable document.

The absence of a stated expiration date will be of no significance. What will always be important is your awareness of the date of the principal debtor's failure to make a required payment. The date of that failure is what will start the clock ticking (the statute of limitations will begin to run) against your ability to collect from the guarantor.

Additionally, you will want to make certain that your actions following such a failure to pay by the principal debtor do not give the guarantor some other kind of excuse to avoid its guarantee obligation. Reference is being made here to defenses that a guarantor might raise against you, such as waiver, estoppel, or laches. Waiver is the intentional or voluntary relinquishment of a known right.

Estoppel is a legal theory under which one party's acts or conduct preclude it from asserting rights that it otherwise had. If, for example, upon the debtor's default, you led the guarantor to justifiably believe that you would pursue collection against the debtor, as opposed to the guarantor, and the guarantor relied upon this to his detriment, you might well be "estopped" from turning around and collecting from the guarantor.

Laches is an equitable statute of limitations and is intended to cut off old, "stale" claims, the enforcement of which have been unreasonably and inexcusably delayed by the claimant. Laches will bar the enforcement of such "stale" claims if enforcement would be unfair to the guarantor.

OTHER METHODS TO SECURE ACCOUNTS

Although not specifically defined as "security instruments", the following practices can be described as "credit enhancements" which provide the same result or minimize the credit risk from a legal standpoint:

- *Net Out/Offset/Setoff.* These terms describe a situation where one party withholds money, services, or goods it owes or is obligated to provide another party to "offset" what the other party owes them.
- *Invoice Net Out.* A situation whereby two parties who owe each other money agree to establish the net amount due one or the other party, and transmit only the difference due to the party owed the net balance amount on a specific date in time. The agreement to invoice net out will occur only after actual performance of the contractual obligations of both parties and should be accompanied by a written or telegraphic agreement setting forth the terms and conditions of the invoice net out.
- *Net Scheduling.* Agreement of two parties to physically schedule a commodity for delivery such that only the net volume difference between the two parties actually is physically delivered. Each party will make payment to the other for the full (i.e., net) amount due the other party, unless invoice netting out has also been agreed to.
- *Book Outs/Book Transfer.* Similar to net scheduling, but usually involving a situation where two or more partners owe each other, via a chain sequence, an equal volume quantity of a similar commodity and agree to complete the delivery obligations without making physical delivery. Each party will make payment to its supplier for the full amount due on a specific day.

- *Business Credit Insurance.* A guarantee that the seller will be reimbursed by the insurance company for credit losses. Claims against the policy are established in either of two ways:
  a. Insolvency
  b. If uncollectible, a past due account is treated as a loss

The actual cost of this policy will depend on many factors: the size of your sales volume, the quality and quantity of your accounts, terms of sale, etc.

Exhibit 10: Letter of Credit Format

We hereby issue our Irrevocable Standby Letter of Credit no. (_____) in favor of:

Beneficiary Name
Beneficiary Address
Beneficiary City, State Zip
SWIFT Address:
Telex:
Fax:

Attention: Beneficiary contact person

By order and for account of (company name) for an amount of approximately (amount spelled out) U.S. dollars, available at sight, but not prior to (effective date), by presentation of the following documents:

1. A copy of Beneficiary's invoice(s) marked unpaid.
2. A statement purportedly signed by an authorized representative of "Beneficiary" stating that the amount being drawn hereunder is due and unpaid.

The expiration of this Letter of Credit is (expiration date).

Special Conditions:

A. Partial shipments and/or partial drawings are acceptable.
B. All banking charges are for the applicant's account.
C. Telex, telefax, or photocopy documents acceptable.
D. Invoices exceeding the total amount of this Letter of Credit are acceptable, provided the issuing bank's liability shall not exceed the total amount permitted by this Credit.

E. Combined documents are acceptable.

F. Documents received 21 days after the date of delivery, and prior to the date of expiry of this Letter of Credit are acceptable.

G. Typographical and spelling errors, with the exception of quantity and amount, are not to be considered as discrepancies as long as meaning is consistent with the other documents presented.

H. This telex is the operative instrument.

Except as otherwise expressly provided herein this Letter of Credit is subject to the Uniform Customs and Practices for Documentary Credits (1993 Revision) International Chamber of Commerce Publication No. 500.

We hereby agree with you that presentation of the documents in compliance with the terms of this Letter of Credit will be duly honored on presentation to us no later than the expiry date of this Credit.

NAME
Authorized Signatory
ISSUING BANK

Chapter 15

CREDIT SCORING MODELS

INTRODUCTION

Most firms sell on credit. The terms on which products are sold varies by industry and the type of product being sold. When extending credit, the selling firm undertakes the risk of nonpayment by the customer. What if the customer is financially unable to pay the invoice on the date it is due? Yet, unless the firm takes the risk, it will lose the opportunity to sell and profit from the sale. This raises the question of how much risk is acceptable and where is the tradeoff between credit risk and lost profit opportunities? The resulting balancing act leads to the process of determining credit limits.

Credit limits for a specific customer reflect the tradeoff that the credit manager has been able to determine a credit limit that appropriately reflects the level of risk, and the lost opportunity in not trading with that specific customer.

Therefore, the basic goal of the credit granting process is to balance the risk of loss of nonpayment against the lost profit opportunity from not granting credit. The prescriptions of modern finance theory in credit granting theory can be summarized as follows:

1. Estimate the probability of nonpayment using statistical procedures.
2. Determine the extent of credit investigation by the tradeoff between the incremental costs of investigation and the amount of credit involved.
3. Estimate the benefits and losses from granting credit for all the periods in the planning horizon.
4. Integrate the probability of nonpayment with the benefits and losses of each period.
5. Grant credit, if net present value is positive and reject full credit, otherwise.

Statistical procedures refer to the process of systematically looking for underlying patterns in the characteristics of customers that humans cannot find with their limited processing power. There are two types of statistical models that can be used to assess credit risk:

1. Simultaneous models
2. Sequential models

The basic motivation underlying the use of statistical models is that there are sets of characteristics that systematically contribute to a given set of outcomes that form the scope of our analysis. In the credit context, we are interested in determining the level of credit risk that a customer represents. Put differently, we may be interested in determining the likelihood that a customer will be unable to meet the financial obligations when they become due.

If we believe that the ability to meet financial obligations is indeed related to some underlying characteristics (financial or nonfinancial), then it follows that a systematic study of customer characteristics should reveal some information about the identity of such factors.

Since the human mind is inherently limited in its ability to grapple with large numbers of customers and their characteristics, a statistical model will more rapidly and effectively uncover these significant characteristics.

The use of statistical models does not mean that they represent an infallible solution to the problem of estimating credit risk. It is merely another means of extracting information from a mass of data regarding customer characteristics. It is also important that the use of such models be complemented by a good understanding of the assumptions inherent in the use of specific models and algorithms.

In building a model, you should ask yourself what are the important factors for a credit-scoring model to be considered accurate and credible? For example, there are industry differences: retailers have different characteristics than manufacturers. Also, the economic environment can differ by geographic region. We could easily add to this list. The point again is that statistical models are not able to successfully capture all the effects that differentiate firms into different levels of pending financial difficulty. So don't rely on them excessively.

There is a place for scoring models in your credit toolkit. Just don't expect it to provide the right answer all the time. Use of scoring models to quickly analyze those accounts that your company has relatively low exposure. In these instances, use the scoring model to indicate possible problems and then conduct a more detailed analysis. Second, for high exposure accounts do a detailed analysis and then run the scoring model to buttress your findings.

There are many professionals that would like to use a scoring model on all accounts—large and small—because they don't have time to analyze them. This is not a very convincing argument. If one of your large accounts files bankruptcy, and the scoring model failed to note it, you will wish that you had taken the time to do the analysis. At a minimum, the analysis should encompass a detailed reading of the annual report. Such a reading often reveals insights that ratio analysis or scoring models don't uncover.

In summary and before preceding any further, financial scorings aren't perfect. They are based on many simplifying assumptions and may be derived on a sampling of firms that isn't representative of your accounts.

SCORING MODEL PARAMETERS

Major rating agencies such as Standard and Poor's, Moody's, and Fitch, may not provide the most reliable estimate but they can be used in conjunction with other parameters within an in-house credit scoring model that may include:

- Agency ratings
- Financial monitors
- Market-based information
- Rumor mill

Agency Ratings

Agencies offer an advantage, in large part, because they have access to company management and financial information not available in the public domain. This is a dual-edged sword as the agencies have been criticized for relying too extensively on company management's projections and outlook. Nevertheless, their ratings are an important input in credit scoring and available to the public at a minimal cost.

Characteristics of Rating Agency Approach

- Industry analysts normally focus on a specific industry.
- The rating assigned is a compilation of a variety of factors. Deficiency in any one category can be made up in another.
- Overall methodology generally weighs qualitative measures over quantitative measures.

- Financial ratios are a guide rather than a benchmark. The numbers must be understood.

Rating agencies (which are independent of the companies that they rate) provide a key piece of information to the markets which enables an estimation of credit risk.

The agencies use a variety of factors in determining a credit rating, both quantitative and qualitative (qualitative generally outweighs quantitative) raw numbers aren't as important as understanding the context of those numbers (industry dynamics, firm's position within an industry, etc.). At the end of the evaluation process, they will assign the company a specific rating category, such as AA or A-.

As an analyst, we can appreciate knowing about the analytical process associated with a given agency's rating for a couple of reasons. First, we gain a better idea of what areas are considered before an agency assigns their final rating. Second, it provides us with a good outline and reminder of the areas we should also be reviewing in conducting our independent assessments and scoring model development.

The agencies first look at industry trends. They concentrate on trends that affect the firm, including but not limited to:

- Economic cycles
- Competition
- Regulatory issues
- Technological changes in the industry
- Cost factors

Management capabilities are an important factor. The agencies want to evaluate these aspects so they drill down a bit and look at the following:

- Strategic outlook
- Funding approach
- General business approach
- Historical record
- Key man planning
- Systems

The firm's competitive position is an important factor. Agencies want to ascertain the company's position relative to its industry and assess their market share and trends, diversification, and overall economic efficiency.

Analyzing financial ratios and estimates is a critical part of the evaluation. Agencies review historical financial information, including:

- Projected cash flow and profitability for the next five to eight years
- Short- and long-term liquidity
- Back-up financial plans (credit, etc.)
- Other financial information

The agencies will also examine other factors, including:

- Parent/subsidiary issues
- General financial issues
- Legal issues
- Other activities

There are strengths and weaknesses to the rating agency approach. The strengths come from the fact that there are a large number of companies being looked at, the risk ratings applied are easy to understand, the agencies conduct periodic reassessments of the assigned ratings and they provide us with default information by rating category.

The weaknesses stem from the fact that their universe is limited (only publicly listed companies are assessed), their analysis takes on a subjective rather than objective approach, and the ratings assigned are not comparable across industries.

Financial Monitors

Published financial reports and SEC filings (10-Ks), although historic in perspective, are still an important source for information on a company's financial health. Of course, in recent years the credibility of audited statements has been eroded by a series of disclosures. The authenticity of revenue, quality of earnings, the potential for off-balance sheet obligations, etc., all make an unquestioning acceptance of financial report an unwise approach. That's why we need to continue to develop our analytical skills for both the art and science aspects. We need to learn how to dive deeper and ask probing questions.

Market-Based Information

Market-based indicators can be thought of as reflecting the market's view of company risk. As so, unlike historic information such as financial ratios that are backward-looking, market indicators are forward-looking in their perspective. Market inputs might include:

- Bond spreads
- Pricing of default swaps
- Beta values
- LIBOR or lending spreads

Rumor Mill

The value of casual intelligence that comes simply from operating in the same business lines with the company should not be underestimated. Information on energy counterparties flows to company business units: trading, marketing, operations, and management. For example, changes in trading behaviors, altered marketing focus or operating procedures, resumes, and job candidate interviews, etc., all provide a depth of intelligence not even available to the rating agencies.

Scoring

By assimilating both forward and backward-looking information and data, a more immediate picture can be drawn. Systematized and/or modeled, they can be translated to a higher-powered credit rating or scoring system that can also quantify changing default probabilities. Many firms are users of internally developed scoring systems, but increasingly energy companies are developing their own internal systems. Additionally there are outside vendors (e.g., KMV) who can offer such analysis.

A question needs to be raised about internally developed scoring systems. Can in-house credit scoring models withstand the challenges of the "real world"?

In-house credit scoring models offer companies a number of benefits. For example, they can provide credit assessments on otherwise unrated counterparties. And the scores can be used to price credit risk into your product. However, in the real world; these models must be able to withstand a number of business and legal challenges.

Anytime non-public models are used in a third-party credit decision it opens the door for third-party challenges. The decision to extend credit initially can come up against discrimination challenges, market manipulation challenges, and fraudulent conveyance challenges. And then the decision to reduce or withdraw credit could be challenged with a wrongful termination assertion.

What are some of the parameters associated with scoring models? Credit scoring models must be reasonable. This means that they must generate consistent results for a similar exposure term and that they are actually better than independent models in some way. All in-house developed scoring models need to be clearly documented and aligned with relevant credit related policies.

In addition, credit scoring must be done in accordance with policies that are consistently applied across all counterparties and linked to expected loss, not just a score or probability of default.

Rating Agencies vs. Credit Scoring

The immediacy of using a well-designed scoring system can provide learning information about a counterparty's credit standing, often before the rating agencies. One good example can be seen during the Enron implosion. By incorporating forward looking indicators, the third party KMV's scoring system (calibrated in default probabilities) was able to give strong caution signals months prior to actual downgrades.

Turning back to the subject of market-based indicators (discussed above), an analysis of lending spreads is a key forward-looking indicator as it represents market expectations of the future credit quality of a borrower.

SPREAD TYPES

There are two principal credit spreads that are analyzed. Both tend to be discussed as "basis points," with one basis point equaling 0.01%, or 1.00% equaling 100 basis points.

1. **Bond spreads.** The margin by which the corporate bond yield exceeds the current yield on a U.S. Treasury Note of comparable duration.
2. **LIBOR spread.** Margin over the London Interbank **Bor**rowing rate that a borrower would have to pay to borrow money currently.

Using Credit Spreads to Measure Credit Risk

In theory, you can use the market credit spreads to determine credit risk or to calculate the overall expected credit loss. The presumption is that a credit grantor would require a spread that at least compensates them for the expected default losses. The question is which spread (Bond or Libor) is a better measure for determining expected default losses?

1. *Bond spread.* The bond spread is extremely useful for learning market sentiment. However, it may not be that useful in actually measuring credit risk. This is because there are several non-credit factors that contribute to the yield differential between corporate and government bonds.

2. ***Libor spread.*** The spread over LIBOR is seen as a closer proxy to a true credit differential spread. LIBOR is a common and very liquid reference used as a benchmark by international banks for its own short-term (one to six months) funding as well as to make corporate loans at a spread over LIBOR.

Using Credit Default Pricing for Measuring Credit Risk

Another approach to measuring credit risk utilizes the pricing of default swaps. As with credit spreads, default prices are forward-looking measures that should reflect market expectations of credit risk for a given counterparty. Default swaps can be thought of as insurance against default losses wherein the premium paid is an "actuarial" measure of expected rates of default coupled with expected recovery rates. A note of caution about the derivative market related to default swaps. This market for any single borrower can be somewhat illiquid. This illiquidity brings into question the efficiency of the market and how good it might be as a barometer of market expectations.

ALTMAN Z SCORE

Many credit professionals are familiar with credit scoring models developed by Edward I. Altman in 1968. The Altman Z Model uses a statistical technique known as multiple discriminant analysis (MDA).

There are four general steps involved in using MDA. First, one must determine a sample group. Second, one must establish explicit group classifications (two or more). Third, one has to collect data on all objects in the sample group. Fourth, one allows MDA to derive a linear combination of these particular characteristics which "best discriminates between the group classifications established in step two."

Altman's research followed the same four steps. First, he selected 66 manufacturing corporations as his initial sample group. He also made sure that one-half of these manufacturing companies had actually filed bankruptcy petitions. The remaining one-half of the companies were solvent manufacturing firms chosen at random. He, therefore, had established his two group classifications as bankrupt/non-bankrupt. Third, he reviewed a number of characteristics of a corporation (i.e., profitability, liquidity, etc.) by examining many different financial ratios. Eventually, he concluded that there were five ratios that were *statistically* significant in delineating between a company heading for bankruptcy and one, which was financially sound. With this data, he applied MDA to formulate the actual equation, which optimally weighted these five variables in a linear equation.

The result is the well-known Z equation as shown below:

$$Z = .012X1 + .014X2 + .033X3 + .006X4 + .999X5$$

Where: X1 = Net Working Capital ÷ Total Assets
X2 = Retained Earnings ÷ Total Assets
X3 = Earnings before Interest and Taxes ÷ Total Assets
X4= Market Value Equity ÷ Book Value of Total Debt
X5 = Sales ÷ Total Assets

Altman's formula utilizes five factors, four of which—Net Working Capital, Retained Earnings, Pre-Tax Earnings, and Sales—are divided by the fifth (Total Assets). Market Value (equity plus preferred stock), is divided by Total Liabilities. Each of these factors is then multiplied by an individual assigned weight. The five equations are then totaled to produce a "Z" score, which would indicate that the company may be a candidate for bankruptcy if the Z score falls below 1.81.[9]

1. $\dfrac{\text{Net Working Capital}}{\text{Assets}}$ × 1.2 = _____

2. $\dfrac{\text{Retained Earnings}}{\text{Assets}}$ × 1.4 = _____

3. $\dfrac{\text{Pre-Tax Earnings}}{\text{Assets}}$ × 3.3 = _____

4. $\dfrac{\text{Market Value}}{\text{Liabilities}}$ × 0.6 = _____

5. $\dfrac{\text{Sales}}{\text{Assets}}$ × 1.0 = _____

TOTAL "Z" SCORE   = _____

Z greater than 2.99 indicates a non-bankrupt company.
Z between 1.81 and 2.99 indicates the Zone of Ignorance.
Z less than 1.81 indicates a bankruptcy prone corporation.

[9]Edward I. Altman, *Corporate Financial Distress and Bankruptcy* (Hoboken, NJ: Wiley & Sons, 1993), 20.

Note that a score between 1.81 and 2.99 falls into what Altman described as a Zone of Ignorance. This gray area represents scores that are not statistically significant in terms of predicting whether a company is solvent or insolvent.

The model's advantages are obvious. It is fast, inexpensive, provides consistency between analysts, and offers a predictive value of approximately two years with approximately an 83 percent accuracy rate. Nonetheless, there are a number of significant disadvantages and/or pitfalls associated with the model's use. The most important are listed below:

1. Outdated: Altman's original model was based on information from 1945-1965. Aware of this potential weakness, Altman introduced a "new and improved" model in 1977. However, unlike the first version, this one is copyrighted and must be purchased from Altman's company.
2. Limitations in applications: Altman's original model is only valid with similar sized manufacturing companies.
3. Failure to discriminate between inherently weak firms and firms that are currently in a depressed industry.
4. Large zone of ignorance (roughly 20 percent).
5. Liquidity is based on working capital and not cash.
6. Four out of the five ratios are based on "total assets," which could possibly result in a bias against certain industries such as service companies.
7. Market value of a company's stock is not always available.
8. There have been significant accounting changes since Altman introduced his model (i.e., capitalization of leases).

A word of caution to the reader: this model should be used only in concept with other analytical tools.

LAMBDA

Measuring short-term liquidity is an important financial management task. A wide variety of familiar ratios have traditionally been used, however, none of these traditional ratios relate a firm's cash flow to its stock of liquid reserves. Nor do they recognize uncertainty and different time horizons. Traditional liquidity ratios have been used in nearly all of the credit scoring models but results have often been disappointing. One could argue that the traditional ratios are deficient for both theoretical and practical reasons.[10]

Lambda is a liquidity measurement ratio that predicts the probability of bankruptcy based upon historical cash flow analysis. It indicates the probability of being out of cash. Lambda is defined as:

$$\text{Lambda} = \frac{\text{Initial liquid reserve} + \begin{array}{c}\text{Total anticipated net cash}\\\text{flow during the analysis horizon}\end{array}}{\text{Uncertainty about net cash flow during analysis horizon}}$$

The larger the value of Lambda, the more liquid is the firm. A firm with a Lambda value of 3.0, for example, has liquid resources equal to three times its typical unexpected requirements for cash. Lambda can be described as a ratio of cash flow resources to potential cash flow requirements.

Any ratio that is used to measure short-term liquidity must have five characteristics if it is to perform well. These characteristics are:

1. The ratio must be related to the likelihood the firm will be able to meet its cash requirement
2. It must include only liquid resources
3. It must incorporate cash flow
4. It must recognize the effect of uncertainty
5. It must be adaptable to different time horizons

The traditional measures of working capital position, working capital activity, and leverage do not have these characteristics.

Three factors that determine a firm's ability to meet its cash obligations are as follows:

1. Size of the firm's liquid reserve
2. Characteristics of its cash flow
3. The length of the analysis horizon

Lambda is a coverage ratio that describes that extent to which the firm's potential cash obligations are covered by both its stock and liquid resources. Lambda not only incorporates the factors that determine a firm's ability to pay, but also meets the five conditions described above. Lambda has been demonstrated as an accurate measurer of both long-term and short-term solvency. The Lambda model is a big improvement over the Z score model because it directly addresses the issue of cash flow. After all, it takes cash to pay the bills. The Z score doesn't directly address cash flow.

---

[10]Gary W. Emery, "The Lambda Index: Beyond the Current Ratio," *Business Credit* (1991), 97.

ABC Company

Liquid Reserve

Cash	$ 59
Marketable Securities	100
Line of Credit (Bank Line)	515
Total	**$ 674**

Cash Flow from Operations

1995	$ 254
1996	$ 221
1997	$ 72
1998	$ 265
1999	$ 276
Anticipated Net Cash Flow	$ 198
(Add 5 years and divide by 5)	
Uncertainty about net cash flow	94

ABC Company: Lambda 674 + 198 = 9.3

They hint at the issue through the use of the net working capital-to-asset ratio... however, there are many shortcomings associated with the traditional liquidity ratios in my estimation. Therefore, working capital is an inadequate measure of liquidity.

The model's outcome, called Lambda, is simply a ratio. The numerator of the ratio is the firm's cash and marketable securities, as shown on the balance sheet. To this number is added any unused lines of credit that are available to the firm. You need to look into the notes to the financial statement to find this number. When added together, these two numbers represent the "liquid reserve".

Next, you add or subtract the firm's average free cash flow to the "liquid reserve." Free cash flow is the operating cash flow less capital expenditures. Both of these items are found in the Statement of Cash Flows. They are normally called cash flow from operations and cash flow from investing activities, respectively. The average free cash flow is based on the free cash flows for that and preceding years. By adding the average free cash flow number to the liquid reserve number, the result is called the "net liquid reserve." This number represents the numerator of the Lambda ratio.

The denominator of the ratio is the standard deviation of the free cash flow numbers. Standard deviation represents the variability of free cash flow during the historical period. If you want to know how to calculate standard deviations, ask your son or daughter in college... otherwise, just rely on the model to do it for you.

When the numerator (the expected cash resources) is divided by the denominator (the variability of cash flows), the resulting ratio is used to provide an estimate of the probability that the firm will be out of cash within the next year. As the lambda score becomes smaller, the probability of being out of cash becomes larger.

The Lambda model uses operating cash flow in the numerator—not free cash flow—so the model ignores capital expenditures. Many managers spend money on questionable assets under the guise that the investment is needed to grow the business. And many firms that file bankruptcy often do so because they grew too quickly. The true probability of a firm becoming bankrupt is most likely somewhere between these two probability measures. You need to interpret these scores in terms of any given situation and other opinions you have formed about the company. There is no magic cutoff score similar to the Altman model. If a company operates with high profit margins, you can take more risk in extending a credit line than companies with low margins.

The following is Lambda applied to a hypothetical situation:

BOND RATING

This predictive model is based on the academic research of two financial economists by the names of Kaplan and Urwitz. Their study appeared in an academic literature several years ago and does a reasonably good job of forecasting a company's bond rating. This model is dependent on the company's asset size (the bigger the better), whether it has debt that is subordinated (bad) or unsubordinated (good), the long-term debt-to-total asset ratio (the smaller the better), the profitability of the company as measured by net income divided by sales (the higher the better), the variability in net income as measured by a statistic called the coefficient of variation (the lower the better) and the interest coverage ratio (the higher the better). If you stop to think about each of these elements, you will agree that their impact on the bond rating is in the direction you would expect. For example, if the company has a high level of debt relative to total assets, it is riskier than a firm with a low debt level.

MODEL FORMATS:

ALTMAN Z SCORE, EMERY LAMBDA INDEX (TWO MODELS), KAPLAN-URWITZ BOND RATE PREDICTION

Altman's Z Score Bankruptcy Prediction
Cash & Marketable securities
Unused lines of credit
Liquid reserve
Free cash flow
Net liquid reserve
Standard deviation of expected cash flows

Liquid reserve
Operating cash flow
Net liquid reserve
Standard deviation of expected OCF
Emery's Lambda Index of Cash Insolvency

Cash & Marketable securities
Unused lines of credit
Liquid reserve
Free cash flow
Net liquid reserve
Standard deviation of expected cash flows
Emery's Adjusted Lambda Index to Include FCF

Kaplan-Urwitz Bond Rate Prediction
Private & Non-manufacturing firms
EBIT/Total assets
Net working capital ÷ Total assets
Book value equity ÷ Book value debt
Retained earnings ÷ Total assets
Total Score

Chapter 16

RATING AGENCIES AND DEFAULT PROBABILITIES

A credit rating agency is a firm that provides its opinion on the creditworthiness of an entity and the financial obligations (such as, bonds, preferred stock, and commercial paper) issued by an entity. Generally, credit ratings distinguish between investment grade and non-investment grade. For example, a credit rating agency may assign a "triple A" credit rating as its top "investment grade" rating for corporate bonds and a "double B" credit rating or below for "non-investment grade" or "high-yield" corporate bonds.

Some credit rating agencies whose credit ratings are used under the SEC's regulations are known as Nationally Recognized Statistical Rating Organizations or NRSROs. There are currently four NRSROs—Dominion Bond Rating Service Ltd., Fitch, Inc., Moody's Investors Service, and the Standard & Poor's Division of the McGraw Hill Companies Inc.

Default risk is the uncertainty surrounding a firm's ability to service its debts and obligations. Prior to default, there is no way to discriminate unambiguously between firms that will default and those that will not. At best we can only make probabilistic assessments of the likelihood of default. As a result, firms generally pay a spread over the default-free rate of interest that is proportional to their probability to compensate lenders for this uncertainty.

Default is a deceptively rare event. The typical firm has a default probability of around 2 percent in any year. However, there is considerable variation in default probabilities across firms. For example, the odds of a firm with a AAA rating defaulting are only about 2 in 10,000 per annum. A single A-rated firm has odds of around 10 in 10,000 per annum, five times higher than a AAA. At the bottom of the rating scale, a CCC-rated firm's odds of defaulting are 4 in 100 (4%), 200 times the odds of a AAA-rated firm.

There are three main elements that determine the default probability of a firm:

1. *Value of Assets:* The market value of the firm's assets. This is a measure of the present value of the future free cash flows produced by the firm's assets discounted back at the appropriate discount rate. This measures the firm's prospects and incorporates relevant information about the firm's industry and the economy.

2. *Asset Risk:* The uncertainty or risk of the asset value. This is measure of the firm's business and industry risk. The value of the firm's assets is an estimate and is thus uncertain. As a result, the value of the firm's assets should always be understood in the context of the firm's business or asset risk.

3. *Leverage:* The extent of the firm's contractual liabilities. Whereas the relevant measure of the firm's assets is always their market value, the book value of liabilities relative to the market value of assets is the pertinent measure of the firm's leverage, since that is the amount the firm must repay.

The default risk of the firm increases as the value of the assets approaches the book value of the liabilities, until finally the firm defaults when the market value of the assets is insufficient to repay the liabilities. Studies have indicated that, in general, firms do not default when their asset value reaches the book value of their total liabilities. While some firms certainly default at this point, many continue to trade and service their debts. The long-term nature of some of their liabilities provides these firms with some breathing space. Certain studies have found that the default point, the asset value at which the firm will default, generally lies somewhere between total liabilities and current, or short-term liabilities.

MEASURING DEFAULT PROBABILITY: A PRACTICAL APPROACH

There are three basic types of information available that are relevant to the default probability of a firm: financial statements, market prices of the firm's debt and equity, and subjective appraisals of the firm's prospects and risk. Recall that default probability is the probability that the counterparty or borrower will fail to service its obligations.

Financial statements, by their nature, are inherently backward looking. They are reports of the past. Prices, by their nature, are inherently forward looking. Investors form debt and equity prices as they anticipate the firm's future. In determining the market prices, investors use, among many other things, subjective appraisals of the firm's prospects and risk, financial statements, and other market prices. This information is combined using their own analysis and synthesis and results in their willingness to buy and sell the debt and equity securities of the firm. Market prices are the result of the combined willingness of many investors to buy and sell so prices reflect the synthesized views and forecasts of many investors. As a result of this combined effect, the most effective default measurement derives from models that utilize both market prices and financial statements. Default analysts will typically want to use market prices in the determination of default risk because prices add considerably to the predictive power of the estimates.

Oldrich Vasicek and Stephen Kealhofer have extended the Black-Scholes-Merton framework to produce a model of default probability known as the Vasicek-Kealhofer (VK) model.[11] This model assumes the firm's equity is a perpetual option with the default point acting as the absorbing barrier for the firm's asset value. When the asset value hits the default point, the firm is assumed to default. Multiple classes of liabilities are modeled: short-term liabilities, long-term items convertible debt, preferred equity and common equity. When the firm's asset value becomes very large, the convertible securities are assumed to convert and dilute the existing equity. In addition, cash payouts such as dividends are explicitly used in the VK model. A default database is used to derive an empirical distribution relating the distance-to-default to a default probability. In this way, the relationship between asset value and liabilities can be captured without resorting to a substantially more complex model characterizing a firm's liability process. A predictor model called KMV has implemented the VK model to calculate an Expected Default Frequency (EDF) credit measure which is the probability of default during the forthcoming year, or years for firms with publicly traded equity (this model can also be modified to produce EDF values for firms without publicly traded equity.) The EDF value requires equity prices and certain items from financial statements as inputs. EDF credit measures can be viewed and analyzed within the context of a software product called Credit Monitor (CM). CM calculates EDF values for years 1 through 5 allowing the user to see a term structure EDF values. KMV's EDF credit measure assumes that default is defined as the nonpayment of any scheduled payment, interest or principal.

Default risk cannot be hedged or "structured" away. The government cannot insure it away. It is a reflection of the substantial risk in a company's future. Various schemes exist—and more are coming—which can shift risk, but in the end, someone must bear this risk. It does not "net out" in the aggregate.

---

[11]Peter J. Crosbie, *Modeling Default Risk* (KMV LLC, 2002).

How does the KMV's EDF model deal with off-balance sheet liabilities? This is a critical question (Enron) for many firms, particularly financial institutions where these liabilities can obviously be quite significant. Fortunately, the model is surprisingly robust to the precise level of the liabilities.

Why isn't information from the bond or credit derivatives market included? There is a whole class of models, usually called reduced-form models that relate credit spreads and default probabilities. There is nothing wrong with the models per se. However, the data required to calibrate and implement reduced-form models is not yet widely available. In most cases credit risk simply is not an activity and cleanly traded as equities at the moment.

There are essentially three steps in the determination of the default probability of a firm:

1. *Estimate asset value and volatility*. In this step the asset value and asset volatility of the firm is estimated from the market value and volatility of equity and the book value of liabilities.
2. *Calculate the distance-to-default*. The distance-to-default (DD) is calculated from the asset value and asset volatility (estimated in the first step) and the book value of liabilities.
3. *Calculate the default probability*. The default probability is determined directly from the distance-to-default and the default rate for given levels of distance-to-default.

KMV Scoring Model Overview

In estimation, Credit Scoring and Financial Analysis are not interchangeable. Each provides a different value. Both have strengths and weaknesses.

Credit scoring promotes consistency and allows you to rank-order counterparties using common predictors. It is a very efficient and automated approach. It's also easy to train credit personnel to use a model.

With regards to financial analysis, efficacy can vary based on the analyst skill and information availability. The trick is to look for red flags or changes that may have a material adverse affect on credit quality going forward. One must interpret subjective factors and this may require a lot of manual effort. Personal expertise and industry knowledge are essential in making the call. However, credit scoring and financial analysis do not fully cover the credit analysis continuum. The past is covered by credit scoring as it uses actual quantitative data to rank-order a population of counterparties by risk (i.e., expected default probability). This is the Credit

Science approach. Financial analysis is the Credit Art portion. You rely on expert analysis of the current state of a counterparty (plus industry, macroeconomic factors, etc.) to identify changes or emerging trends that could affect that counterparty's creditworthiness (for good or bad).

Taking this one step further, the credit science and art are integrated and the future is evaluated with cash flow forecasting and bankruptcy modeling based on cash flows (Lambda model). Cash flow forecasting provides a forward look of potential creditworthiness extrapolated from historical financial performance and remaining portions of existing bank lines, as refined through insights gained from prospective analysis.

Specifically, with regards to KMV, it can be a good scoring tool but only one piece of the overall analytical process as described above. There are advantages and disadvantages or imperfections with the KMV model.

1. The model is good only for publicly rated, traded companies. However, a new model is being developed by KMV that will be established for non-publicly traded companies.
2. The model puts too much emphasis on short-term nature of indicators such as stock price. We know how profoundly stock prices get affected by information flow.
3. Pricing of a firm's debt is influenced by interest rates.
4. Not sure how the model treats off-balance sheet liabilities and other commitments.
5. There is a suggestion with the KMV model that bond market and its spreads play a role in estimating default probability of a firm. However, the bond or credit derivatives market is not explicitly included in the model.
6. KMV must assume a lot of information about a given counterparty and then adjust for these assumptions with default spreads and credit derivatives.
7. KMV uses Equity Value (market value) vs. Book Value. Stock analysts would not take this approach.
8. It's more about having a database of experience not the model itself.

In summary, KMV is an important piece of information but certainly not the only piece. There are weaknesses that should not be ignored. Your analysis should incorporate a full counterparty assessment that combines credit scoring, financial analysis as well as cash flow forecasting.

The ultimate call on creditworthiness lies with the analysts and credit managers. The objective here is to supplement that process and to provide a standardizing or calibrating measure that can be used to validate the analyst's call, and equate a risk rank and probability of default with counterparties—particularly using the S&P scale and P(d)'s. As long as you can bucket your exposures meaningfully into the S&P categories, and "check" those calls using another measure such as Z score, Lambda, S&P Credit Scores or Moody's "Risk Calc", we will have the desired P(d)'s usable for portfolio management and other aggregation objectives.

Mentioned earlier was the work performed by Oldrich Vasicek and Stephen Kealhofer that extended the Black-Scholes-Merton framework to produce a model of default probability known as the Vasicek-Kealhofer (VK) model. Black-Scholes, then Black-Scholes-Merton models as they relate directly to the KMV VK model just discussed, follow.

The Black and Scholes Option Pricing Model didn't appear overnight, in fact, Fisher Black started out working to create a valuation model for stock warrants. This work involved calculating a derivative to measure how the discount rate of a warrant varies with time and stock price. The result of this calculation held a striking resemblance to a well-known heat transfer equation. Soon after this discovery, Myron Scholes joined Black and the result of their work is a startlingly accurate option-pricing model. Black and Scholes can't take all credit for their work, in fact their model is actually an improved version of a previous model developed by A. James Boness in his Ph.D. dissertation at the University of Chicago. Black and Scholes' improvements on the Boness model come in the form of a proof that the risk-free interest rate is the correct discount factor, and with the absence of assumptions regarding investor's risk preferences.

In order to understand the model itself, we divide it into two parts. The first part, $SN(d_1)$, derives the expected benefit from acquiring a stock outright. This is found by multiplying stock price [S] by the change in the call premium with respect to a change in the underlying stock price [$N(d_1)$]. The second part of the model, $Ke^{(-rt)}N(d_2)$, gives the present value of paying the exercise price on the expiration day. The fair market value of the call option is then calculated by taking the difference between these two parts.

Assumptions of the Black and Scholes Model

1. *The stock pays no dividends during the option's life.* Most companies pay dividends to their shareholders, so this might seem a serious limitation to the model considering the observation that higher dividend yields elicit lower call premiums. A common way of adjusting the model for this situation is to subtract the discounted value of a future dividend from the stock price.

2. *European exercise terms are used.* European exercise terms
    dictate that the option can only be exercised on the expiration
    date. American exercise terms allow the option to be exercised at
    any time during the life of the option, making American options
    more valuable due to their greater flexibility. This limitation is not
    a major concern because very few calls are ever exercised before
    the last few days of their life. This is true because when you
    exercise a call early, you forfeit the remaining time value on the
    call and collect the intrinsic value. Towards the end of the life of a
    call, the remaining time value is very small, but the intrinsic value
    is the same.

3. *Markets are efficient.* This assumption suggests that people cannot
    consistently predict the direction of the market or an individual
    stock. The market operates continuously with share prices
    following a continuous Itô process. To understand what a
    continuous Itô process is, you must first know that a Markov
    process is "one where the observation in time period "t" depends
    only on the preceding observation." An Itô process is simply a
    Markov process in continuous time. If you were to draw a
    continuous process you would do so without picking the pen up
    from the piece of paper.

4. *No commissions are charged.* Usually market participants do have
    to pay a commission to buy or sell options. Even floor traders pay
    some kind of fee, but it is usually very small. The fees that
    Individual investor's pay is more substantial and can often distort
    the output of the model.

5. *Interest rates remain constant and known.* The Black and Scholes
    model uses the risk-free rate to represent this constant and known
    rate. In reality there is no such thing as the risk-free rate, but the
    discount rate on U.S. Government Treasury Bills with 30 days left
    until maturity is usually used to represent it. During periods of
    rapidly changing interest rates, these 30-day rates are often subject
    to change, thereby violating one of the assumptions of the model.

6. *Returns are lognormally distributed.* This assumption suggests,
    returns on the underlying stock are normally distributed, which is
    reasonable for most assets that offer options.

Since 1973, the original Black and Scholes Option Pricing Model has
been the subject of much attention. Many financial scholars have
expanded upon the original work. In 1973, Robert Merton relaxed the

assumption of no dividends. In 1976, Jonathan Ingerson went one step further and relaxed the assumption of no taxes or transaction costs. In 1976, Merton responded by removing the restriction of constant interest rates. The results of all of this attention that originated in the autumn of 1969 are alarmingly accurate valuation models for stock options.

In summary, KMV's Portfolio Manager uses a Merton approach, in which loans are valued as call options on a borrower firm's asset values, using a Black-Scholes pricing framework. Asset values are assumed to be closely related to a firm's market equity values, so that stock prices and stock price volatilities can be used as the key inputs to the model. The default point is derived from the firm's balance sheet. Once a distribution for future asset values has been generated it is translated into an expected default frequency (EFD) distribution by comparison with a large historical database of default incidents.

Pros: Forward-looking since it uses stock prices as its major input. Able to model any listed company. Strong theoretical model, which also accounts for cyclical conditions.

Cons: Not able to model unlisted companies. Theoretical approach to modeling loans of large size relative to a firm's asset value and therefore not relevant to trade credit. Assumes constant debt structure in borrowing firm. Inaccurate when used to model short-term exposures—BSM pricing model predicts almost zero risk over short times.

Black and Scholes Model

$C = SN(d_1) - Ke^{(-rt)}N(d_2)$

C = Theoretical Call Premium

S = Current Stock Price

t = Time Until Option Expiration

K = Option Striking Price

r = Risk-Free Interest Rate

N = Cumulative Standard Normal Distribution

e = Exponential Term (2.7183)

$$d_1 = \frac{\ln(S \div K) + (r + \frac{s^2}{2})t}{s\sqrt{t}}$$

$d_2 = d_1 - s\sqrt{t}$

s = Standard Deviation of Stock Returns

ln = Natural Logarithm

Chapter 17

PORTFOLIO RISK ANALYSIS

Credit risk measurement has evolved over time. Fewer companies are analyzing risk at a single point and are using techniques based on projecting risk factors over specific time periods. Included among the most popular of these techniques are CVAR and Monte Carlo. Both methods enable assessment of default and/or credit migration (downgrades) probabilities.

Credit risk measurement methodologies must allow for time and market and position/transaction dynamics.

Each step in Figure 17-1 represents increasing levels of sophistication in risk measurement methodologies. Notional credit risk is the easiest to measure. Current mark-to-market requires analysis of asset liquidity. Potential exposure at the transaction level requires quantification of cost entailed in asset replacement.

Exposure at the portfolio level must include the correlation of assets; exposure at the portfolio level is not the same thing as exposure at the transaction level. For example, each individual deal might be creditworthy, but since they're all in the same industry, exposure to an adverse credit event could be excessive. On the other hand, if various transactions within a portfolio offset each other it would reduce the overall credit exposure.

Finally Value at Risk incorporates the volatility of assets held within the portfolio and includes the probability of loss (CVAR includes the probability of an adverse credit event).

This chapter will cover three specific concepts related to portfolio analysis. They are:

- Value-at-Risk (VAR)
- Volatility
- Capital at Risk (CAR)

Value-at-Risk (VAR) provides companies with a valuable tool to measure and control market risk. Premier trading and marketing

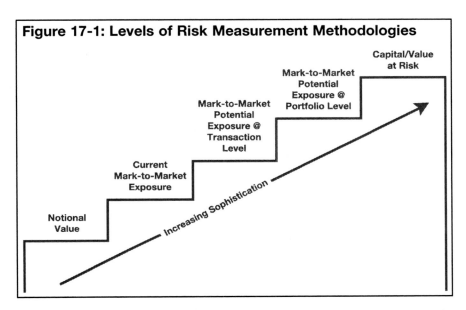

Figure 17-1: Levels of Risk Measurement Methodologies

companies around the world use Value-at-Risk to maximize profit opportunities and minimize costly positioning mistakes.

VAR is a statistical estimation of the potential effect of market movements on a portfolio, with a defined probability. VAR is a powerful measurement tool and represents a consistent yardstick to estimate and quantify the market risk associated with a diverse portfolio of exposures. One of the measure's greatest benefits is that it results in a simple statement that is easy to understand.

Capital at Risk (CAR) is a tool to measure and control credit risk. No prescribed methodology exists for quantifying the capital required by an energy company to back credit risk positions. The intent of any such calculation should be to measure the expected loss from a default probability which is qualified by the magnitude of the statistical measure of the counterparty's credit strength.

Before getting into the specifics related to VAR and CAR measurements, let us first turn our attention to the concept of **Volatility**. This is a measure of how uncertain we are about the future values that will be taken by a variable. In other words, how dispersed are the likely deviations from expectations. This is an important concept in measuring risk in that it is a measure of the speed of the market given your current position. Markets which move slowly are low-volatility markets; markets which move quickly are high-volatility markets. For example, high technology stocks tend to be more volatile than utility stocks. Natural gas

Figure 17-2: Risk Capital

Market Risk	Credit Risk	Operational Risk
Flat Price	Default Risk	Human
Volatility	Rating Downgrade	Processes
Open Positions	Sovereign Risk	Systems
Holding Period	Concentration Risk	External
How to capture market liquidity risk in VAR?	Rating systems and credit risk models.	Quantitative and qualitative approaches will be developed further.

Risk Management
- Market Risk is measured by M VaR.
- Credit Risk is monitored by multi-faceted measurements, including net credit exposure, potential future exposure, expected loss and unexpected loss. The most relevant measurement to a Financial Framework is unexpected loss.
- Quantitative and Qualitative Operational Risk approaches must be defined.

has higher volatility than coal, so it has a higher probability of achieving very good or very bad performance.

Volatility greatly impacts credit exposure. The effect of different volatilities has important impacts on credit risk measurements. Natural gas, with its higher volatility has a greater chance of moving far into the money than coal. This larger unrealized gain represents a larger potential credit exposure.

PROBABILITY DISTRIBUTION

When statistical methods are used to quantify the relative likelihood of an event, the result is a probability distribution. A probability distribution used extensively in risk analytics is the Normal Distribution. Normal distribution curves are used to describe the likely outcomes of random events. Fortunately, a normal distribution curve can be fully described with two numbers, the mean and the standard deviation. If we know that a distribution is normal, and we also know these two numbers, then we know all the characteristics of the distribution. Graphically, we can interpret the mean as the location of the peak of the curve, and the standard deviation as a measure of how fast the curve spreads out. The mean is nothing more than the average outcome. Add up all the outcomes and

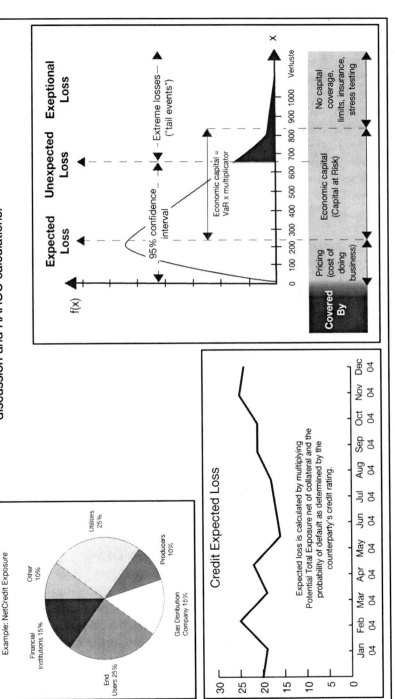

Figure 17-3: Risk Capital (credit risk)

The development of unexpected loss is most relevant to economic capital allocation purpose. Thus use the UL for Financial Framework discussion and RAROC calculations.

divide by the number of occurrences will give you the mean number. The speed of change or standard deviation not only describes how fast the distribution spreads out; it also tells us something about the likelihood of an occurrence ending in a particular distance from the mean. For example, if the mean is calculated to be 7.50 and the standard deviation is 3.00; what does this tell us about the distribution? How far from the mean will the occurrence actually take place? One standard deviation from the mean is 7.50 +/– 3 = 4.50 to 10.50. We also know that one standard deviation takes in about 2/3 of all occurrences. A +/– two standard deviations would represents about 95.4% of all occurrences.

KEY RISK PARAMETERS

In summary of the above, there are two key numbers necessary for the statistical analysis used in credit exposure measurement:

1. Expected Value (Mean: generally assumed to be the market price)
2. Standard Deviation (Dispersion around the Mean given by Volatility)

Relationship between Volatility and Standard Deviation

Volatility is standard deviation expressed as a percentage of the market price.

$$\text{Volatility} = \frac{\text{Standard Deviation}}{\text{Market Price}}$$

If the average (mean) price is: $40 and the standard deviation is $8 (one standard deviation) then the volatility would be:

$$= \frac{\$8}{\$40} = .20 \text{ or } 20\%$$

The expected value is the value (e.g., forward price) in which we would expect half the likely outcomes (e.g., future spot price) to be above the value and half the likely outcomes to be below that value. In other words, it is the average or mean of the expected likely outcomes.

The standard deviation allows us to determine where the values of a frequency distribution are located in relation to the mean. With a normal distribution, we know that 68 percent of the values in a population will fall within +/– one standard deviation as indicated in Figure 17-4.

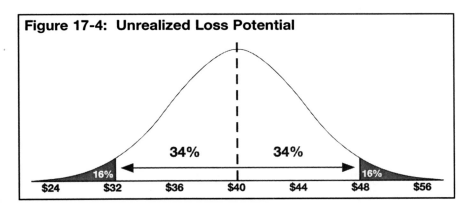

Figure 17-4: Unrealized Loss Potential

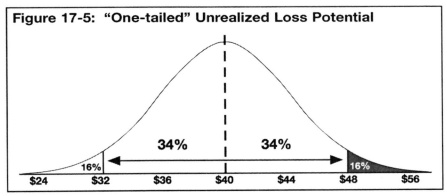

Figure 17-5: "One-tailed" Unrealized Loss Potential

In the analysis of counterparty credit exposure, the focus is on the potential for unrealized gains that may not be realized due to counterparty default. The potential for unrealized losses from a price risk position, while an obvious concern, it is not relevant to default risk (no loss would result from a counterparty default if a transaction is in a loss position). Credit exposure focuses only on upside (gain) risk. Analysis therefore will be "one-tailed," examining the probability of price movements in the favorable direction as indicated in Figure 17-5.

RISK AND CAPITAL ALLOCATION

The conservative tendency to overstate risk may appear prudent. But the consequences of overstating risk is to require more excessive capital backing, reducing apparent expected returns and thus resulting in poor business decisions and inefficient capital allocation. In some cases, the results using 100 percent confidence are unworkable since it can result in infinitely large risk.

If you impose a requirement of 100 percent, VAR would probably destroy established businesses. For example, insurance could not be provided since there would be the possibility that all policyholders would make a claim at the same time. And commercial banks could not make loans from its customer deposits since there would be the possibility that all their customers would want to withdraw their funds at the same time. There would be the possibility that all their loans would default at the same time.

Types of Volatility

Several forms of volatility are commonly referenced.

Historic Volatility

The measure of a time series of historic prices results in a backward-looking quantification of what volatility was in the past. Although this is useful information, it is not an indication of volatility of future prices. The measure of credit exposures relies on estimates of volatility in future periods.

Forecast Volatility

A forward-looking estimate, forecast volatility is an expectation of future volatility. Credit exposure analysis relies on the use of an appropriate forecast of volatility.

Implied Volatility

This is a specialized forecast of volatility. It reflects market expectations of future period volatility.

Capital Value at Risk (CVAR)

Unlike the methodology in worst-case loss VAR, in which the holding period relates not to the term of the transactions, but the time required to liquidate the position, CVAR must generally assume the credit risk position is held for the full term of the transaction.

Three variables are applied against the transaction amount to get CVAR:

1. Current total market value of the transaction
2. Annual volatility
3. Period over which the exposure will be held
4. Desired confidence level

Carrying the CVAR concept one step further, the maximum potential exposure (MPE) calculation of any given transaction will have two components:

1) mark-to-market value, if in-the-money; which is your current exposure; plus
2) the maximum CVAR based on the current market price, volatility and remaining term of the contract (potential exposure).

Written as a formula:

MPE = Current (MTM) Exposure + CVAR (Potential Exposure)

Credit risk dynamics come into play with CVAR calculations when we consider that the MPE credit exposure is not an amount fixed at the inception of a transaction. Mark-to-market value will change with prices. CVAR will change with time, market volatility, and prices. This gives rise to the possibility that, without changing a portfolio of deals that originally fit under an existing credit exposure limit, the unchanged portfolio could subsequently exceed those limits without any new trades.

Capital at Risk

This leads to a discussion about Capital at Risk. As stated earlier, no prescribed methodology exists for quantifying the capital required by an energy company to back credit risk positions. The intent of any calculation made should be to measure the expected loss from a default position which will be qualified by the magnitude of the statistical measure of the counterparty's credit strength.

One of the more straightforward approaches to measuring Capital at Risk (CAR) is to begin with the largest exposure (CVAR) that would be anticipated of the life of the transaction. This potential loss is qualified by credit quality by multiplying it by the default rate and the recovery rate. As with CVAR this will vary with the forward term length.

$$\text{CAR} = \frac{\text{CVAR}}{\text{Variable}} \times \frac{\text{Default Probability}}{\text{Constant}} \times \frac{(1 - \text{Recovery Rate})}{\text{Constant}}$$

CAR or any given transaction can be thought of as the maximum expected default (i.e., maximum credit risk value) over the projected term of the deal.

An alternative method for determining CAR involves modifying the capital measure. To offset the methods overstatement of risk and capital, a firm might:

• Reduce the confidence level (e.g., to 84 percent or only 1.0 standard deviation)

- Use average credit risk over the term rather than the maximum credit risk
- Apply marginal default rates to period-specific exposures

The above approach will definitely offset the overstated method for risk and capital calculations.

DEFAULT MODEL PARADIGMS

In these models, the only two states of interest are default or no default. No credit loss is recognized until default occurs. The model depends only on the default probability distribution and the credit exposure.

Credit limits are eventually set for each counterparty dealt with while taking into account their creditworthiness, the likely volume of business and your business unit's risk tolerance. Most effort will be spent on the mid tier counterparty risk (Categories 3–7 in Figure 17-6).

Any exposure calculation is net of the credit risk mitigating tools used (discussed in a subsequent chapter). The main methods used are letters of credit, confirmed if necessary, netting agreements, and perhaps credit derivatives (covered in subsequent chapters).

Now, lets try to quantify the annual expected losses based on the following methodology:

- Open credit counterparties should be placed into nine risk categories.
- A default probability, largely derived from S&P annual default tables, is then applied to each risk category.
- This default probability is then multiplied by the credit exposure for each counterparty to produce expected default values.

In general, the result from this methodology is most useful for indicating relative levels of risk in your debt portfolio, rather than absolute levels. It will become more useful as the exercise is repeated so that trends can be established. As a result, you have developed a credit value at risk methodology that calculates a possible expected loss scenario. However, primarily due to the very short-term nature of one's risk, the calculation will overstate the real expected loss and, therefore, why the outcome will be considerably higher than your actual credit loss experience.

After completing the exercise, you will probably find that the calculations are conservative as a result of the assumptions made and described above, therefore, you should be capable of taking higher levels of credit risk where

Figure 17-6: Risk Categories

S&P Rating	Moody's Rating	Internal Credit Rating	Credit Rating 1-Year P(d) Risk
AAA to AA–	Aaa to Aa3	1	0.02%
A+ to A–	A1 to A3	2	0.03%
BBB+ to BBB	Baa1 to Baa2	3	0.26%
BB+	Ba1	4	0.67%
BB–	Ba3	5	2.34%
B+	B1	6	3.22%
B to B–	B2 to B3	7	9.05%
CCC	Caa	8	23.49%
Other	—	9	27.87%

Internal Credit Rating Explanations

1   Extremely strong counterparty, strong balance sheet and profitable. Compares favorably with the upper quartile of market sector. Survivability of business deemed strong, no signs of insolvency. Organization likely to be operating for foreseeable future.

2   Strong but more susceptible to changes in circumstances and prevailing economic conditions. Strong balance sheet in the short- and long-term and are profitable. Compares with upper quartile of the market sector. Can also be weak but part of a group with strong balance sheet and $ performance. Survivability strong.

3   Adequate profile but vulnerable to adverse moves in conditions and circumstances. Moderate balance sheet in short- and long-term or some weakness in the short term which is consistent with industry averages. Profitable but margins under pressure. Compares with average performers in industry sector. Survivability: < 1 year.

4   Less vulnerable than grades 5-9 but faces ongoing uncertainties. Moderate balance sheet which compares with worst performers in market sector. Some pressure evident on business with evidence of cash flow weakness, consistently deteriorating profile and pressure on margins. Survivability: at least 1 year.

5   Uncertainties increase in materiality and could affect counterparty's ability to repay. Balance sheet is worse than poorest performers in market sector. Poor leverage and an adverse cash flow. Pressure from creditors could be evident. Losses will be seen with a deteriorating profile. Survivability: 1 year.

6   Currently has ability to repay but marginal adverse moves in macro/micro position will put this in doubt. Balance sheet tends towards an insolvent position. Judgments registered and unfavorable comparisons made with market sector. Deteriorating profile. Survivability: potentially < 1 year.

7   Doubt about current ability to repay exists. Insolvent balance sheet, judgments registered performing worse than majority of performers in market sector. Losses occurring and imminent insolvency proceedings anticipated. Survivability: < 6 months.

8   Highly vulnerable to nonpayment, ongoing viability depends on favorable conditions. An entity with an insolvent balance sheet, judgments registered performing significantly worse than poorer performers in market sector. Losses occurring and insolvency proceedings imminent. Survivability: < 6 months.

9   Near bankruptcy.

it provides a suitable return and supports the business objectives. It is recommended to take the risks in a focused way to optimize the risk/return ratio, rather than as a general relaxation of credit standards.

How can we use this Agency information to assess your overall customer portfolio? Try using the risk ranking technique in Figure 17-6.

The credit professional may choose to assign a probability of default assessment to specific counterparties irrespective of the public or internal rating. Such an assessment should be based on market information or an internal review. In other words, you may not always agree with the assigned agency rating.

S&P Rating Definitions

Long-Term Credit Ratings

AAA. An obligation rated "AAA" has the highest rating assigned by Standard and Poor's. The obligor's capacity to meet its financial commitment on the obligation is extremely strong.

AA. An obligation rated "AA" differs from the highest rated obligations only in small degree. The obligor's capacity to meet its financial commitment on the obligation is very strong.

A. An obligation rated "A" is somewhat more susceptible to adverse effects of changes in circumstances and economic conditions than obligations in higher rated categories. However, the obligor's capacity to meet its financial obligations is still strong.

BBB. An obligation rated "BBB" exhibits adequate protection parameters. However, adverse economic conditions, or changing circumstances are more likely to lead to a weakened capacity of the obligor to meet its financial commitment to the obligation.

Obligations rated "BB" through "C" are regarded as having significant speculative characteristics. "BB" indicates the least degree of speculation and "C" the highest. While such obligations will likely have some quality and protective characteristics, these may be outweighed by large uncertainties or major exposures to adverse conditions.

BB. An obligation rated "BB" is less vulnerable to nonpayment than other speculative issues. However, it faces major ongoing uncertainties or exposure to adverse business, financial, or economic conditions, which could lead to the obligor's inadequate capacity to meet financial commitment on the obligation.

B. An obligation rated "B" is more vulnerable to nonpayment than obligations rated "BB," but the obligor currently has the capacity to meet its financial obligation. Adverse business, financial, or economic conditions will likely impair the obligor's capacity to or willingness to meet its financial commitment on the obligation.

CCC. An obligation rated "CCC" is currently vulnerable to nonpayment, and is dependent upon favorable business, financial and economic conditions for the obligor to meet its financial commitment on the obligation. In case of adverse business, financial, or economic conditions, the obligor is not likely to have the capacity to meet its financial commitment on the obligation.

CC. An obligation rated "CC" is currently highly vulnerable to nonpayment.

C. The "C" rating may be used to cover a situation where a bankruptcy petition has been filed or similar action has been taken, but payments on the obligation are being continued.

D. The "D" rating, unlike other Standard & Poor's ratings, is not prospective; rather, it is used to only where a default has actually occurred —and not where a default is only expected.

The ratings from "AA" to "CCC" may be modified by the addition of a plus (+) or minus (–) sign to show relative standing within the major categories.

POTENTIAL FUTURE EXPOSURE (PFE)

A high-level explanation of a PFE calculation is as follows: Potential Future Exposure (PFE) is the estimated future mark-to-market value of a portfolio of deals with a given counterparty, described as probability distribution (i.e., a function assigning a probability of occurrence to a range of possible future exposure values at time t).

Where a commercial arrangement extends beyond normal payment terms, it is important to consider whether your company is exposed to an increased level of credit at some point in the future. Credit risk managers traditionally remain focused on current exposure measurement (i.e., current mark-to-market exposure, plus outstanding receivables) and collateral management. The problem with this focus is that it places excessive emphasis on the present and fails to provide an acceptable indication of credit risk at some point in the future. Because losses from credit risk take a relatively long time to evolve, a more useful measure of exposure is potential exposure. Potential exposure is not like current exposure. It exists in the future and therefore represents a range or distribution of outcomes rather than a single point estimate.

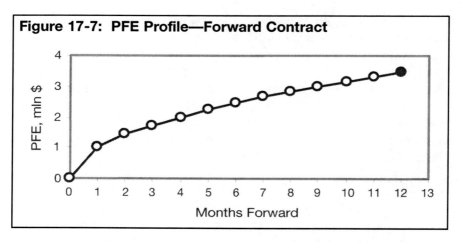

Figure 17-7: PFE Profile—Forward Contract

For all contracts, a qualitative process assessing the tenor and legal rights within the contract and an estimate of PFE under a range of possible price scenarios should be signed off by the Segment Executive before commitment. When possible, PFE should be estimated using statistical simulation techniques that incorporate the "Monte Carlo" model, at least for large financial mark-to-market contracts. PFE can be removed or considerably reduced through clear credit rights in the legal documentation (e.g., termination clauses, collateral rights, etc.).

Potential Future Exposure (PFE) is defined as maximum credit exposures over a specified period of time calculated at some level of confidence. This maximum is not to be confused with the maximum credit exposure possible. Instead, the maximum credit exposure indicated by the PFE analysis is an upper bound on a confidence interval for future credit exposure.

For example, a risk analyst finds that PFE for a swap transaction with XYZ Corp. is $10 million at a 70 percent confidence level. This means that there is a 70 percent chance that our credit exposure to XYZ Corp. over the entire life of the swap will not exceed $10 million. Of course the actual credit exposure in the future might exceed $10 million however the PFE analysis indicates that this is not very likely to happen.

Potential future exposure is not constant over the life of a contract. It is typically reported as a single number, which corresponds to a maximum point on the PFE profile. The shape of the PFE profile depends on the type of a contact in question and portfolio composition. Two PFE profiles are particularly instructive.

A **forward contract** profile has a monotonically increasing PFE curve (Figure 17-7). The initial mark-to-market value of a forward contract is

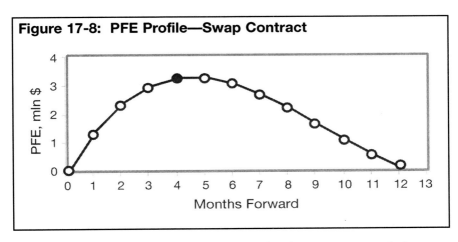

Figure 17-8: PFE Profile—Swap Contract

zero, hence there is no credit exposure. As time progresses, it is more likely that the forward contract will have either positive or negative mark-to-market value and hence the credit exposure. PFE for a forward contract reaches a maximum at the time of contract maturity.

A **swap contract** profile has a different PFE profile (Figure 17-8). The initial mark-to-market value of a swap is zero, hence there is no credit exposure. The swap PFE steadily increases until the beginning of the pricing period. This point corresponds to a maximum in the swap PFE profile. Once the swap pricing period is reached, the potential future exposure starts to decline as the swap payments are settled between the parties, eliminating the outstanding credit risk.

As illustrated by Figure 17-9, this credit management process is enabled by the PFE model, in conjunction with a thorough credit analysis of the counterparty. Currently there are several steps involved in this process as follows:

1. Traders or marketers send the deal request in the agreed format to the Trade Finance Executive to run PFE for the potential deals.
2. Trade Finance Executive and the Credit Analyst review the counterparty credit quality.
3. Trade Finance and Credit manager provides credit guide based on the PFE result and credit analysis.
4. Traders and marketers conduct the deals based on the credit guide.
5. Trade Finance Executive tracks the executed deals with a particular counterparty by running retrospective PFE and sends alert if the deal exceeds the agreed limit.

Figure 17-9: Credit Management Process

PFE serves as a crucial tool for the credit approval of each deal and the track of executed deals.

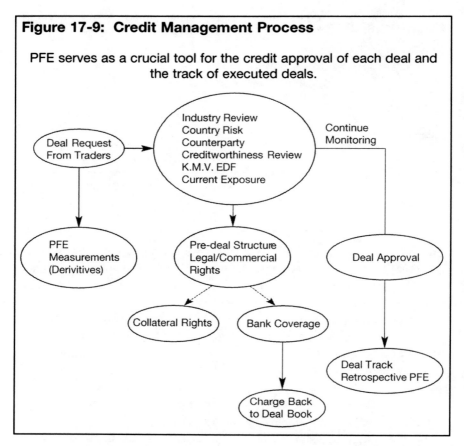

6. If the bank guarantee is sought, the cost of the guarantee can be charged to the book that generates the deal. This should be discussed in depth once the first few deals are executed, as you are moving from central credit risk towards a deal based charging out model.

Counterparty Credit Review

From day one, the trade finance and credit team should be very clear that the PFE is a rough estimation of the future credit exposure for a certain deal with a given counterparty. The ability to assess the counterparty credit quality by using some of the techniques outlined in this book along with outside rating agencies is invaluable at this point. To get an expected default frequency of a listed counterparty, the Moody's KMV scoring model could be used. Improving upon this model and identifying

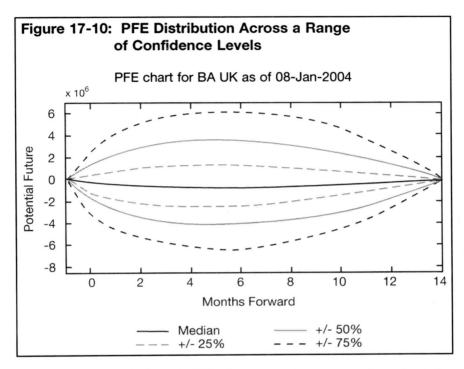

Figure 17-10: PFE Distribution Across a Range of Confidence Levels

PFE chart for BA UK as of 08-Jan-2004

the appropriate default probability is an ongoing process throughout the life of a given deal.

Credit Risk Mitigation Strategy

Having identified the potential credit future exposures and the level of credit quality of the given counterparty, the trade finance and credit team can then develop a credit risk mitigation strategy and recommend different forms of solutions to traders. You should still regard collateral rights as the primary means to provide credit support for those counterparties, which exceed the credit limit. You could also suggest the utilization of a Trade Finance Derivative, a silent bank guarantee, at an acceptable cost to the traders. Other mitigation techniques to consider are as follows: netting agreements, cash collateral, margin calls and deposits, prepayments and early payments, parent company guarantees, letters of credit, credit insurance, surety bonds and termination clauses.

Figure 17-10 shows the output for a whole deal data file, across a range of confidence levels at 25, 50 and 75 percent. The 75 percent line is at the top and bottom (+/-).

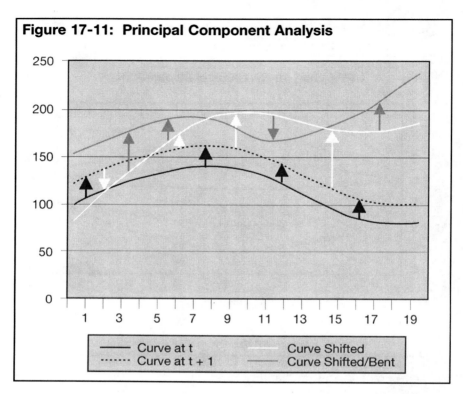

Figure 17-11: Principal Component Analysis

The forward curve PFE model can be split into two stages. First, Principal Component Analysis (PCA) takes the historical forward curve data and computes various components. It assists in the selection of required components, and rescales them to yield "shock functions." Second, the PFE model receives the shock functions as manual input along with the current deal data and latest forward curve information and then computes the PFE profile using Monte Carlo simulation.

PCA describes changes in the forward curve from one period to the next through a limited number of factors which plots any curve shift, tilt or bend as illustrated in Figure 17-11.

Information required to do the above calculation is a daily history of forward curves. In essence, you can model the forward curve directly, using PCA to capture the dynamics of the forward curve.

A word of caution, beware of the GIGO principle—Garbage In, Garbage Out.

PCA calculations place higher demands on the market data than simple spot models, so it is more sensitive to data errors, hence, data cleaning is required, it is not an option.

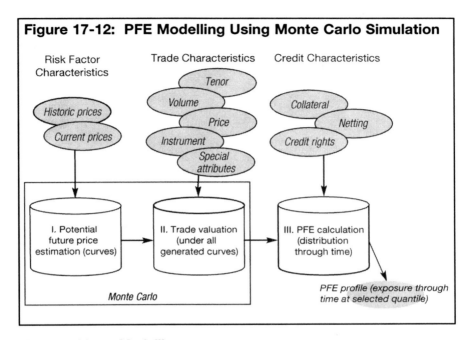

Figure 17-12: PFE Modelling Using Monte Carlo Simulation

Expected Loss Modelling

The difficulty with Expected Loss is not the modelling, but in deriving the 'default probability' and 'recovery rates.' The logical sequence of events in calculating the expected loss can be summarized as follows: **Commodity Price Characteristics (simulate future possible prices) + Deal Characteristics (calculate PFE) + counterparty Characteristics (simulate default events) = the calculated expected loss.**

In conclusion, PFE should be used in conjunction with thorough credit analysis of the given counterparty. Regular review of PFE controlled counterparties is necessary in managing the risks.

Remember that Potential Future Exposure (PFE) is the estimated future mark-to-market value of a set of positions/contracts with a given counterparty, described as a probability distribution—i.e., a function assigning a probability of occurrence to a range of possible future exposure values at time t.

In Figure 17-12, the diagram summarizes the principle of PFE modelling using Monte Carlo simulation.

Figure 17-13: D&B Financial Stress Score v. S&P Default Rates

S&P Bond Rating	Default Rate	D&B Financial Stress
AAA	0.0	1539-1875
AA	0.1	1504-1538
A	0.1	1467-1503
BBB	0.4	1367-1466
BB	2.2	1353-1366
B	4.0	1315-1352
CCC	7.0	1001-1314

Figure 17-14: Comparison of Three Rating Agencies

Quality	Moody's	S&P	Fitch	Fitch (IND)	Credit Quality Category	1-Year Default Risk %
	Long-Term Debt Ratings					
Exceptional	Aaa	AAA	AAA	A	1	0.00
Excellent	Aa1	AA+	AA+	A/B	1	0.01
	Aa2	AA	AA			
	Aa3	AA-	AA-	B	1	
Good	A1	A+	A+	B/C	2	0.05
	A2	A	A			
	A3	A-	A-	C	2	
Adequate	Baa1	BBB+	BBB+		3	0.37
	Baa2	BBB	BBB	C/D2		
	Baa3	BBB-	BBB-		4	
Questionable	Ba1	BB+	BB+		5	1.38
	Ba2	BB	BB	D		
	Ba3	BB-	BB-		6	
Poor	B1	B+	B+		7	6.20
	B2	B	B			
	B3	B-	B-		8	
Very Poor	Caa1	CCC+	CCC+		9	27.87
	Caa2	CCC	CCC			
	Caa3	CCC-	CCC-			

Chapter 18

FASB Updates
and the Sarbanes-Oxley Act

FAS-105

Disclosure of information about financial instruments with off-balance sheet risk and financial instruments with concentrations of credit risk.

Introduction

The Financial Accounting Standards Board (FASB) has issued a pronouncement dealing with off-balance sheet risk and concentrations of credit risk. Its purpose was, for statements ending June 15, 1990, to force disclosure to users of financial statements those risks that were formerly omitted. FASB adopted GAAP to standardize the way financial statements are prepared and presented so that users would have a common point of reference for their interpretation. As the number varied and complex business transactions have increased, the need to properly disclose the risk associated with each has been addressed in FAS-105. What the disclosures are and how the analyst treats them is the discussion that follows.

Instruments with Off-Balance Sheet Risk

A. Companies have made concerted efforts to shift risk to those areas not usually reported on financial statements.
B. FASB is stopping that effort by requiring disclosure.
C. Types of transactions requiring disclosure:
   a. "Financial guarantees, letters of credit written, outstanding loan commitments written, options written, interest rate caps and floors, recourse obligations on sold receivables, futures contracts, interest rate and foreign currency swaps, and obligations arising from financial instruments sold short." This quote is from FAS 105.
   b. Most of these transactions are ones bankers and brokers deal with, but with increasing frequency, industry is utilizing these tools to achieve corporate objectives.

179

FASB Uses Two Types of Risk Reporting

A. *Market Risk.* "The possibility that future changes in market prices may make the financial instrument less valuable or more onerous."
B. *Credit Risk.* "The possibility that loss may occur from the failure of another party to perform according to the terms of a contract."

Disclosures

A. Either in the financial statements or in the notes, "the amount of the accounting loss."
B. The entity's collateralization policy including "information about the entity's access to that collateral or security and a brief discussion about the specific nature of the collateral or other security supporting those financial instruments."

Concentrations of Credit Risk

A. Group Concentrations. If one or more financial instruments share common characteristics, which would significantly affect all instruments of their kind, such as counterparties engaged in similar activities, sharing similar economic characteristics or within a specific region, which would tie their fates together, they are said to have a group concentration.
B. FAS 30 already addresses the situation where a large portion (10 percent) of a company's sales are to a single customer.

Disclosures

A. "Information about the shared activity region or economic characteristic that identifies the concentration."
B. "The *amount* of the accounting loss due to credit risk the entity would incur if parties to the financial instruments that make up the concentration failed completely to perform according to the terms of the contracts and the collateral or other security, if any, for the amount due proved to be of no value to the entity."
C. The entity's policy of requiring collateral or other security, etc.

Conclusion

The disclosures were aimed primarily at people who evaluate credit using financial statements (that's us). Increased disclosure is a double-edged sword. It means the information for analysis will be enhanced, but it also means that to avail ourselves of it, we must wade through more verbiage in the notes. This will mean more time spent on each evaluation, but each evaluation will represent a better credit decision.

FAS-133

As of January 1st, 2001, this pronouncement requires that derivatives be market-to-market to reflect the value at the date of the financial report. Fluctuations in value are reflected in per-share earnings. Under the treatment being scrapped, companies have been allowed to record options on their balance sheets at historical cost, and this cost is amortized over the option's life.

Options are an increasingly popular way for corporations to hedge exposures to fluctuations in interest rates, foreign currencies or commodity prices. But options themselves can display fairly volatile swings in day-to-day prices. Now the difference between the cost at which the company obtained its derivatives and their current fair market value at time of filing could have a significant impact on the earnings number.

From an analyst's point of view, it's about time. It's preferable to have everything in front rather than dig through the third footnote on some back page to eventually back into this information.

Expect to see the following take place:

- Hedge documentation will require much more specificity and detail as compared to current GAAP requirements.
- Systems changes in order to comply with this new requirement, for all but the modest derivative users, could be extensive.
- Contracts, even standard inventory purchase or sale contracts, might well be derivatives under FAS 133.

This activity will require current risk management policies and procedures to be reassessed. A call for the redesign or development of new risk management programs such as risk tolerance, new hedging strategies and techniques will certainly be in order.

We should now be asking if the business under review has taken the necessary steps to capture and report derivative contracts and related exposures in order to comply with FAS 133. Have they developed the necessary systems environment or are they in the process of developing something that can assess their hedge program's effectiveness along with tracking on exposures and derivative positions?

Pooling of Interest

In 2001, FASB voted to eliminate pooling of interest, so all future acquisitions must follow the purchase accounting rules. In addition, goodwill derived from a purchase will no longer be automatically subject to systematic amortization each period. Instead, goodwill amortization will be required only if the assets acquired have become impaired.

The new amortization rules are likely to lead to new accounting tricks that attempt to allocate much of the acquisition price to goodwill. And, of course, the plan will be not to amortize any of it, but rather to claim that no impairment has taken place. This trick will allow companies to keep most of the cost of an acquisition on the balance sheet, rather than charging those costs against income.

When companies use the pooling-of-interest method to account for acquisitions, prior-period financial reports generally are adjusted to reflect "pro forma" results so that current-period results will not appear inflated and misleading because of the later acquisition. There is one exception, however: companies are permitted to not restate prior periods if the pooling is deemed to be immaterial and it is management's final decision. The decision not to restate could result in an overstatement of year-to-year revenue growth.

THE SARBANES-OXLEY ACT OF 2002

The Sarbanes-Oxley Act of 2002, signed into law by President Bush, provides the most sweeping reform of public reporting and corporate governance in decades. The Act makes significant changes to the existing laws. These changes were in direct response to the Enron Bankruptcy and the host of financial restatements made by many publicly traded companies shortly thereafter. A summary of the significant changes is listed below[12]:

1. CEO and CFO must certify the financial statements of their companies.
2. Requires a true auditor independent from the company.
3. Mandates that the majority of the board be independent.
4. Mandates that the audit committee formed at the company act independently from the company's operating officers.
5. Imposes harsher sentencing.
6. Mandates that Wall Street analysts certify their report and that they have some independence from the investment banking side of their firm.

One thing missing which has yet to be addressed is any restraints on executive compensation. So, the CEO can still get paid 400 times the average worker.

---

[12]Chamberlain Hrdlicka, Attorneys at Law, Corporate Governance Update, Legislation July 39, 2002.

Chapter 19

FINANCIAL PLANNING

OVERVIEW

Financial Planning can be defined as a forward-looking variant of financial analysis. The focus of financial planning is on constructing a financial statement that will achieve a desired set of objectives. In the process of constructing this statement, concepts related to break even analysis and sustainable growth will be a part of this exercise. Understanding these concepts will provide you with another set of tools to measure a company's overall success.

In this chapter, you will be introduced to the concept of break-even analysis, which allows you to ascertain the minimum level of unit volume/sales revenues that you must generate to be viable.

You will become familiar with the concept of sustainable growth rates, which allow you to determine the rate of growth you can sustain without additional financing.

BREAK EVEN ANALYSIS

Break even analysis determines the level of sales activity that will allow a firm to cover its costs and the firm's profits or losses if sales surpass or fall below that point. The fundamental concept in break even analysis is that of understanding the differential impact of Fixed and Variable costs on a firm's financial performance.

In conventional terms, break even implies zero profit or loss. However, an expanded definition of break even could imply a situation where the firm earns exactly its desired level of profit. In other words, one could compute break even levels that would produce a pre-specified level of profits.

Fixed costs refer to costs that remain fixed (do not increase or decrease) in response to a change in sales revenues. A significant fixed cost in most firms is the level of salaries (not commissions)

Note that fixed costs do not imply that these costs will not change. They only mean that as sales revenues change, these costs will remain fixed. An example is the level of interest expenses. Interest expenses may not change directly as a result of changes in sales. But interest will change if the firm increases/decreases its level of borrowing.

A fundamental fact is that higher levels of fixed costs will result in a higher break even point.

	Scenario 1	Scenario 2	Scenario 3
Sales Price per Unit	100.00	100.00	100.00
Variable Costs per Unit	60.00	60.00	60.00
Contribution Margin per Unit	40.00	40.00	40.00
Fixed Costs ($)	100.00	150.00	200.00
Break Even Level in $	250,000	375,000	500,000

Formula = Fixed Cost/Contribution Margin per Unit

Variable costs refer to costs that change proportionately with changes in sales. Examples of such costs are sales commissions, etc. Theoretically, since the level of sales directly influences these costs, zero sales will result in zero variable costs.

Break even analysis can be computed at various levels of activity:

Operating Break Even. Refers to break even at the operating profit level. This break even calculation does not consider any financing costs.

Profit Break Even. Refers to break even at the net profit level. This computation considers financing costs.

Cash Flow Break Even. Refers to the break even point on a cash flow basis. In many instances, profits are computed after deducting many non-cash expenses such as depreciation. Since these are not actual cash outflows, the operating and profit break even points are overstated to the extent of such non-cash outflows.

The future holds a great deal of uncertainty. As a result, point estimates are never precise. Most often, managers have an estimate of a range of possible values for various costs and revenues. To get a better grip on the effects of significant deviations in point estimates, one needs to perform sensitivity analysis using best and worst case scenarios. If there are a large number of variables, a more sophisticated approach to conducting sensitivity analysis is to perform a Monte Carlo simulation.

Monte Carlo simulation could be thought of as an attempt to generate a large number of "What-if" analyses by drawing randomly from a range of estimates provided by the decision maker. Each "What-if" analysis is referred to as a trial. For each trial, an estimate of costs and revenues is drawn randomly from the range specified by the decision maker. For example, the decision maker could specify a range of 60-70 percent as an estimate for operating costs. In each trial, the operating cost percentage is chosen randomly between 60 and 70 percent. Since a large number of trials are generated, the decision maker can gain insight on the effects of uncertainty in his/her point estimates by plotting the results, say, net profits, of various trials and observing the frequency of unfavorable outcomes.

Break Even Analysis - An Example

	Most Optimistic	Likely	Pessimistic
Selling Price Per Unit	400	300	250
Variable Operating Cost Per Unit	140	150	160
Fixed Op. Costs (cash costs only)	75,000	80,000	77,000
Noncash Costs (Depreciation, etc)	10,000	20,000	15,000
Financing Costs	20,000	25,000	20,000
Operating Break Even	32,692	66,666	102,222
Profit Break Even	40,384	83,333	124,444
Cash Flow Break Even	36,538	70,000	107,777

SUSTAINABLE GROWTH

The Concept

Sustainable growth is the rate of growth a company can sustain with currently available financial resources. A rate of growth higher than a corporation's sustainable growth rate will require incremental financing from either internal or external sources. Or, to put this another way, it is the rate of growth in sales, assets, debt, and equity that can be sustained indefinitely without management altering the debt-to-equity relationship, the return on equity performance or the dividend payout rate.

Several years ago, a study conducted by a professor at the Harvard Business School concluded that management's ability to manage growth of the company is an important factor of differentiating value-enhancing companies from companies that destroy shareholder values. You will find that understanding a firm's sustainable growth rate provides a peek into whether the firm is likely to encounter financial distress in the future. Firms that file bankruptcy do so, with minor exceptions, because they grow too quickly. Their profits and cash flow fail to follow their strong sales growth. The analysis of sustainable growth will tie directly to analysis of cash flows in the company.

Increasing leverage raises the risk of financial failure. If a firm grows faster than their LTSGR, then there will have to be a correction period eventually.

Some firms end up going the opposite direction with slow growth and high profits. If they reinvest all the profits, they will pay off all the debt, take all the discounts, buy assets for cash and accumulate cash to invest in securities. A private firm like this would go to a sub-S corporation and pay out the excess profits to shareholders and only get taxed once.

Growth is a positive thing if it is done with matching, reinvested profitability that complies with the LTSGR formula. The problem is with rapid growth goals usually set for ego reasons and supported by obsolete rationalizations such as: needing clout and visibility with suppliers achieving low-cost economics with economies of scale; and needing to be #1 to impress customers. Today volume is vanity and profits are sanity. If suppliers are pushing for volume increases, ask them to stop wishful thinking and suggest where and how additional, profitable market share can be found. By best serving targeted customers, a firm will grow faster than mediocre competitors by retaining satisfied customers at a greater rate than the competition. Make customer satisfaction and retention the first priority and growth will occur as a by-product.

Sustainable growth can be calculated in different ways. The most prevalent approach is to multiply the return on equity ratio by the firm's profit retention rate. The retention rate is 1 − (Dividends Paid ÷ Net Income), stated as a percentage number. Excluded are the non-operating effects. After all, by definition, the non-operating effects should not be ongoing. Thus, sustainable growth is return on equity (excluding special items) multiplied by the retention ratio. You need to compare sustainable growth rate number to actual growth performance to draw conclusions about growth.

If sustainable growth is less than both actual growths in sales and assets over two or three consecutive years, then maybe management is missing opportunities in the firm's markets to capture more sales, profits and cash flows. The firm is possibly losing market share to competitors. If this situation is not corrected, the firm may become the target of a takeover or merger.

By continuing with this breakdown of the problem process into several parts, you should have a good understanding of the financial performance of a company and its likelihood of sustaining growth into the future without financial problems arising. Whatever your conclusions about the company's profitability, they are transferable to your analysis of growth. The reason is that sustainable growth analysis is nothing more than the extension of analyzing the company's return on equity performance.

Relationship between Sales and Funds Needed

To understand the concept of sustainable growth, the first thing we should do is examine and understand the relationship between sales and funds needed.

Think about a typical manufacturing firm that is just starting up its operations. One of the first decisions made by such a firm is to invest in a manufacturing plant. Subsequently, as the plant comes on line, and the rate of capacity utilization increases, the need for working capital also increases proportionately. This relationship can be shown graphically as follows:

As you can see in the graph below, the level of fixed assets is assumed to be fixed, at least in the short run. When the firm starts up its plant, it has already invested the monies required to build and operate the plant. As sales increase, total assets also increase due to the firm's investments in inventories, receivables, and other working capital requirements.

Relationship between Assets and Sales

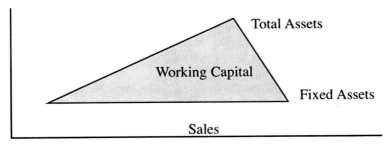

In the Short Run...

The reason we say, in the short run, is because fixed assets will not remain constant at all levels of sales. When sales exceed the output that can be produced by the existing plant the firm will have to think in terms of setting up another plant. However, this will most likely take some time.

Therefore, in the long run, fixed assets will also increase. The increase in fixed assets is likely to exhibit a stair-step characteristic (i.e., it will go up in spurts and will not increase in a continuous fashion as will working capital).

The graphical portrayal above leads us to a logical conclusion. As sales increase, total asset investments are going to increase and therefore, the firm's financing needs will also increase. Some of these needs can be met through internal generation of funds as we will see but typically, internal generation of funds can only support a normal level of sales growth. At very high levels of sales growth, the firm will need external financing.

To reiterate, three key ideas that underline the relationship between sales, assets, and financing needs are:

- The relationship between sales and working capital is proportional. This is more or less true for most manufacturing corporations. The levels of inventories, the outstanding balance of receivables and payables are all related to the level of sales and purchases.
- The relationship between sales and fixed assets is likely to be less proportional. This relationship is likely at best to follow a stair-step characteristic. The current level of fixed assets constitutes a certain level of productive capacity for the firm. Only when the level of sales starts to exceed such productive capacity, will the firm contemplate increasing its productive capacity and hence its level of investments in fixed assets.
- The maintenance of the existing productive capacity (repairs, routine maintenance, etc.) is assumed to be insignificant.
- If your firm is a trading firm with relatively little fixed assets, the relationship between working capital and financing needs are going to be directly related to the firm's working capital needs.

Steps to Compute the Sustainable Growth Rate for a Firm

We are now ready to walk through the computations involved in deriving the sustainable growth rate for a firm. These computations can be broken down into the following three steps:

1. Establish the Asset Intensity Ratio
2. Establish the Retention Ratio
3. Determine the Sustainable Growth Rate

The Asset Intensity Ratio is the overall proportional relationship that various balance sheet items have with sales. We have discussed how many of the working capital items on the balance sheet have a proportional relationship with sales. The asset intensity ratio is an aggregate measurement that is the sum of the proportional relationships that each individual balance sheet item has with sales.

The Retention Ratio refers to the ratio of profits that the firm retains in the business. These are the internal funds that are available for supporting future growth. Consequently, the retention ratio is the profit margin less the dividends that the firm pays out to its shareholders. In many private firms, dividends are often paid out in the form of salaries to the owners.

Example:

Company Name: **Dean Oil Company**

$4,910.00	Sales
4,532.00	Costs
87.00	Taxes
291.00	Net Income

Balance Sheet

		% of Sales			% of Sales
Current Assets	1586	32.30%	Accounts Payable	575	11.71
Fixed Assets	2413	N/A	Debt & Equity	3544	N/A
Total Assets	4119	N/A	Total Liab. & Eq.	4119	N/A

From the above example, we can calculate the following:

Profit Margin $\boxed{5.93}$
Asset Intensity Ratio $\quad 32.30 - 11.71 = \boxed{20.59}$

So, for every $100 increase in sales, assets will increase by $32.20 and payables will increase by $11.71. The net increase in assets will be $20.59.

Example:

Total Financing Needs for Estimated Growth:

Estimated growth $\boxed{2\%}$
Estimated financing needs $\boxed{\$20}$ = Additional investments in assets

Some of the financing necessary to cover the increase in asset requirements will come from retaining the profits that the company expects to generate. Since we have assumed that dividends are paid out in the form of salaries, the retention ratio in this case is the same as the net profit margin.

Retention next year = Profit margin × Estimated sales next year = $\boxed{\$297}$

We need $20 in additional investments in assets and have $297. The firm can sustain the estimated growth of 2%.

Using the example above, try different rates of growth and see if you can iteratively converge to the firm's sustainable growth rate.

We have seen how external financing needs directly depend on the estimated growth rate in sales. The higher this growth rate is, the higher the need for external financing. At some rate of growth, financing needs are going to outstrip the firm's internal retention dollars necessitating external financing.

A key conclusion for most normal situations:

There is only a finite rate of growth that a firm can achieve without reliance on external financing.

$$\frac{\text{Retention Ratio} \times \text{Current Year's Sales}}{\text{Asset Intensity Ratio} \times \text{Current Year's Sales} - \text{Retention Ratio} \times \text{Current Year's Sales}}$$

The sustainable growth rate for Dean Oil Company is 40.450%

The sustainable growth rate calculated previously relies on a number of assumptions regarding the firm's policy as reflected in the financial statements.

By focusing on these assumptions, we can understand the key determinants of sustainable growth:

- *The Asset Intensity Ratio is at normal/optional levels.* This means that the relationships observed on the financial statements between assets and sales is indeed normal/optimal for the firm. If this is not true, then you should adjust the asset intensity rations appropriately before computing the sustainable growth rate.
- *The firm has no incremental debt capacity.* In the computations completed so far, we have assumed that the firm has no incremental borrowing power. This may not be true. There are two ways of adjusting for this assumption:

1. We can use the interest coverage ratio as a gauge of the relative adequacy of the firm's debt servicing capacity. If a firm's interest coverage is substantially below the median interest coverage in the industry, all other things being the same, we can conclude that the firm has additional borrowing power.
2. Another approach is to assume that an optimal debt/equity ratio can be specified for firms in the industry and that the firm will be able to maintain the existing/given level of debt/equity ratio. We will cover this in the next section on Building a Financial Plan.

Obviously, both sets of assumptions need not be valid. We can appropriately modify the computation of the sustainable growth rate to relax these assumptions.

SUSTAINABLE GROWTH AND THE DUPONT MODEL

Sustainable growth has a close relationship with the DuPont model. In fact, if we assume that the current debt/equity ratio of the firm is at optimal levels, the sustainable growth rate can be restated in terms of the DuPont model identity:

$$\text{Sustainable Growth Rate} = \frac{\text{Return on Equity} \times \text{Retention Ratio}}{1 - (\text{Return on Equity} \times \text{Retention Ratio})}$$

Therefore, a firm can increase its sustainable growth rate by focusing on any/all of the three critical components of financial performance: Profitability, Operating efficiency, and Financial leverage.

You can clearly see a company's alternatives for increasing its sustainable growth rate by using the DuPont formula in the formula G (Sustainable Growth Rate) = ROE × RET × RET. This is equal to LEV × TAT × PM × RE. Written this way, the formula says that a company can increase its sustainable growth rate by:

*   using more borrowed money to increase its leverage ratio,
*   using assets more intensively to increase its total asset turnover ratio,
*   reducing costs to increase its profit margin, or
*   investing more of the owner's money in the business to increase its retention ratio.

Increasing the value of these ratios or some combination of them is the only alternative for increasing the sustainable growth rate.

By using alternative two and three above, these improvements are viable alternatives if the company's operations are below capacity or not cost effective. Some companies are in this situation and can improve operations to increase their sustainable growth rates while others are not. Consequently, there is no general tendency for companies to use an improvement in operations to increase their growth rates.

A company can also increase its sustainable growth rate by using more borrowed money or by investing more of the owner's money in the business. There are two ways to increase the owner's investment: the company can reduce its dividends to increase retained earnings or issue additional common stock.

In summary, this discussion demonstrates that companies must change their operating or financing policies to achieve growth targets that exceed their sustainable growth rates.

BUILDING A FINANCIAL PLAN

A sound financial plan achieves the firm's objectives with respect to providing a desired return to its investors while treating all other constituents like employees, creditors, etc., fairly. The following steps form a paradigm for building a sound financial plan:

1. Establish overall objectives in terms of the required Return on Equity over the planning horizon.
2. Understand past performance both over time and in relation to industry aggregates.
3. Understand critical performance drivers.
4. Estimate and input an initial financial profile.
5. Generate Pro Forma statements and examine.
6. Repeat the above steps until satisfied.

Shown below is a graphical representation of the six steps outlined previously:

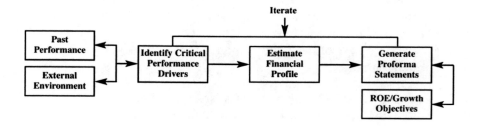

Chapter 20

ECONOMIC VALUE ADDED (EVA) AND RISK ADJUSTED RETURN ON CAPITOL (RAROC)

One of the jobs of corporate managers is to raise capital. The only reason investors will make that capital available is the belief that the managers can turn their money invested into a positive return. After all, the shareholders own the company, and to keep capital flowing into the company, the managers must provide them with an appropriate rate of return. The return to shareholders is the yardstick for measuring corporate success.

Many of the traditional corporate performance measures have been found to poorly correlate, or even conflict, with management's job of maximizing the market value of a firm's stock. One measure that seems to have received a great deal of notice and acceptance is Economic Value Added (EVA), developed by Joel M. Stern and G. Bennett Stewart III of Stern Stewart & Co.[13]

Economic value-added (EVA) is the after-tax cash flow generated by a business minus the cost of the capital it has deployed to generate that cash flow. Representing real profit versus paper profit, EVA, underlines shareholder value. Shareholders are the players who provide the firm with its capital; they invest to gain a return on that capital.

EVA simply balances a company's profitability against the capital it employs to generate this profitability. If a company's earnings, after tax, exceed the cost of the capital employed in the business, EVA is positive. Market studies have indicated that a company that continually generates an increasingly positive EVA will be rewarded by a higher stock price.

A definition of EVA is net operating profit after taxes (NOPAT) less an internal charge for the capital employed in the business (i.e., opportunity cost of capital). To illustrate the intuitive nature of EVA, a company with $1 million of net operating profit after tax may not have necessarily performed well. It depends upon how much capital the company uses to

---

[13]Thomas P. Jones, Stern Stewart & Company, "The Economic Value Added Approach to Corporate Investment," *The Journal of Business* (1997).

generate the profit. If this were General Electric, the results would be abysmal. If this business were run from a telephone in a small office, the EVA would be extraordinary.

When computing EVA, there are adjustments to both NOPAT and capital employed to reduce what could be considered non-economic accounting and financing conventions on the income statement and on the balance sheet. In computing NOPAT, certain expenses that do not affect cash are added back to the income statement. These non-cash entries are not believed to affect value. Some of the adjustments required include those for last in, first out (LIFO), bad debts, deferred taxes, inventory obsolescence, and warranty. Depreciation is not included among these adjustments because it is considered a proxy for a true economic cost in the EVA model. Interest expense after tax, on the other hand, is added back to income to eliminate the effect of leverage on the income statement. The result of these adjustments is that NOPAT is unaffected by material, non-cash accounting adjustments or by the financial composition of capital.

On the balance sheet, the reserves associated with the aforementioned adjustments to NOPAT are considered to be "equity equivalents" in that they are included as part and parcel of capital employed. The argument is that if the reserves had not been recorded for accounting purposes, they would be included as part of the income included in equity. Another important adjustment to the balance sheet to arrive at capital employed is the capitalization of operating leases. The net present value of operating leases is considered an asset, and the future payments are considered a debt equivalent. These adjustments are intended to restate the balance sheet to its "economic" book value. Adjustments are designed to address the distortions suffered by traditional measures, such as return on equity, earnings per share and earnings growth, that change depending upon the generally accepted accounting principles adopted or the mix of financing employed.

To illustrate an adjustment to both balance sheet and income statement, a LIFO reserve is added back to inventory on the balance sheet to bring the valuation back to what would have been paid for the inventory if it had been bought today. The net increase to the LIFO reserve from one year to the next would be added back to net income to arrive at NOPAT. A decrease in the LIFO reserve would be subtracted from net income. The tax effect of LIFO in NOPAT is not adjusted because the cash flow from the tax benefit or loss was, in fact, realized. Figure 1 shows the mechanics of calculating EVA.

In Figure 20-1, both the operating and financing perspectives are shown in the capital-employed calculation. The result is the same. The

Figure 20-1: Calculating EVA

Net Operating Profit After Tax:

Sales	$800
Cost of Goods Sold	500
Gross Profit	$300
SG&A	100
Net Operating Profit	$200
Taxes @ 40% Federal & State	80
Net Operating Profit After Tax	$120
Adjustments:	
Add: LIFO Reserve Increase	10
Net Operating Profit After Tax	$130

Capital Employed:

Operating Perspective	
Cash	$20
Accounts Receivable	100
Inventory (Net of LIFO Reserve)	300
Add: LIFO Reserve	50
Accounts Payable	(200)
Net Working Capital	$270
Net Fixed Assets	530
Capital Employed	$800

Cost of Capital @ 12%	.12
Capital Employed Charge	$96

Net Operating Profit After Taxes	$130
Less: Capital-Employed Charge	96
Economic Value Added	$34

Financing Perspective	
Debt (Interest Bearing)	500
Add: LIFO Reserve	50
Common Stock	20
Retained Earnings	230
	$800

operating perspective is particularly useful for a division or subsidiary that has inter-company and inter-plant control accounts rather than a complete owners' equity section.

Calculating the cost of capital is one of the more technical aspects of EVA, but understanding this dimension of EVA is one of the key areas

Figure 20-2: Weighted Average Cost of Capital

(40% Tax Rate)

	Pre-Tax Cost	Post-Tax Cost	% of Total	Contribution to WACC
Debt	9.0%	5.4%	30%	1.6%
Equity	14.9%	14.9%	70%	10.4%
WACC				12.0%

where the financial organization can significantly improve their results from using EVA, cost of capital, also known as the weighted average cost of capital (WACC), represents the expected returns of debt and equity holders of the firm, weighted for the proportionate share each holds in the business (*see* Figure 20-2).

The cost of debt varies by firm, depending upon the term and overall creditworthiness of the company. The cost of equity also varies by firm and reflects both the firm's investment opportunities and its degree of leverage. The balance of debt and equity represents the capital structure of a company, and it is frequently the role of the treasury function to establish a target capital structure. In the example shown above, the WACC is 12 percent, or for simplicity, 12 percent per month.

When a company's net operating profit after tax exceeds its capital-employed charge, its EVA is positive and value has been created. If the result equals zero, the firm's management merely met the expected returns of debt and equity holders.

EVA is a powerful tool for several reasons: it aligns employee behavior with stockholder value generation, separates employee incentive compensation from the traditional performance measurement that compares actual to budgeted results, and it's easy to communicate and understand.

Like EVA, corporate governance has become a widely discussed topic over the past several years. There are numerous situations where management's obligation to act on behalf of shareholders is in conflict with their own best interests. Growth, either internally generated or through acquisition, is typically in the best interests of management because compensation is often based upon such factors as sales volume, size of department and size of budget. Yet, only growth that provides increasingly positive EVA contributes to shareholder value. When EVA becomes the basis for management incentive compensation, management's decision making is aligned with shareholder value creation.

Management is more highly focused on growth that generates a positive EVA. There is also the added benefit of decoupling the budgeting process from incentive compensation. Most practitioners have participated in budgeting processes where the best negotiators end up with the most achievable budgets, and therefore the highest incentive payouts. Not only is there a fairness issue, there is also the issue of providing incentive compensation for results that do not necessarily create shareholder value. Using budgets as a basis for incentive compensation institutionalizes payment for mediocre performance. Incentive compensation under EVA is formula driven, and is automatically adjusted annually for the current year's performance, as well as for performance improvement factor. The budget process becomes one of maximizing EVA through increasing profitability and balance sheet management.

A further benefit of EVA is that it can be boiled down into a message that all parts of the organization can understand and apply to their daily activities. Simply said, the message is to increase overall profitability, while reducing the capital tied-up in the business.

THE EVA MESSAGE

EVA properly motivates the financial organization. Problems on the balance sheet must be dealt with sooner rather than later. Why carry an impaired asset (excess or obsolete inventory or problem receivables) month-after-month, with the associated capital-employed charge, only to write it off at some later date? It makes sense to avoid the cost of capital charge and gain the tax benefit sooner. The longer such a decision is deferred, the lower the net present value of the tax benefit of the ultimate write-off.[14]

Publicly traded firms are under intense pressure to meet Wall Street's quarterly earnings projections. This often results in pushing manufacturing to rush orders to completion in order to "make the quarter." Higher operating expenses attributable to quarter-end shipments result in lower NOPAT. In addition, the capital employed charge is higher because inventory is converted to receivables, which includes the gross margin on the product. EVA discourages this behavior and encourages more even production and shipments throughout a quarter.

From a strategic perspective, management will direct resources to grow the parts of the company that can generate positive EVA results. Those

---

[14]Kenneth Stephens, CPA, "What Is Economic Value Added?", *Business Credit* (1997).

parts of the business that are not contributing a positive EVA get closer scrutiny—and may become candidates for divestiture.

The message of EVA is equally clear for other parts of the organization and can be readily translated to the various functions within the organization. The message to the sales organization is that extended payment terms result in higher receivables, and consignment inventory results in a higher inventory. Balance the incremental sales against the higher capital-employed charge. For industries that require long production times, the message is that progress billings and advance payments can have a huge EVA benefit. Work on the customer's money. This is not today's news, but there is now an economic incentive to do the right thing for the organization and its shareholders. To the marketing organization, the message is that products provided on trial to key customers have an EVA cost. The asset, once used, will likely need to be written down and it will sit on the balance sheet, incurring the monthly capital-employed charge. To the manufacturing and materials organization, the message is to invest in productive machine tools rather than in brick and mortar to reduce cycle times, improve throughput and reduce inventory levels. EVA increases if capital investments return more than the cost of capital. Those investments that return less than the cost of capital should be rejected.

Not all companies will calculate EVA in precisely the same way, so it must be customized for the company involved. Industries also differ, and some of the adjustments recommended may not apply or may be considered immaterial. This means that once EVA is defined for a company to exclude designated immaterial adjustments, one must reexamine the calculation to determine if what had been immaterial yesterday has not become material today.

THE INCENTIVE TO TURN RECEIVABLES FOR CREDIT MANAGEMENT

Credit managers have always been motivated by traditional measures to improve receivables turnover. Looking at net working capital in the capital-employed calculation, both cash and receivables are treated alike. Cash should be excluded from the calculation. Otherwise, there is no direct "incentive" to credit management to convert receivables to cash, other than the general motivation to provide cash for investment in projects or activities that earn a positive EVA.

One way of handling this is by having corporate treasuries, as part of their centralized cash management, "sweep" divisions and subsidiaries of cash. Inter-company receivables and payables used to record the cash transfers to the parent company are excluded from the capital-employed calculation. This leaves outstanding trade receivables directly subject to the cost of capital-employed charge. The subsidiary or division is motivated to collect the cash, leaving the corporate treasury to ensure that cash is available for the appropriate investments. This practice acts as a direct motivator to the credit manager, because the failure to collect receivables can be translated into a measure that all can understand—capital-employed charge. But with EVA, the credit manager will no longer be alone in the collection process. Once the general managers understand that uncollected receivables reduce EVA and their incentive bonus, there will be a heightened interest in supporting the collection effort.

The concept of EVA is well established in financial theory, but only recently has the term moved into the mainstream of corporate finance, as more firms are adopting it as the base for business planning and performance monitoring. There is growing evidence that EVA, not earnings, determines the value of a firm. The chairman of AT&T was quoted as saying that they had found an almost perfect correlation over a five-year period between its market value and EVA. The effective use of capital is the key to value and that message applies to all business processes as well.

What are the main differences between the various performance measures represented by EVA, earnings per share, return on assets and discounted cash flow (the most common model calculations)? To summarize some of the critics:

- Earnings per share tells nothing about the cost of generating the firm's profits. If the cost of capital (loans, bonds, equity) is, say, 15 percent, then a 14 percent earning is actually a reduction, not a gain, in economic value. Profits also increase taxes, thereby reducing cash flow, so that engineering profits through accounting tricks can drain economic value. The real earnings are the equivalent of the money that owners of a well-run mom-and-pop business stash away in the cigar box. Renowned investor Warren Buffett calls these "owners' earnings": real cash flow after all taxes, interest and other obligations have been paid.

- Return on assets is a more realistic measure of economic performance, but it ignores the cost of capital. In its more profitable year, for instance, IBM's return on assets was over 11 percent, but its cost of capital was almost 13 percent. Leading firms can obtain capital at low costs, via favorable interest rates and high stock prices, which they can then invest in their operations at decent rates of return on assets. That tempts them to expand without paying attention to the real return, economic value-added.
- Discounted cash flow is very close to economic value-added, with the discount rate being the cost of capital.

As stated earlier, determining a firm's cost of capital requires making two calculations, one simple and one complex. The simple one figures the cost of debt, which is the after-tax interest rate on loans and bonds. The more complex one estimates the cost of equity and involves analyzing shareholders' expected return implicit in the price they have paid to buy or sold their shares. Investors have the choice of buying risk-free Treasury bonds or investing in other, riskier securities. They would obviously expect a higher return for higher risk. Ironically and to attract investors, weak firms must offer a premium in the form of a lower stock price than stronger firms can command. This lower price amounts to the equivalent of a higher interest rate on loans and bonds; the investor's premium increases the firm's cost of capital.

Earnings per share can be misleading or even create a damaging target for strategy and investment. For example, when a firm switches from FIFO (first in, first out) to LIFO (last in, first out), its cost of goods assumes the price of the most recent purchases of materials in inventory. This typically reduces its profits because the older purchases cost less than the more recent ones. Yet the firm's stock price will rise, even though its reported profits drop, because it pays less in taxes, thus increasing its after-tax cash flow. The money spent to acquire the goods in inventory is exactly the same regardless of which method is used, but LIFO increases economic value-added.

The key business processes of the firm are capital. That fact is obscured by accounting systems that expense salaries, software development, rent, training, and other ongoing costs that are integral to a process capability and that treat the cost of displacing workers, a frequent by-product of process reengineering, downsizing, and the like, as an "extraordinary item" on the income statement. By treating processes as capital assets or liabilities, firms can and should ensure that they directly contribute to economic value-added. The following quotation summarizes the issues here.

How much capital is tied up in your operations? Even if you don't know the answer, you know what it consists of: what you paid for real estate, machines, vehicles and the like, plus working capital. But proponents of EVA say there's more. What about the money your company spends on R&D? On employee training? Those are investments meant to pay off for years, but accounting rules say you can't treat them that way, you have to call them expenses, like the amounts you spend on electricity. EVA proponents say forget the accounting rules. For internal purposes, call these things what they are: capital investment. No one can say what his or her useful life is, so make your best guess—say five years. It's truer than calling them expenses. ("The Real Key to Creating Wealth," *Fortune*, September 1993.)

Any company that implements one of these measures, such as EVA, can fundamentally change the behavior of an entire organization. The new measure focuses the behavior of individuals throughout all parts of the organization in a way that is better aligned with creating stockholder wealth. If compensation incentives are based upon the new measure, employees and stockholders mutually benefit.

CONCLUSION

What is the best way to maximize shareholder value, and what is the best way to measure those efforts? Profits alone do not increase value if they do not represent a return on the invested capital greater than the cost of the capital, so maximizing profits is not sufficient. Maximizing return on investment alone also will not increase value, as the Coca-Cola example demonstrated. EVA does not, by itself, prescribe a strategy for raising market value; it is a measure of operations that relates to market value.

The EVA equation reveals several ways to effect continuous improvements in the EVA number, all of which will lead to maximizing shareholder returns and, therefore, market value.

The EVA approach is useful in numerous applications. It can be used to measure, for any company or acquisition, the capital of the company(ies), which is one component of value, and the present value of the expected EVA's, which is the other component of the value. Those two components will define total value and, therefore, what an investor should be willing to pay for an equity investment.

EVA can also be applied to capital budgeting. Analysts have been told to choose any project whose net present value is greater than zero, and discounted EVA streams are equal to the NPV of a project; therefore, if the project NPV is greater than zero, so is its EVA. In fact, they are the same number.

EVA can be used for performance review, for goal setting, and as the basis for compensation. A major benefit of EVA is providing a common language for communicating performance and goals. Corporations often use different terms for different purposes or audiences. They report to the market in terms of earnings, for example, often manage in terms of investment returns on capital, and often use DCF and NPV terms for capital budgeting and acquisitions. These different, competing measures can lead to different conclusions about the same project; the use of EVA eliminates that problem.

The EVA approach is good news for a company's shareholders and for analysts because it relates company performance directly to shareholder value. If a company maximizes EVA, it will improve earnings and all the traditional measures of value.

WHAT EVA IS

- EVA is the single best-integrated measure of growth in operating profits and operating efficiency. As such, it is a measure, which holds management accountable for all economic outlays whether they are recorded on the income statement, balance sheet, or in the footnotes of the financial statements.
- EVA measures the value created during a single period through increased margin, improved asset management, profitable incremental investment, or redeployment of underutilized assets. EVA creates a common language for making capital budgeting decisions, evaluating performance, and measuring the value—creating potential of strategic and tactical options.[15]

WHAT EVA IS NOT

- EVA is not a holy grail. EVA does not solve problems; managers do. EVA is a good instrument on the dashboard that tells management how much shareholder value they have created. However, it does not make difficult decisions easier.
- EVA is distorted by historical cost accounting. EVA is computed from historical accounting information, or sunk costs. From an

---

[15]The Financial Manager's Report, A Periodic Update for CPAs in Management, *Business & Industry* (1995).

economic viewpoint, sunk costs are irrelevant to the generation of future free cash flow, and hence share value. Without adjustments, an old factory will report higher EVA than a new one, even though both have the same net present value of free cash flows. On the other hand, adjusting historical costs to economic reality is not a perfect science and can add a layer of administrative complexity and confusion to reduce distortions caused by historical cost accounting, management should focus on the change in EVA.

• EVA is not directional. Because it is a single period measure, it provides no direction about the future. For example, negative EVA is not necessarily indicative of a company that should be sold or liquidated. The imbedded capital may be worth little, but new capital may generate positive EVA. Likewise, a positive EVA business is not necessarily one that shouldn't be sold. If the offer price exceeds the value management can achieve, a sale of the business is in the best interests of shareholders.

Some companies have modified the DuPont Formula to include a capital charge. The DuPont model is covered in Chapter 7, but briefly, the DuPont Formula separates the return on capital into three components—margin, capital turnover, and taxes—to assist managers in identifying specific areas for improvement. (*See* Figure 20-3.)

For stable and predictable businesses, this approach works well because it provides managers a complete picture of the interrelationship of capital, margin and EVA. Also, this approach contributes millions in shareholder value to its subscribers by making managers conscious of every dollar they spend. The long-term value-added comes from changing traditional patterns of behavior. Briggs and Stratton, a major manufacturer of small horsepower engines, observed that inventory and receivables tended to move in lock step with sales. This increased market share but did not improve returns to shareholders. After the company installed an EVA system, that pattern was broken. EVA increased, because less capital was tied up in working capital even as sales grew and the company's stock price began to outperform its competitors.

RISK CAPITAL AND RAROC

RAROC (risk-adjusted return on capital) is a managerial tool which enables the firm's management to allocate capital more efficiently in a risk-based decision-making framework. It can be used for two main purposes: (1) strategic decisions (i.e., efficient capital allocation), and (2)

Figure 20-3: Modified DuPont Formula

Return on Capital = Margin × Capital Turnover × (1 – Cash Tax Rate)
ROC   = EBIT/Sales × Sales/Capital × (1 – Cash Tax Rate)
Less: Cost of Capital (C)
Equals: (ROC – C)
Times: Capital Employed
Equals: EVA

EBIT	$2,000	$4,000	$6,000	$2,809
Sales	$50,000	$50,000	$50,000	$50,000
Margin	4.0%	8.0%	12.0%	9.25%
Capital	$12,000	$12,000	$12,000	$12,000
Capital/Turnover	4.17	4.17	4.17	4.17
Cash Tax Rate	46.00%	46.00%	46.00%	46.00%
Cost of Debt	10.00%	10.00%	10.00%	8.75%
Cost of Equity	20.00%	20.00%	20.00%	6.67%
Debt/Equity	4.0:1	4.0:1	4.0:1	4.0:1
EVA	($360)	$720	$1,800	($466)

for the measurement of performance. RAROC can be viewed as a critical measure related to the development of a financial framework.

What is a financial framework? It's the set of policies, procedures, regulations, and standing orders which ensure effective stewardship of funds across the group. Its purpose is to set boundaries around how firms make financial decisions. It can be viewed as a way to ensure that the funds are spent accountably with regard to economy, efficiency, and effectiveness for each level of expenditure. This framework enables a firm to better articulate what and how their inputs (economic capital) generate economic value.

The methodologies described so far in this book have covered market, credit, and operational risk. In each case, the distribution of profits and losses reveals a number of essential insights. First, the expected loss is a measure of the reserves necessary to guard against future losses. At the very least, the pricing of products should provide a buffer against expected losses. Second, the unexpected loss is a measure of the amount of economic capital required to support the firm's financial risk. This capital, also called risk capital, is basically a value-at-risk (VAR) measure.

Knowing the above, a firm can make better-informed decisions about business lines. Each business activity should provide sufficient profit to compensate for the calculated risks involved. Thus, product pricing should account not only for expected losses but also for the remuneration of risk capital.

Some activities may require large amounts of risk capital, which in turn requires higher returns. This is the essence of risk-adjusted return on capital (RAROC) measures. The central objective is to establish benchmarks to evaluate the economic return of business activities. These activities would include transactions, products, customer trades, and business lines, as well as the entire business.

RAROC is also related to concepts such as shareholder value analysis and economic value added (EVA) covered earlier. In the past, performance was measured by yardsticks such as return on assets (ROA), which adjusts profits for the associated book value of assets, or return on equity (ROE), which adjusts profits for the associated book value of equity. None of these measures is satisfactory for evaluating the performance of business lines because they ignore risks.

RAROC was actually developed by Bankers Trust in the late 1970s. The bank was faced with the problem of evaluating traders involved in activities with different risk profiles. Two traders may bring in the same revenue results for the year but how do you compare their performance? Which trader added the most value when you factor in the risk/reward scenario? RAROC is a part of the family of risk-adjusted performance measures that helps answer these types of questions.

RAROC Methodology

The RAROC methodology process has three steps:

1. *Risk measurement.* This requires the measurement of portfolio exposures, of the volatility and correlations of the risk factors.
2. *Capital allocation.* This requires the choice of a confidence level and horizon for the VAR measure, which translates into an economic capital.
3. *Performance measurement.* This requires the adjustment of performance for the risk capital.

Performance measurement can be based on an RAPM method or one of its variants. For instance, economic value added (EVA) focuses on the creation of value during a particular period in excess of the required return on capital. EVA measures residual economic profits as:

$$EVA = Profit - (Capital \times k)$$

This is where profits are adjusted for the cost of economic capital, with k defined as a discount rate. Assuming the whole worth is captured by the EVA, the higher the EVA, the better the project or product.

RAROC is formally defined as:

$$\text{RAROC} = \frac{\text{Profit} - (\text{Capital} \times k\,)}{\text{Capital}}$$

This is a rate of return, obtained by dividing the dollar EVA return by the dollar amount of capital.

Another popular performance measure is shareholder value analysis (SVA), whose purpose is to maximize the total value to shareholders. The framework is that of a net present value (NPV) analysis, where the worth of a project is computed by taking the present value of future cash flows, discounted at the appropriate interest rate k, minus the up-front capital. A project that has positive NPV creates positive shareholder value.

Although SVA is a prospective multi-period measure whereas EVA is a one-period measure, EVA and SVA are consistent with each other provided the same inputs are used.

Chapter 21

WARNING SIGNS AND FINANCIAL SHENANIGANS

ALWAYS LOOK FOR THE WARNING SIGNS

The analyst's ability to pick up on financial distress warning signs is a critical part of the entire analytical process. If available, quarterly financial results certainly provide the interim trends that may indicate either a positive or negative financial development. But even beyond the numbers, you should watch for the behavioral signs that could signify the need for further investigation:

1. Unwillingness to submit financial information.
2. Indication of slowness in collection of customer's account.
3. Expansion to new areas of the business unfamiliar to the customer.
4. Bank overdrafts or NSF checks—No matter how convincingly they are explained, this is an indication of poor record keeping or inadequate financing.
5. Lack of records for proper control—This could manifest itself by way of complaints.
6. Expenditures for capital investment such as new buildings, equipment, fixtures, etc.
7. Financial trends—No company is stagnant, they are either improving or deteriorating. The trick is to find out which way they are headed with proper financial reviews.
8. Marketing has picked up something from the street on an account—Check it out.
9. Customer changes accounting firms or year-ends—May not be negative but always ask the question why.
10. Field visits are invaluable—Fill out a field trip report for filing sighting both positives and negative activity.

Warning signs can be categorized into Operational, Managerial, and Financial signals.

Operational Signals:
1. Change in senior management
2. High employee turnover
3. Board of Directors resignation
4. Strike or unusual fire or theft
5. Market changes
6. A change in suppliers or payment to suppliers
7. Pricing issues and quality control problems
8. One-time events such as a large bad debt claim

Managerial Signals:
1. Reliance on one individual for decision making
2. Inexperienced management team with weak financial and organizational skills
3. Frivolous spending
4. Not returning phone calls
5. Personal problems
6. Working long hours

Financial Signals:
1. Decline in sales
2. Lower profit margins
3. Sustained losses
4. Growth at faster rate than inventory and accounts receivable
5. Increased debt
6. Highly leveraged balance sheet
7. Reduced cash flow or negative FCF
8. Working capital decline and becomes negative as accounts payable grows at faster rate than inventory and accounts receivable
9. Change in company's bank relationship—Reduced availability on a company's operating line or change in borrowing patterns without any change in the business
10. Increase in loan security or a bank's request for security on a previously unsecured loan
11. Breach of loan covenants or missed loan payments

A decline in cash flow, which is key to any business, is the most important bell weather of financial distress. Unfortunately, approximately 80 percent of all companies are privately held and do not provide detailed financial information. As a result, suppliers must rely on their customer's payment patterns, their competitor's experience with the customer and the customer's actions as a means of assessing their customer's financial health. This means that businesses must be aware of Operational and Managerial Signals that warn of impending financial problems, which may result in a bankruptcy.

With regards to the Enron bankruptcy, financial analysts should be wary whenever a company dramatically changes its business model, particularly from one easily understood by investors to another, far more obtuse and difficult to evaluate and monitor. Moreover, analysts should assume the use of special-purpose entities, and other off-balance sheet entities can be used to create phantom profits and hide liabilities. The absence of detailed disclosure about such entities raises additional red flags. Other warning signs in the Enron debacle include numerous related-party activities and self-dealing by senior executives, large stock sales by directors and officers, and the mysterious resignation of a rather young CEO. Also, the company showed arrogance in its treatment of financial analysts who were asking probing questions about its accounting and disclosure policies.

ACCRUALS AND STRUCTURED FINANCE

Earnings are composed of cash flows and accruals, and the manipulation of either component will affect the earnings number. Earnings management occurs when managers use judgment in financial reporting and in structuring transactions to alter financial reports to either mislead stockholders about the underlying economic performance of the company or to influence contractual outcomes that depend on reported accounting numbers. Given that brief introduction, let's look at this method where companies don't change their activities but, rather opportunistically report income for an existing activity. Examples that increase income are as follows: reducing the allowance for doubtful accounts, capitalizing rather than expensing costs, and avoiding write-offs of assets.

Accruals create the opportunity for earnings management because they require managers to make forecasts, estimates and judgments. With a greater degree of discretion in an accrual, you can see a greater opportunity for earnings management to take place. In what this author likes to call "garden-variety" earnings management, an activity found in almost any major corporation, a manager may increase or decrease the levels of accounting accruals in order to reach a desired profit. The following examples will serve to highlight typical accrual adjustments to assets and liability accounts:

- *Accounts receivable*. Managers forecast the proportion of customers that will not pay.
- *Inventory*. Managers capitalize some costs in inventory and expense other costs as periodic expenses. They forecast expected demand in order to determine if a write-down is necessary.
- *Other current assets*. This is usually a catchall category for capitalized costs
- *Property, plant and equipment (PP&E)*. Managers capitalize a multitude of costs and depreciate them in arbitrary ways.
- *Accounts or interest payable*. These accounts are amounts owed in dollars to suppliers or debtors. There is low discretion here.
- *Pension liabilities and post-retirement benefits*. Managers must forecast the expected return on plan assets, obtain actuarial assumptions on life expectancies and so forth.
- *Long-term debt*. Low discretion here. Manager's value is based on the amount received at issuance of long-term debt, and the premium is amortized under specific rules.

As an example of such an accruals management, let us assume that a manager reports a cash expenditure of, say, $90,000 on a marketing campaign as an asset called "deferred subscriber acquisition cost" instead of an expense. The result of this accounting decision is to boost the bottom line of the division by $90,000. Generally accepted accounting principles define assets as economic resources that provide *future* benefits to the company. It may well be that the above manager is convinced that the marketing expenditure will result in future benefits, and is simply trying to report the transaction properly as an asset. On the other hand, it may be that the manager is really trying to manipulate reported earnings using an accounting decision. Perhaps he or she is trying to meet a quarterly earnings target for the division, and the capitalization of the marketing expenditure is just the boost in earnings needed to tip the reported earnings from a deficit to a surplus relative to the division's target. The investor, and often the external auditor of the company, is usually not in a position to distinguish between the two alternative scenarios because doing so requires second guessing the manager's business judgment as to whether the expenditure will result in future benefits.

But there is good news for investors and financial analysts. While the above earnings management decision increased reported earnings, it also resulted in a very visible balance sheet "accrual" item, specifically, an asset item called "deferred subscriber acquisition cost." Unfortunately for the manager, this accrual is not a permanent item. Over time, this accrual item will be amortized and will result in expenses in future periods, thus reversing the beneficial income effect realized in the current period. In fact, the above accrual will reverse completely over time. This reversal of accruals over time is in fact a general property of all "operating" accrual items, such as inventory, accounts receivable, accounts payable, capitalized costs, and so on.

More generally, we can define accruals as the difference between cash flow from operations and net income. Over time, managers would be forced to make up earnings shortfalls with real cash earnings. By carefully studying the level of accruals reported by companies and the changes in them over time, analysts and corporate leaders can hope to identify companies that are building up accruals.

Accruals management affects only the timing of the recognition of earnings. An overstatement of earnings in one period implies an understatement of earnings in another. Earnings management by opportunistically reporting accruals is not necessarily a violation of GAAP. The firm is free to choose among methods without economic justification (e.g., using straight-line depreciation instead of accelerated depreciation). One result found in many studies is that high accruals are a potential "red flag" that companies are engaging in earnings management. A continued build-up in accruals could be masking financial stress. "The overstatement of revenues is the most common type of earnings management."[16]

In summary, the goal of accruals management is the management of the income statement. Any additional effect on other financial statements, such as the effect on assets and liabilities, is viewed by the manager as secondary or irrelevant. Second, accruals management is done easily through accounting decisions, and does not require the creation of a new business transaction. In the capitalization case, one could assume that the $90,000 expenditure would have been made anyway for business reasons,

---

[16]SEC Accounting and Auditing Enforcement Release (AAER).

and that the capitalization decision was additionally made to manage earnings. Third, and most important, accruals management is usually done by a lone manager or a small group of managers.

By contrast, the structure of financial engineering transactions of the kind employed by Enron is inherently complex, requiring the formation of legal entities, and creation of financing arrangements between the company, its lenders, and new outside investors. These financial arrangements are sometimes referred to as **"structured finance."** For example, consider a complex structured finance arrangement for a "special purpose entity" (SPE) undertaken by Enron, apparently to book a large gain from the "sale" of an unprofitable start-up venture. In the venture with Blockbuster, Inc., digitized video entertainment from Blockbuster would be piped to customers' television sets over an Enron-provided broadband fiber network. By late 2000, this venture had neither paying customers nor profits. But Enron nevertheless apparently wanted to report the venture as a success. It formed an SPE called "Braveheart," with $115 million financing from CIBC, a Canadian investment bank, and $10 million equity from two small entities, one of which was a 72 percent owned subsidiary of Enron. The funds were then channeled to a second SPE, which then paid the funds to Enron in exchange for the Braveheart venture. The bottom line from these very complex set of transactions was that Enron "sold" a revenueless and profitless venture to an SPE controlled by itself for $125.8 million and booked a $111 million profit.

Unlike accrual decisions which can be planned and executed by small groups of individuals, financial engineering transactions like the one above require significant legal planning, including the proper creation of legal entities, and additionally often requires raising new long-term capital in the form of loans or equity. A comparison of the simplicity of accruals management with the complexity found in financial engineering arrangements thus shows that financial engineering requires an *organizational commitment* to earnings management. In other words, in addition to middle managers desiring higher earnings etc., financial engineering requires the commitment of senior management and the company board of directors in the decisions to create the needed financial commitments and structures.

Financial Analysis of Financial Engineering

As noted earlier, accruals generally reverse over time, providing the analyst with tell-tale signs of earnings management. By contrast, financial engineering is often designed specifically with the goal of hiding and removing accruals (such as operating assets and liabilities) from financial reports forever. Once taken off the balance sheet, these accruals are impossible for the investor to track. There would be no expectation that the accruals will reappear or reverse in a future period. For example, if debt is held off-balance sheet, there is not much an investor or even a corporate manager can do to predict when and whether the debt will affect the reported financial performance of the company. There is also no assurance that the income effects will reverse in some definite time frame. For example, off-balance sheet debt can be refinanced indefinitely through the creation of additional SPEs.

To summarize, the financial reporting management opportunities presented by financial engineering potentially fall in a different class altogether from the traditional accounting accruals-based earnings management. Moreover, there are currently few developed tools of financial analysis currently available to senior managers and investors to monitor the income and balance sheet effects of financial engineering. Financial engineering, of course, is good for the company if it achieves any of the standard goals of corporate finance—raise capital at the lowest cost, reduce the risk exposure and manage or spread risk, and make funds available for value creating projects—just as accounting accruals management is supposed to convey information to investors about managers' expectations of future cash flows. Still, the lack of transparency inherent in financial engineering means that the potential to misuse it as a powerful tool of earnings management is high, especially where an organizational commitment to earnings management exists. It is thus imperative for corporations now, more than ever, to recommit to developing and enforcing corporate governance systems that create a corporate climate of transparency and full disclosure to investors. Any structural weakness in corporate controls and governance could easily lead to large-scale management of earnings through financial engineering, and ultimately to shareholder value destruction. This is the main lesson of Enron.

FINANCIAL SHENANIGANS

The great Sherlock Holmes and other outstanding detectives, like Colombo, all search for the clues, examine all the evidence, and deduce what actually happened. The hat, cigar, and raincoat are optional during this process. Similarly, successful investors, lenders, and financial analysts read financial reports and other information, searching for clues and deducing just how the company actually performed in the past and how it is likely to perform in the future.

An essential skill for analysts is the ability to detect early signs that a firm is using financial shenanigans to camouflage problems.

Not all financial shenanigans are illegal or violations of generally accepted accounting principles (GAAP), or what is referred to as GAP (games accountants play). They can range from the fairly benign (amortizing costs too slowly) to outright fraud (recording bogus revenue). Like most folks, managers are motivated by rewards and punishments. Many companies offer bonuses and stock options based on financial results and, as a result, managers are inclined to report more favorable financial results. Because of this pressure to report higher results than the previous year or quarter, managers get creative with their interpretation of GAAP.

Look for the shenanigan warning signs in the following type companies: fast-growth companies whose real growth is beginning to slow, basket-case companies that are struggling to survive, newly public companies, and private companies.

Always look at the footnotes to get an indication of the integrity of management. Companies that fail to use conservative accounting methods may be demonstrating a lack of integrity in the financial reporting process.

For example, watch for the inventory valuation method used. This can substantially affect a company's reported profits. The most popular methods are last in, first out (LIFO) and first in, first out (FIFO). LIFO charges the latest inventory costs as an expense first; conversely, FIFO charges the earliest costs first. So, during inflationary periods, as when inventory costs are rising, the difference between LIFO and FIFO can affect profits substantially. Under these circumstances, LIFO generally produces lower reported profits for a company than does FIFO (this also results in lower taxes and therefore in higher cash flows).

Look for changes in accounting principles for no apparent reason, which could signal the GAP principle mentioned earlier. Slowing down a company's depreciation schedule or changing its depreciation method can dress up earnings.

Always read the president's message but do it for the current as well as the previous two years. You know the president will put a positive spin on things so looking at past messages will tell you how things really turned out. Along with this reading, look at the Management Discussion and Analysis section where specific issues are discussed in order to assess the company's current financial condition. See just how candid the president happens to be. If the company is clearly having financial difficulty, will the president level with the reader or try to sugar coat the problem.

Common-size analysis (both Vertical and Horizontal) is used to detect possible shenanigans. Vertical analysis spots structural changes and horizontal identifies organizational trends. In vertical analysis, all balance sheet items are expressed as a percentage of total assets and all income statement items as a percentage of net sales. In horizontal analysis, a particular year is designated as the base year and percentage change in subsequent years are computed.

Warning signs that could be found using vertical analysis:

- There was a big improvement in selling expense relative to sales.
- Cash and equivalents represent a much smaller percentage of total assets.
- Receivables represent a much larger percentage of total assets over previous period.
- Gross margins expanded by an astounding amount.

The point here is that dramatic changes can be spotted rather easily when the numbers are laid out in this fashion.

Warning signs that could be found using horizontal analysis:

- SG&A grew much more slowly than sales. Are we capitalizing operational costs?
- Other current assets and other assets growing much faster than sales. Perhaps another sign of capitalizing operating costs.
- Accounts payable growing much faster than inventory.
- A big decline in the cash balance while sales jumped. Increased sales should translate into increasing cash and equivalents.

There are other warning signs general in nature such as:

- The company made loans to its officers.
- The company is facing pending litigation.
- There were related party transactions.
- Cash flow from operations materially lags behind net income.
- Cash flow generated mainly from sale of assets, additional borrowing and selling of stock.

Houston-based Enron started as a natural gas pipeline company in the 1980s, with a stock price virtually flat for the decade. In the 1990s, Enron became a global trading behemoth and, by 2001, had 21,000 employees and an $80 billion market capitalization. The stock price grew more than sevenfold.

Enron effectively operated like other Wall Street trading companies. It bought, resold, and invested in commodities future contracts—gambling on future prices and market conditions. It traded in a wide variety of products such as natural gas and electricity contracts, complex derivatives, broadband capacity futures, and weather derivatives.

The old Enron generated consistent (although sluggish) revenue and profit growth from selling products to customers. It had real assets on its balance sheet that investors and creditors value. In contrast, the new Enron generated revenue and profits from risky and unpredictable trading and asset sales to investment partners. Moreover, the new Enron created few tangible assets. In fact, Enron's CEO, Jeffrey Skilling, boasted about the company's absence of hard assets. He described the approach as "asset like," adding, "In the old days, people worked for assets. We've turned it around—what we've said is, the assets work for people." Being "asset like" meant that once Enron announced problems, there was no foundation of hard assets—real product or real value—to fall back on. Creditors braced for a big loss.

An important part of Enron's strategy for growth was through a variety of investment partnerships and special-purpose entities (SPEs). A Houston-based analyst at Prudential Securities estimated that there existed over 3,000 such partnerships. Enron created a series of joint ventures (many involving related parties at Enron) and excluded the results from its consolidated financial statements. As a result, Enron materially inflated its profits and had massive debt from shareholders. Enron failed to disclose details of these ventures until just before the collapse. The joint ventures used a variety of schemes to enrich senior executives, create phantom profits, and drive up Enron's share price. The partnerships were typically initially funded with Enron's own stock. Much of the bogus profits recorded by Enron came either from the continued appreciation in the company's stock or from Enron selling goods or services to these affiliated entities.

Chapter 22

BANKRUPTCY

An all too common disposition of a highly distressed credit is for the company to file for bankruptcy protection.

The Bankruptcy Code deals with all aspects of a debtor's rights and obligations, and a creditor's rights and obligations. The two types of bankruptcies that have the most impact on a company's business are Chapter 7 and Chapter 11 bankruptcy cases.

THE BANKRUPTCY ABUSE PREVENTION AND CONSUMER PROTECTION ACT OF 2005

On April 20, 2005, President George W. Bush signed the Bankruptcy Abuse and Consumer Protection Act of 2005 (Pub. L. No. 109-9) (the "Act") into law. The Act makes significant amendments to the Bankruptcy Code, and generally takes effect with bankruptcy cases commenced 180 days after its enactment, or October 17, 2005, however particular provisions have different effective dates. Although the Act reforms both commercial and consumer bankruptcies, the following summarizes the impact upon only business bankruptcies under Chapter 11 of the Bankruptcy Code and is a summary of some of the more significant changes instituted by the Act from a creditor's perspective.

Topic: Treatment of financial contracts. **Act Section:** 907, 910.

Impact of the Act

The Act expands the definitions of forward contract, repurchase agreement, swap agreement, commodity contract, and securities contract to account for market developments and to create flexible mechanisms that can include similar agreements and new types of transactions developed in the future. The Act also expands the counterparties eligible for securities, forward and commodity contract protections by creating protections for "financial participants" including clearing organizations and entities engaging in identified transactions based on a qualifying transaction size.

217

In addition, the Act permits creditors to close out derivative contracts with debtor-companies. This provision reduces risk by allowing swaps and other financial contracts to be unraveled quickly and without the approval of bankruptcy courts. The Act also restricts a bankruptcy trustee's avoidance powers regarding certain master netting agreement transfers to those transfers which are intentionally fraudulent (subject to a limited exception for transactions included in a master netting agreement that are not "safe harbor" contracts). Also notable is that the expanded definition of "swap agreements," together with the subtle changes to section 546(g), greatly expand the protection from avoidance actions provided to non-debtor counterparties. The Act adds section 561, which provides for bilateral cross-product netting across forward contracts, repurchase agreements, swap agreements, commodity contracts, and securities contracts, and by participants of master netting agreements. Further, the Act's addition of section 562 clarifies the measure of damages when debtors reject securities contracts, forward contracts, commodity contracts, repurchase agreements, swap agreements or master netting agreements. Section 562 provides that damages are measured as of the earlier of the rejection date or the liquidation/termination/acceleration date(s).

Topic: Administrative expenses-limitations on KERP payments and committee member's expenses. **Act Section:** 331; 1208.

Impact of the Act

Limits the ability of a debtor to pay officer and director retention bonuses (a three-part test must be satisfied), severance pay (a two-part test must be satisfied), and certain other key employee retention programs. Limits payments outside the ordinary course of business to officers, managers or consultants hired postpetition by requiring that such payments be justified by the facts and circumstances of the case. Excludes from compensable professional services any expenses incurred for any attorney or an accountant by an individual member of a creditors' or equity security holders' committee.

Topic: Reclamation rights and administrative expense claim. **Act Section:** 546(c); 503(b).

Impact of the Act

The Act expands the right to reclaim goods sold to a debtor in the ordinary course of business where the debtor received such goods while insolvent within 45 days prior to the petition date. A seller may not reclaim goods unless a demand in writing is made: (i) within 45 days after receipt of such goods by the debtor, or (ii) within 20 days after the petition date if the 45-day period expires after the petition date. The Act also supplements 503(b) of the Bankruptcy Code by granting an administrative expense claim for the value of goods sold to a debtor in the ordinary course of business and received by the debtor within 20 days prior to the petition date.

Topic: Increased look-back period for fraudulent conveyances; Increased inclusion in fraudulent conveyances. **Act Section:** 1402.

Impact of the Act

The Act increases the look-back period for fraudulent conveyances from one year to two years prior to the petition date. This provision will apply only to cases commenced more than one year after the enactment of the Act. The Act also expands fraudulent conveyances to include payments to an insider under an employment contract, outside of the debtor's ordinary course of business, where the debtor did not receive reasonably equivalent value in exchange for such payment. This provision will apply to causes commenced immediately on or after the enactment of the Act.

Topic: Limitation on debtor's exclusivity to file and solicit a plan. **Act Section:** 411.

Impact of the Act

This Act limits a court's ability to extend a debtor-in-possession's exclusive right to file a plan of reorganization beyond the prescribed 120-day period commencing on the petition date by providing that exclusivity cannot exceed beyond the periods of 18 months postpetition for filing a plan and 20 months postpetition for solicitation of a plan.

From a credit risk trading perspective, relevant changes addressed above fall into the following four primary categories.

1. Safe harbor definition
2. Netting and setoff
3. Preferential transfers
4. Administrative priority

From a **Safe Harbor** definition change, the definition of a forward and swap contract has broadened. Contracts such as options and credit derivatives are now expressly included.

Master Netting Agreements (MNAs) have been added as a defined term. Along with this, security agreements and credit enhancements have been expressly addressed as part of the contracts (e.g., CSAs, LCs and guarantees).

Provisions now apply to governmental units such as municipal bankruptcies.

Netting and Setoff arrangements are affected by making it clear with regards to one's ability to net/set-off across product contracts. It was previously only clear within the product contracts. You can net physical against financial, however, the contract must be in place, for example, an MNA. In addition, there is now ability to net/set-off across affiliates not addressed in the agreement. With this comes the issue of "mutuality" which can be resolved by requiring all parties to sign the contract.

With **preference payments**, any payments made within a 90-day period prior to filing could be challenged as "excessive" and potentially "avoided." The creditor's defense was previously defined as payments made in the "ordinary course of business," *and* according to ordinary business terms were acceptable. Now, payments made in ordinary course of business *or* according to ordinary business terms are acceptable which makes it much easier to prove your argument.

With regards to **administrative priority**, it would get paid before any postpetition claims. Now, deliveries made within 20 days of filing will be accorded this status provided it meets the "ordinary course of business" test. So, there is a greater probability these days of getting more back and quicker.

Another interesting development was the aforementioned Act limiting a court's ability to extend a debtor-in-possession's exclusive right to file a plan of reorganization beyond the prescribed 120-day period commencing on the petition date. Exclusivity cannot exceed beyond the periods of 18 months postpetition which stops the usual drawing out of proceedings caused by bankrupt firm's applying for and receiving extensions.

CHAPTER 7

Chapter 7 of the Bankruptcy Code provides the framework for the orderly liquidation of a company. In a Chapter 7 case, a trustee is appointed and the trustee is given the power to arrange for the collection, liquidation and distribution of the assets to creditors of the debtor according to the priority status of each creditor. Some creditors (usually banks and insurance companies) have loaned money against specific assets of the bankrupt estate. These creditors are called "secured" creditors. Normally, their claims must be satisfied before any distribution can be made to "unsecured" creditors.

CHAPTER 11

Chapter 11 of the Bankruptcy Code was designed to be a single, unified way of dealing with the reorganization of a business. The objective of Chapter 11 is to reorganize a financially troubled debtor while maximizing the return to the creditors. Another objective is to retain the employees and other economic benefits that the community derives from the business. Two major provisions of Chapter 11 are:

1. The debtor will continue in control of its business.
2. Normally, the debtor will prepare a plan of reorganization, which is submitted for approval by all classes of creditors.

The key players in a Chapter 11 case include the judge, who decides the relevant legal issues; the U.S. Trustee, who appoints the committee and has general oversight responsibility over the creditors; equity security holders; the debtor; and, of course, the creditors' committee.

A case starts with the filing of a voluntary or involuntary bankruptcy petition. This results in an automatic stay, which prevents creditors from enforcing prepetition claims or from seeking recourse against the debtor's assets without first obtaining permission from the court.

During the Chapter 11 case, the debtor continues to operate its business as a "debtor-in-possession" (DIP), unless a Chapter 11 Trustee is appointed due to mismanagement or fraud by the debtor's management, or the case is converted to a Chapter 7 liquidation. The ultimate objective of a Chapter 11 case is the confirmation of a plan of reorganization, which provides for the amount and manner which creditors will be paid.[17]

Creditors are typically divided into separate classes; each class of creditors must be treated in a fair, equitable and nondiscriminatory manner.

The debtor initially has a period of 120 days within which it has the exclusive right to file a plan. This time may be lengthened or shortened by a court order. All classes of creditors that are impaired (negatively affected) by the plan may vote in favor of or against the plan. Creditors of a class are deemed to accept the plan if both a majority in number, and two-thirds in dollar amount of those voting concur. If the plan is accepted

[17] James S. Carr, Attorney, Kelly Dry and Warren LLP, New York, NY.

by at least one but not all classes impaired by the plan, it nevertheless can be confirmed in some circumstances through a process called "cram down." Now that's a real technical term you can relate to.

Critical First Days

Chapter 11 cases often move very quickly during the first several days. While some of the pressure on the debtor is relieved by the automatic stay that goes into effect upon the filing of the bankruptcy petition, there are a number of things that the debtor normally must do at the inception of the case to get its house in order.

In most Chapter 11 cases, the debtor will need to arrange for the financing of its operations through an agreement for postpetition borrowing or use of the cash collateral securing its bank debt. Sometimes, the debtor cannot obtain such an agreement and will file a motion to use cash collateral over the objection of the bank. Other pleadings may be filed with the court in the first few days of the case, such as a motion to pay prepetition wages, a motion to allow the debtor to maintain its bank accounts and cash management system, a motion to compel utilities to continue to provide utility services to the debtor, a motion to pay critical vendor claims, a motion to sell assets, and/or file complaints for the turnover of property or for injunctive relief critical to the debtor's survival.

Immediate Actions to Be Taken

1. *Gather Documents:* Begin gathering all documents relating to the customer and keep them in one place. Also, actively gather all bankruptcy related documents that were sent to your company by the bankruptcy court or the customer. Don't wait for these documents to work their way to your desk. Frequently, they are sent to the same address that the customer uses to send its payments. Forward all bankruptcy related documents directly to your company's law department or whoever is responsible for making decisions and taking action in bankruptcy cases.

2. *Send Reclamation Letter:* Stop delivery of goods in transit before the customer takes possession. If the customer is already in possession of your recently delivered goods when you become aware of the bankruptcy filing, send a letter to the customer immediately demanding the return of your goods. Obtain wording for the letter from the law department or legal counsel. All such letters should be sent so that you have proof of mailing, such as return-receipt requested, facsimile or overnight mail.

3. *Communicate:* Check your systems data and inform all business units that deal with the customer of the bankruptcy filing. This includes every department! You need to coordinate your strategy in dealing with the customer, and you want to make sure your company doesn't violate any bankruptcy laws.
4. *Don't Make Any Payments:* Assess the amount of your claim against the customer and whether your company owes any money to the customer for any reason, don't pay it to the customer, and don't apply any of the customer's funds you are holding to satisfy your company's claims. Wait for instructions from you law department or legal counsel.
5. *Open a New Account:* If you plan on continuing to conduct business with the customer after the customer files for bankruptcy (and in some instances you have no choice), close the customer's account as of the day the customer filed for bankruptcy and open a new account. Every transaction from the date the customer filed for bankruptcy should be billed to the new account.
6. *Contact Legal:* Upon learning of the bankruptcy filing, contact your law department or legal counsel.

Other Actions to Be Taken
1. Assess the Situation:
   a. Discontinue credit sales by calling appropriate internal personnel immediately.
   b. Assess exposure by viewing accounts and contacting all delivery points.
   c. Locate contracts, security agreements and Letters of Credit.
2. File a Proof of Claim once notified by the bankruptcy court.

If you end up being one of the largest creditors of the debtor, your company may be asked to serve on the unsecured creditors' committee.

This author advocates the development of a formal procedure that establishes a **financial crisis event response plan**, which proposes a three-tiered approach: (1) Incident Management Team, (2) Business Impact Team and (3) Group Crisis Team.

The procedure to handle distressed situations or credit events would include a core group of individuals that will be tasked to deal directly with both the external and internal constituencies within the three-tiered approach noted above. Those nominated individuals are as follows:

- **Relationship Manager, Trading/Supply Manager**
  - *Definition of Role:*
    - Incident Commander
    - Identification of commercial options
    - Risk mitigation through position replacement cost measurement using both market and estimate liquidation value

- **CFO**
  - *Definition of Role:*
    - Incident Facilitator
    - Convener of distressed management process
    - Communication Strategist—within the Business Group
    - Conveyor of credit risk tolerance levels

- **Credit Manager**
  - *Definition of Role:*
    - Incident originator
    - Provide aggregate exposure to counterparty that should include both on and off-balance sheet exposures
    - Exposure should be measured under conservative assumptions as to the efficacy of netting and collateral arrangements
    - Provide ongoing analysis and support

- **Legal**
  - *Definition of Role:*
    - Payment netting documentation and practices
    - Coordination procedures between documentation control and credit risk management
    - Support the distressed situation

PREFERENCE PAYMENTS

A preference payment is a concern because it may involve the return to the bankrupt estate of any money collected on a past-due debt during the 90 days preceding the date of the bankruptcy filing. The theory here is that the creditor who accepts a preferential payment may be receiving a larger share of the bankrupt's estate than the creditor would have received with a pro-rata liquidation under Chapter 7 of the Bankruptcy Code.

Certain defenses to preferential payments exist. Some of the more common defenses are:

1. Payments intended to be contemporaneous with the exchange of the product.
2. Payments of debts incurred in the ordinary course of business of the debtor and the creditor, payments made in the ordinary course of business of both the debtor and the creditor, and payments made according to ordinary business terms.
3. Payments made where the creditor gives new value, after such transfer, to or for the benefit of the debtor.

FREQUENTLY REFERENCED GLOSSARY OF TERMS

Automatic Stay. When a bankruptcy petition is filed, creditors are automatically prohibited from attempting to collect their pre-petition claims from the debtor or proceeding against the property of the debtor without first obtaining permission from the court to do so.

Debtor. The entity undergoing reorganization.

Debtor-in-Possession. Unless and until a Chapter 11 Trustee is appointed, a debtor remains in possession of its assets and will manage its own business affairs. The debtor-in-possession has a fiduciary obligation to the creditors, much the same as a court-appointed trustee.

Petition. The document filed with the court that initiates a bankruptcy case.

Plan of Reorganization. Sometimes referred to by the shortened term "plan," the document that, when approved by the court, specifies the treatment of the claims of the debtor's creditors. A confirmed plan is binding on all creditors, even those who did not vote in favor of the plan. Where the debtor's assets are liquidated in a Chapter 11 case, this document may be called a plan of liquidation.

Preference. Payments made by a debtor to creditors within 90 days prior to the filing of the petition on account of pre-existing debts may, under some circumstances, be avoided by the debtor-in-possession or trustee. The 90-day preference period is extended to one year if the creditor is an insider of the debtor. The committee may be instrumental in pursuing preference claims, particularly preference claims against insiders of the debtor.

Chapter 23

SERVING ON A CREDITORS'
COMMITTEE: WHAT TO KNOW

This author, having served as chairman of a Creditors' Committee in a case where the debtor had over $2 billion in debt, will tell you that it is an unfortunate time-consuming experience of a lifetime. However, it certainly can be a $1 million dollar education and an experience you will not soon forget.

WHY SERVE ON THE COMMITTEE?

The existence and proper functioning of a committee is a key determinant to how unsecured creditors will be treated in a Chapter 11 case. Service on a committee can give a creditor a direct role in the outcome of the case through the committee's monitoring of the debtor's business, participation in plan negotiations and other committee activities. A committee member will obtain knowledge and have influence on the plan negotiation and reorganization process. Committee members also may gain valuable insight into the debtor's industry that could be helpful in their future business dealings. Further, some people gain a sense of personal satisfaction from participating in the Chapter 11 process.

Not everyone should serve on a committee. Don't serve unless you are prepared to make the commitment of time and energy to do the job. Don't serve unless you will act fairly for the benefit of all unsecured creditors. Remember, a bad committee is probably worse than no committee at all. A dysfunctional committee can give the court and the creditors the false impression that creditor interests are represented when, in fact, they are not. But effective participation on a committee can make a positive difference in the case.

COMMITTEE POWERS AND DUTIES

The committee is the watchdog for the unsecured creditors' interests, protecting the rights of all unsecured creditors. It acts as a check-and-balance system against the exercise of unrestrained discretion of the debtor. It can form alliances with the debtor to realize value from the secured creditors. It can form alliances with secured creditors to maximize recoveries from the debtor. It can act independently. Under some circumstances, it can control the flow of a case. On the other hand, if its powers are not utilized effectively, it could be of no value to the unsecured creditors it is supposed to represent. Ultimately, the committee must determine whether creditors will receive more through a plan of reorganization or through liquidation.

What Should the Committee Do?

One of the most important powers of the committee is to investigate the debtor's affairs. A committee cannot decide whether reorganization, liquidation or any other action, such as sale of a debtor's business, is in order without sufficient reliable information about the debtor. The committee should evaluate the ability of the debtor's management and recommend whether any changes need to be made. The committee should gain full understanding of the debtor's assets and liabilities, cash flow and profitability. It should gain an understanding of the debtor's operations.

It should ascertain whether the debtor has any claims against third parties and whether they should be pursued. The committee, subject to first obtaining court approval, has the right to sue third parties if the debtor fails to do so. A debtor might not pursue preferences or claims against insiders, yet the committee has the power and might chose to do so. It should review and gain a thorough understanding of the debtor's schedules, statement of affairs, monthly operating reports and other court filings.

The committee has the ongoing right and duty to consult with the debtor concerning the administration of the case. If necessary, the committee can seek court appointment of a Chapter 11 Trustee to run the debtor's business or a portion thereof, or an examiner to examine an important issue in the case and provide a report to the court. The committee can be heard in court on any matter.

Fiduciary Obligations

In performing its duties, the committee and its members have fiduciary obligations to all general unsecured creditors. They must at all times act in good faith, honestly and reasonably. The committee members must set aside their individual interests in connection with committee matters. They must act and make decisions based on what is best for all general unsecured creditors. The committee, therefore, must try to maximize the return for all general unsecured creditors as a whole.

COMMITTEE ORGANIZATION AND OPERATION

A committee operates most effectively when it is well organized and its members abide by clearly defined rules. The minimum requirement for any committee is to select an effective chair and establish procedures by which the committee can most effectively accomplish its goals.

The first task normally performed by any committee is to select a chair. The chair should have both leadership and communications skills. Leadership skills are necessary to harmonize the divergent elements of the committee members, each of whom could have conflicting viewpoints. Communication skills are necessary to ensure that all members, as well as other interested parties, clearly understand the committee's positions and objectives.

The chair will be the focal point of communication between the committee members and the other interests in the case. In many cases, the chair is often given decision-making authority on certain issues, especially if quick action is required. For these reasons, the chair must be willing to devote the time necessary to the tasks and ought to be accessible to the committee's members and its counsel.

Defining and Achieving Objectives

From the outset, the goal of a committee in any Chapter 11 case is to maximize the value received by the unsecured creditors. To do this, the committee must formulate and stick to a game plan, while always recognizing the need to be flexible as conditions change. Having developed its game plan, the committee must engage in timely and purposeful activity to achieve its goals such as weekly teleconference calls and in-person meetings with the debtor, when appropriate.

Initially, the committee should focus on the nature of the debtor's business. What caused the financial problem? Was it caused by human error, changes in the economy, obsolescence in the debtor's product or service, liability claims, or some other reason? Is the debtor's management worthy of trust? Can the problems be solved so that the debtor can be profitable as a going concern in the future? Can the debtor be successfully reorganized? Should the debtor be liquidated?

While making these critical strategic evaluations, the committee must be sure that the assets of the debtor are preserved. Are the debtor's operations at least breaking even in the short term? Are there immediate problems to be solved? Can they be solved? Are the debtor's key personnel still employed with the company? Is there adequate working capital and access to credit?

The committee does have the power to engage professionals as it sees the need to do so in performing its duties and to obtain answers to the questions raised above. The cost of these professionals will be paid by the debtor's estate as an administrative expense, with court's approval. In virtually all cases, the committee will select an attorney or law firm and possibly hire an accountant or financial advisor. In appropriate cases, the committee may also hire business consultants, appraisers, brokers, engineers, investment bankers, and others.

CONCLUSION

Chapter 11 is a complex process. It is a crisis for both debtors and creditors alike. Indeed, failure to successfully reorganize in a Chapter 11 case can be as devastating to creditors as it is to the debtor. The committee should get organized as soon as possible, establish its leadership and lines of communication within the committee and with other parties, get the facts, and establish a plan of action and execute that plan with competent, dedicated professional assistance. Committees that do so will be rewarded with results for their membership and for all unsecured creditors.

Chapter 24

COLLATERAL DOCUMENT GUIDELINES

WHEN IS COLLATERAL NECESSARY
OR WHEN SHOULD IT BE CONSIDERED?

When the weighted risk classification yielded by your scoring model indicates a shortfall in required credit exposure or the probability of default exceeds your risk appetite, you may consider extending credit after obtaining a pledge of collateral (something with a value equal to part or all of the credit exposure being granted or considered) from the counterparty. This is referred to as secured credit. Commonly used forms of security are cash collateral/prepayments, pledged assets, parent (corporate) guarantees, personal guarantees, surety bonds, master netting agreements, and letters of credit—all of which are described in this collateral guidance discussion. The reasons for requiring security may be high leverage, weak cash flow, questionable payment history, or just any circumstance where repayment of an unsecured obligation becomes doubtful.

RISK MITIGATION INSTRUMENTS

Cash Collateral/Prepayments

In certain cases, you may decide to require liquid assets be pledged as security for the credit required by a counterparty. These assets generally have readily identifiable value either through their intrinsic value (i.e., cash) or readily identifiable market value (common stock of a blue chip company traded on the New York Stock Exchange). Because these instruments are easily converted to cash and portable, it is essential that a company hold any asset of this type pledged to it as collateral for an obligation. The assets should be recorded in the appropriate ledger and placed in a fireproof safe for safekeeping. These assets do not need to be signed over to the company, merely held by it. This prevents the counterparty from selling the pledged asset without the company's approval as well as precluding its employees from doing the same.

Determining acceptable terms and conditions when requiring cash collateral and/or prepayments would require working with the company's legal department or legal counsel.

Pledged Assets (Security Interests)

In certain cases, you may decide to accept hard, generally illiquid, assets as collateral for an obligation. The list of potential acceptable hard assets is virtually limitless. The key concept behind acceptable collateral is that the value equal or exceed the amount of credit being extended. To determine this value, an appraisal is typically obtained from a third party source. The appraisal may also contain an estimate of the costs of sale so that the 'true' value of collateral can be compared to the credit requested. Because of the variability in equipment types, appraisers, and the documents required to secure the assets, working closely with legal counsel is important to insure that the assets have the value they are supposed to and a lien is properly filed against the collateral on behalf of the company. The secured interest is typically perfected by filing a UCC-1 Financing Statement with the appropriate offices within a particular state.

Parent (Corporate) Guarantees

When extending credit to a financially weak company, a corporate guarantee from a financially stronger entity (related or not) may offer you sufficient protection to provide open terms to an account. Be sure to obtain the signature of an officer of the company that has the capacity to commit the company to such a guarantee. Determining acceptable terms and conditions for a parent (corporate) guarantee would require working with the company legal department or counsel.

Personal Guarantees

A guarantee (in general) is an undertaking on the part of one person (the guarantor) that is collateral to the obligation of another person (the debtor or obligor), and which binds the guarantor to performance of the obligation in the event of default by the debtor or obligor. Often, regardless of the legal issues involved, a guarantor will make every effort possible to satisfy those obligations, which are personally guaranteed. By providing this additional "incentive," the guarantee increases the odds that the credit grantor will be paid.

The guarantee of an individual is only as valuable as the liquid assets they possess and the number of times they have offered a personal guarantee to other creditors (suppliers and banks, etc.). As the number of guarantees provided from the same guarantor increases (i.e., the same guarantor backs promises to pay to multiple creditors at the same time), the value of the guarantee, therefore, diminishes.

Before relying on a personal guarantee, the individual's personal financial statement must be reviewed to determine their Liquid Accessible Net Worth (LANW). To determine the LANW, real estate, antiques stock in the counterparty being evaluated for credit, and any other asset that is not readily liquid should be subtracted from the individual's net worth. Keep in mind that your company does not want to be in the business of liquidating assets at distressed prices.

To fully support a personal financial statement an analyst should confirm an individual's liquid assets by requesting copies of savings, IRA and 401K accounts, and any other verifiable financial asset. Additionally, at least two years of the guarantor's Federal Income Tax Returns must also be submitted with the personal financial statement. If extensions have been applied for and granted, copies of such must be provided. Once taxes are filed, those returns must be provided to your company.

One of the most important purposes of the personal guarantee is that it shows the individual's personal commitment to the business and hopefully provides additional cause for the guarantor to fulfill their business obligations. In the event that your company must file suit to enforce the personal guarantee it must prove to the courts that it relied on the personal guarantee to extend credit to the corporate entity. To prove your company's continuing reliance, you must obtain annual personal financial statements. Also, if the corporation files bankruptcy, the personal guarantor may also file bankruptcy soon thereafter so if you are going to take legal action you must do so quickly. To obtain updated financial statements, reminders should be entered into the relevant ERP system used with a flag for follow-up on a certain date in the future.

A uniform personal financial statement must be provided for proper analysis. If personal financial statements are provided on a form other than yours, each principal must still complete the contingent liabilities section on the personal financial statement as well as read, complete, and sign the form. In addition to the guarantor information contractually required by the guarantee, a list of all other guarantees given by the guarantors, together with the controlling documents for such guarantees, should be provided to you.

Spousal guarantees are required as a condition of any consensual deal *unless* each principal can demonstrate, through a written legal opinion, that the assets supporting the guarantee are not community property, and that the spouses have not filed joint tax returns for any of the last three tax years.

Determining acceptable terms and conditions for a personal guarantee requires working with the company's legal department or counsel.

Surety Bonds

A surety bond is typically a tri-party agreement among the seller, counterparty, and the surety company (insurance company). Under specifically negotiated conditions, the surety bond company will fulfill the debtor's obligations to the seller. Upon payment by the surety company, the debtor becomes obligated to the surety company pursuant to an indemnification agreement. When issued on an unsecured basis, the surety bond will not impact the debtor's existing lines of credit (like a letter of credit) and hence, may free-up working capital. Determining acceptable terms and conditions for a surety bond requires working with legal counsel.

Netting Exposures to Reduce Risk

Netting refers to the ability to offset a payable and receivable so that only the net difference is paid by the party owing the larger amount. Netting can take numerous forms, including (1) Netting Transaction Settlements, and (2) Netting Default Claims.

When cash settlements are both due to and due from the same counterparty on the same day, netting should be employed. Instead of exchanging wire transfers of cash, the amounts are netted and payment is only made by the party owing the larger sum and only for the net difference between the payable and receivable. This eliminates settlement risk.

Settlement risk is incurred when two parties mutually owe each other a cash payment on the same date. Both parties incur the risk that, after delivering cash on the payable it owes, the other party defaults on its payment. Because the non-defaulting party has made its payment, its default loss becomes their entire receivable amount, rather than just the differential between payable and receivable.

Transaction netting is widely used in energy transactions. However not all bilateral settlement amounts can be netted. Transaction netting requires both settlements be due on the same date. However, conventions in the various energy markets are not the same. Conventional settlement dates for monthly power differ from dates for monthly gas that differ from settlements for swap transactions.

A more significant aspect to netting would be its application to default situations. Instead of net settling routine payables and receivables, here the netting is of the mutual claims that are accelerated following an event of default. Upon default, the non-defaulting party will make a claim on its receivable due from the defaulting party (loans, accounts receivable, etc.). Moreover, regardless of the originally contracted due dates on such receivables, upon default, the claims are accelerated and become current claims.

Master Netting Agreements

A master agreement is a document that contains all the legal and documentary terms for a transaction, except initially there are no actual transaction-specific terms. It is sometimes described as an "umbrella" contract...a shell within which subsequent transactions are contained and become governed by the terms spelled out in the umbrella master. Unlimited transactions can be included with the master.

The principle advantage of this documentary structure is that all the transactions contained within the master contract are considered components of that single contract. Each transaction is no longer considered a separate contract.

This master contract is subject to review in a bankruptcy court. But as a single contract, the court can either accept or reject it in its entirety. It cannot cherry pick among the transactions within the master.

In all previous examples and discussion, the netting was bilateral: amounts netted were from commitments between two distinct corporate entities. But the benefits of netting increase exponentially the larger the number of entities in the pool.

Most energy traders buy and sell several different energy commodities, such as electricity, natural gas, and coal. These energy companies trade commodities both in a physical sense, where actual delivery of a product will eventually take place, and in a financial sense, where only money will change hands based on future market value. They often trade these commodities with each other—exchanging different quantities of the same commodity several times during a given month, week, or day.

As a result of this web of trading contracts, the financial exposure between two companies might be millions of dollars on any given day. When one of these companies encounters financial difficulties, causing it to default under an agreement or file for bankruptcy, the stage is set for financial disaster. Under traditional trading agreements a defaulting company might be able to avoid payment of outstanding obligations, yet still collect payments that it is owed. Making matters worse, the company required to make payment without receiving what it is owed might then be forced to default on its obligations to other companies.

Since energy-trading companies do much of their trading with each other, this "domino effect" will continue until it reaches a company with the financial ability to withstand a large loss and still pay everyone that it owes for purchased commodities.

The solution to this dilemma is not new. For years, trading companies have used two simple techniques to reduce their credit risks: collateral and netting (also called set-off).

Based on the financial strength of their trading partners, companies have required the posting of collateral prior to any trading. Generally a security interest is granted in the collateral so that it can be applied to any unpaid obligations.

Trading companies also have included the concept of netting in their trading agreements. Netting allows the parties to set-off any amounts they owe each other and only pay the "net" owed from one party to the other. For example, if Trader A sells $1,000 worth of energy to Trader B and also has a contract to buy $1,500 worth of energy from Trader B, a netting agreement would allow Trader A to secure the difference, $500, if Trader B defaults on its obligations. Importantly, netting allows Trader A to claim a lower amount ($500 vs. $1,500) as its liability, and the reduced risk exposure lowers the amount of collateral the firm needs to operate its business.

However, these basic collateral and netting provisions were not drafted to handle a market meltdown like the one that recently took place (Enron). These provisions were included in separate trading agreements for each commodity, and these agreements were often between different affiliates or subsidiaries of the same parent company. Therefore, when one of these affiliates or subsidiaries defaulted under an agreement, their trading party was not able to apply collateral or set-off amounts that it owed under a different agreement or with a different affiliate or subsidiary.

In an attempt to prevent similar market failures in the future, energy trading attorneys joined together, under the sponsorship of the Edison Electric Institute, to develop a Master Netting, Setoff, Security, and Collateral Agreement. This agreement was drafted with a global view of the energy trading business, recognizing that most of the players were trading multiple commodities between multiple affiliates and subsidiaries.

The final draft of the master netting agreement was released in October 2002. It addresses five important concepts:

1. First, the master netting agreement links all underlying commodity-trading agreements between two companies into a single, integrated agreement. This integration is important because it prevents a bankrupt trading party from choosing and excluding commodity transactions based on whether or not the transactions are favorable to the bankrupt party.

2. Second, the agreement allows the parties to adopt a uniform definition of events that will constitute default under all trading agreements between the parties. Under these provisions, the occurrence of an event of default will allow the non-defaulting party to terminate and liquidate all transactions under all agreements. This is important because it prevents the situation whereby a default under one trading agreement does not necessarily trigger a default under other agreements—leaving the non-defaulting party potentially exposed to a financially struggling counterparty.

3. The agreement also allows the parties to adopt a uniform method by which transactions under all trading agreements will be terminated and liquidated in the event of a default. These provisions bring consistency to this liquidation process, which might otherwise be chaotic as the non-defaulting party tries to apply different calculation provisions for different commodities. This consistency is also important because it prevents uncertainties in the liquidation process from delaying the final closeout of obligations between the parties.

4. Fourth, the agreement encourages the parties to net monthly payments that they owe each other under all of the underlying trading agreements. Such "cross-product" and "cross-affiliate" netting reduces the cash demands on both parties and also greatly reduces their overall credit exposure.

5. Finally, the agreement establishes a single collateral-posting requirement between the parties to cover the total exposure under all of the underlying trading agreements. This provision reduces the total amount of collateral that each party is required to provide and in turn makes more of their "credit" available for trading activities with other companies.

Despite the positive steps taken in the master netting agreement, some uncertainty still remains about how effective this agreement will be in practice. Enron is currently challenging the enforceability of similar agreements based on provisions in the Bankruptcy Code. As that litigation continues, other companies are supporting proposed legislation that would clarify the issues.

Regardless of the outcome of the litigation and legislative proposals, master-netting agreements will play a major role in helping the energy trading industry get back on its feet and regain investor confidence. Companies are no longer willing to accept the risks associated with the old way of doing business. The players recognize that managing credit exposure is now clearly the key to winning the game.

ISDA Credit Support Annex

With the relatively recent explosion of hedging activities in the energy industry, many organizations have begun using privately negotiated over-the-counter (OTC) transactions as part of their overall risk management hedging portfolios. Also known simply as OTC derivatives, these products that derive their value from an underlying asset or index can be extremely useful as risk transfer tools when used in an overall risk management climate designed to implement policies set by an organization's Board of Directors.

It is critical that credit personnel in these organizations be knowledgeable about the ISDA Credit Support Annex, one of a series of tools provided by the International Swaps and Derivatives Association to facilitate OTC transactions and related collateral transfers between trading counterparties.

Letters of Credit

A company may choose to enter into certain transactions that require the use of a Documentary Letter of Credit. Examples of such transactions include the following:

- Transactions involving new counterparties with insufficient financial information to support open credit terms.
- Transactions with highly leveraged or otherwise financially burdened entities.
- Transactions to support a trade investment loan exposure.
- Transactions resulting in debt due from any foreign entity.

A letter of credit essentially puts a bank's guarantee behind a counterparty subject to certain terms and conditions. Please refer to the letter of credit details below for requirements and other important information.

Letters of Credit (Detail)

Clarification of the three primary parties involved:

Issuing Bank. The bank that writes, opens, or establishes a letter of credit is referred to as the issuing bank.

Account Party. The issuing bank's counterparty is called the account party or applicant. By opening a letter of credit, the issuing bank substitutes its credit for that of its counterparty, the account party. In a typical commercial letter of credit transaction, the account party is a buyer/importer of goods/services.

Beneficiary. The addressee of a letter of credit is referred to as the beneficiary. The beneficiary receives the benefit of the issuing bank's financial commitment, provided it (the beneficiary) complies fully with the terms and conditions as stipulated in the letter of credit.

Other parties involved in a letter of credit transaction:

Advising Bank. Typically, issuing banks send their letters of credit to beneficiaries via an advising bank. The advising bank is a correspondent bank with which the issuing bank already has a working relationship. The advising bank verifies that the letter of credit was, in fact, issued by the named issuing bank and then forwards the document(s) to the beneficiary without further responsibility. It is important to note that the advising bank has no financial obligation to honor (pay) the letter of credit. In this sense, the advising bank differs greatly from the confirming bank (*see below*).

Negotiating Bank. A letter of credit can allow the beneficiary the option to engage its local bank to negotiate the beneficiary's draft (demand for payment) under the issuing bank's letter of credit. If the local bank agrees to negotiate (give value to the beneficiary) that bank becomes known as the negotiating bank.

Confirming Bank. A bank, which adds its financial backing to that of the issuing bank to honor a beneficiary's demand for payment is called a confirming bank. Essentially, the confirming bank ensures payment to the beneficiary if the issuing bank is unable satisfy its obligation to pay.

The LC document serves several purposes. First, it is a purchase order, outlining the product, price, and shipping requirements. It is also a financial security document, which guarantees payment upon proper performance. The following is a general summary of objectives/benefits associated with the use on an LC:

1. Reduce risk (provide assurance)
2. Method of payment for goods delivered
3. Promote international trade
4. Backup financial or contractual performance

Types of Letters of Credit
Documentary. A letter of credit, which requires the presentation of specified documents on the part of the beneficiary in order to receive payment.

Sight vs. Time. Under a sight letter of credit, the bank's obligation to pay the beneficiary extends until the expiration date of the sight LC, but not beyond. Sight payments can be made to the beneficiary upon performance at any time during the life of the letter of credit, from its issuance to its expiration. Sight LCs facilitate prompt payment for prompt performance. In contrast, a time letter of credit allows the issuing bank to defer payment beyond the expiration date. However, the beneficiary must still perform prior to expiration of the LC, but instead of immediate payment, the issuing bank can promise deferred payment at some fixed time in the future. The time-span is usually determined by estimating how long it would take the buyer to resell the underlying goods.

Standby. A special purpose letter of credit, which is used to back up the financial or contractual performance of the bank's counterparty. Standby LCs are frequently used in place of guarantees. The use of a standby LC allows a new distributor or business to achieve prompt payment, while also providing complete security. A standby LC can also be used in combination with open account terms to gain incremental volume while balancing a company's risk.

Forms of Letters of Credit

Letters of credit may be issued in either revocable or irrevocable form.

Revocable. A revocable letter of credit may be canceled or amended unilaterally at the applicant's discretion, without the knowledge or consent of the beneficiary.

Irrevocable. An irrevocable letter of credit cannot be canceled or amended without the unanimous agreement of the three primary parties—the account party, the beneficiary and the issuing bank.

Procedure

It is imperative that the following guidelines be followed to ensure adequate security when utilizing letter of credits:

1. All LCs must be *irrevocable*.
2. All LCs must be issued or confirmed by a major correspondent bank or large money center bank located in the United States.
3. Conditions included in the letter of credit document should be limited to a copy the commercial invoice, the draft and a statement indicating that invoice(s) are past due.
4. Funds should be available at *sight* upon presentation of documents.
5. All banking charges and fees should be charged to the buyer's account.

6. Where applicable, the LC security should be in the form of a transference of the beneficiary and not via the assignment of proceeds.

Once the above guidelines are satisfied and an LC is issued, the credit department supervisor must review the document to ensure the following:

1. The product and shipping requirements of the document must be able to be satisfied within the timeframe outlined in the LC, including:
   a. All product items ordered are available and can be shipped as required.
   b. All supporting documents will be available before the expiry date.

Upon notification of approval from the credit department manager and after sufficient credit review due diligence, the credit analyst will release the order to which the LC pertains.

Any changes to the requirements, expiration date or other stipulations require a formal amendment to the letter of credit.

1. Once an irrevocable letter of credit has been established and the beneficiary notified accordingly, any amendment must be fully agreed to by all parties concerned.
   a. An amendment may not be partially accepted or rejected. Partial acceptance constitutes a rejection of the whole document.

The credit department manager and the appropriate credit supervisor must be notified of any transactions requiring a LC. The credit department should retain legal advice if any procedures, terms, or conditions seem unclear.

Document control:

1. Original document must be maintained in a fireproof safe, with a copy kept in the credit file.
2. Expiration of LCs are tracked by setting the expiration date of the account's credit limit 60 days prior to the expiration of letter of credit. This will allow adequate time to either request a renewal from the counterparty or establish an open line of credit.

TRADE CREDIT INSURANCE

Generally, purchased by the seller to minimize risk of nonpayment for goods and/or services supplied on open credit terms (trade accounts receivable). Typically, trade credit insurance is underwritten and priced based upon level of risk. Trade credit insurance minimizes balance sheet fluctuations by substituting a contingent liability with a known premium cost.

SECURITIZATION OF TRADE RECEIVABLES

Securitization can represent a structured or agreed process whereby interests in loans and other receivables are, packaged, underwritten, and sold in the form of Asset Backed Securities (ABS). ABS are the securities, which are issued through a 'Special-Purpose Vehicle' or SPV. (The SPV is usually a trust with an asset/liability structure and legal status that makes its obligations secure even if the parent company goes bankrupt.)[18]

On a broader view, securitization is a process by which any SPV raises funds by the issue of Term Finance Certificates (TFCs)—or any other instrument for such purpose—and uses such funds by making payment to the originator, or through such process, acquires a property or right in the receivables or other assets in the form of actionable claims.

Residential mortgages, home equity loans, manufactured housing loans, automobile loans and leases; credit card receivables; equipment loans and leases; small business loans; student loans; and trade receivables are the examples of securitization.

The foremost benefits of securitization are:

- Trade receivables are moved "off-balance sheet" and interchanged by cash equivalents (less expenses of the securitization), thus improving the originator's balance sheet and resulting in gain (or loss), which it is usually an intended, valuable corollary.
- The securities issued in the securitization are more highly rated by participating rating agencies (due to the isolation of the receivables in a "bankruptcy-remote" entity), thus reducing the cost of funds to the originator when compared to conventional forms of financing. In cases where the receivables bear interest, there is usually a significant spread between the interest paid on the securities and the interest earned on the receivables. Ultimately, the originator receives the benefit of the spread.

---

[18]Robert J. Baldoni, "A Best Practices Approach to Risk Management," *TMA Journal* (1998).

- Another benefit for the originator is—as it usually acts as a 'servicer' and there is normally no need to give any notice to the obligators under the receivables—the transaction is transparent to the Originator's counterparties and other persons with whom it carries out business.

CREDIT DEFAULT SWAP TRANSACTIONS

The most common credit derivative is a **credit default swap**, which are contracts that transfer counterparty credit risk and allow investors to manage credit exposures by separating their credit views from other market variables. I will provide a more in-depth assessment of credit default swaps follow in the chapter entitled Credit Derivatives. A simple credit default swap involves a "buyer" seeking credit protection and is willing to pay a credit spread to do so. The "seller" is the party that sells credit protection and receives a credit spread from the protection buyer. Clearly, this sort of transaction is used for the purchase and sale of protection. Before entering into a transaction, both parties in the credit default swap usually have "a signed ISDA" in place. This is an agreement that sets forth the rights and duties of the two parties under all swap contracts. (ISDA provides a standard template to document a default swap contract). Also, before a credit default swap is executed, credit lines between the counterparties must be in place because each party is taking on credit exposure to the other.

In the event of the occurrence of a "credit event" (circumstance that must occur for the protection buyer (or seller) to require the buyer to exercise its right to exchange a deliverable obligation for the payment of par), the seller will be required to pay par to the buyer in exchange for the deliverable obligation. If such a credit event on the underlying reference entity should occur, the credit default swap is designed to "unwind" in an orderly manner. Determining acceptable terms and conditions of a credit default swap transaction would require working with legal counsel.

Chapter 25

CREDIT DERIVATIVES

The use of credit derivatives is something everyone talks about but no one is really using it. The credit derivatives market or growth potential has been one of the most spoken about topics. However, the credit derivatives years really started in 2000-2003. Major investment banks strengthened their credit derivatives capabilities, most of the time by creating a dedicated product line to support this growing activity. Market growth has also been fueled by the fact that documentation was largely standardized and adopted by the market participants.

However, there are still many credit professionals who are not very familiar with the products and who are reluctant to use them. Credit derivatives are a very efficient way to protect a company from the default of its customers, and presents many advantages over insurance products.

WHAT ARE CREDIT DERIVATIVES?

The most common credit derivatives, called credit default swaps, are financial instruments that can be used to transfer the credit risk of a company (called "the reference entity") from one party to another. The buyer of protection pays a premium or spread to the protection seller in return for protection against predefined credit events experienced by the reference entity. Protection buyers are compensated if and when credit events occur, whether or not they actually incurred a loss. This fundamentally differentiates credit derivatives from insurance policies, which require that the insured suffer a loss before compensation is paid.

The tenor of a credit derivative contract is agreed to in advance between the two parties, and the buyer is compensated if and when a credit event occurs during the tenor of the contract. Protection buyers sometimes request early cancellation of the contracts if, for instance, it is no longer exposed because it stopped selling its goods or services to its clients. The protection seller may agree to terminate the contract, but is not required to do so.

Contrary to credit insurance, which protects only trade receivables, credit derivatives can protect all sources of credit risk exposures such as long-term supply contracts or derivatives exposures. For instance, energy companies are using credit derivatives to protect the potential replacement cost on fixed-price forward contracts. In the event of a supplier or client default, an energy company may have to re-contract its existing "power" contract(s) at a different price.

Different Forms of Credit Derivatives

There are various forms of credit derivatives primarily differentiated by: (1) what credit event(s) trigger the settlement of the contract (i.e., when a protection buyer is paid); and (2) the way the contract is settled upon occurrence of credit events (i.e., how much money a protection buyer receives).

Credit Events

Contrary to an insurance policy, the settlement of a credit derivative is not triggered by an actual loss incurred by the protection buyer but by the occurrence of credit events previously agreed upon. There are typically three main credit events covered: bankruptcy, failure to pay borrowed money obligations, and a restructuring of borrowed money obligations. In theory, the inclusion of a credit event in a credit derivative contract is the result of negotiations between the protection buyer and the protection seller. However, market customs have developed, and most financial institutions have underwriting policies or strategies, which limit the credit events they want to include. Similarly, the precise wording of the credit events is largely standardized. The inclusion or not of certain credit events may affect the price asked by the protection seller. The greater the number of credit events, the more expensive the credit derivative. Also, protection on certain companies might be available only with a limited number of events. The smaller the number of events, the greater the number of companies on which protection may be offered.

What it means for a corporation is that it must carefully analyze the nature and type of its exposures and understand which credit event may coincide with a potential loss. Generally speaking, the restructuring of the debt of a company (e.g., an extension of maturity on a loan) does not affect the ability of a company to pay its suppliers or to honor its long-term supply/purchase contract(s). Most corporations are actually primarily exposed to the bankruptcy of their clients or counterparties. Therefore, bankruptcy is in many cases sufficient to cover corporate exposures.

Settlement

The other important aspect of a credit derivative contract is the way it is settled upon the occurrence of a credit event. Protection sellers are offering three main methods as follows:

1. *Physical settlement* requires the protection buyer to deliver to the protection seller an asset, such as a bond or a loan, meeting criteria specified in the contract, typically any senior unsecured bond or loan. In exchange, the protection buyer will receive the notional amount of the contract. The net amount received by the buyer is therefore the difference between the notional amount of the contract and the value at which it purchased the asset. Physical settlement is a market standard for inter-bank trades but quite inconvenient for many corporates. Corporates often do not own any bonds or loans, and buying one, only for the purpose of delivering it to its protection seller, can be inconvenient.

2. Another method is *cash settlement* whereby the protection buyer receives a payment reflecting the difference between the notional amount of the contract and the market value of a specific asset (typically a bond) called "the reference obligation." Upon occurrence of a credit event, the protection seller usually asks several traders the value of the reference obligation and will then pay the buyer(s) accordingly. The net payment is the same as the physically settled credit derivative contract, but it is more convenient as there is no exchange of assets. Unfortunately, for corporates, many financial institutions do not offer cash-settled credit derivatives.

3. Finally, the most convenient method for corporate needs is a *digital settlement*, whereby both parties agree in advance to the amount to be paid upon occurrence of a credit event. For instance, if a company buys a $10 million digital credit default swap on Wal-Mart Stores Inc., the protection seller will be required to pay $10 million upon occurrence of a covered credit event. With a digital settlement, there are no obligations to be delivered to the seller. A digital credit default swap, with bankruptcy being the sole credit event, can provide credit protection on a company (the reference entity) that many not have a credit rating (i.e., from Moody's or Standard & Poor's) and /or have any bonds or loans outstanding. The digital credit default swap allows credit protection to be sold on a larger universe of companies.

Whatever the mechanism (physical, cash, or digital), settlement is quick and requires only minimal documentation. Since credit derivatives are not insurance products, the protection buyer will not have to prove that it was actually exposed to the company which defaulted or that it lost any money because of the default. In most cases, credit events are public events, which are reported in the press, and press articles are sufficient to notify the protection seller that a credit event has occurred and that the credit derivative contact(s) must be settled. Except in the case of a physical settlement, whereby the protection buyer has to deliver a bond or a loan, the protection buyer will not have to deliver anything except a notice to receive its payment, which normally occurs 10 days after the notification of the credit event. In addition to the settlement of the credit derivative, the buyer can recoup whatever may be collected and keep the benefit of the recovery in respect to the subject reference entity.

Single-Name and Basket

Contrary to all turnover credit insurance policies, buyers of credit derivatives are free to choose the reference entities they may want to cover. Credit default swaps can be purchased on single names whereby only one entity is protected. For instance, a company can buy $10 million protection on Wal-Mart Stores Inc. for 18 months.

Credit derivatives can also be used to protect a basket of multiple credit risk exposures. Basket or portfolio transactions are credit default swaps that are based on a number of reference entities documented in one contract rather than a number of single-name credit default swap contracts. Often, portfolio transactions are structured so that the company retains a certain amount of money and transfers to the protection seller all credit events above an agreed attachment amount. This is similar to the deductible applied to an insurance policy. The main benefit of structuring a portfolio with a "retained layer" is essentially in terms of cost. A portfolio transaction can be significantly cheaper than the sum of transactions on individual reference entities contained within that portfolio. The price level is primarily dependent on two factors: (1) the diversification of the portfolio, in terms of both the number of reference entities and the respective industry sectors represented; and (2) the size of the retained layer.

Portfolio transactions are a powerful way to cap the credit risk exposures on certain names and hence avoid earnings volatility. For example, a company could include in a portfolio transaction its top 20 credit exposures up to a certain amount per name and will thus be assured that its losses will not exceed the size of the retained layer. Portfolio transactions may be multi-year and the substitution of the reference entities may be agreed upon with the protection seller.

<u>Who Are the Sellers of Credit Derivatives?</u>

There are two major categories:

1. Those wishing to assume credit risk, typically insurance and reinsurance companies. Some have started selling credit derivatives online, adding liquidity and transparency into the market.
2. Those seeking to broker credit risk, such as investment banks and brokerage units of commercial banks.

Credit derivatives are marketed by more and more institutions, but corporates interested in purchasing credit derivatives must carefully select the protection seller called "counterparty." Particular attention must be paid to the reputation, the experience, the market position, and the credit quality of the counterparty. Buying protection from a highly rated, e.g. AA and above, experienced counterparty offers the most comfort that the contract will be honored if a credit event were to occur.

LIMITATIONS ON THE USE OF CREDIT DERIVATIVES

Certain aspects of credit derivatives may deter some companies from utilizing credit derivatives. The credit derivatives market is growing, but it is still considered to be in its infancy, and it may not yet offer as many opportunities to outsource credit risk as the insurance market. Following are certain features, which may not make credit derivatives attractive for corporates.

*   According to the Statement of Financial Accounting Standards No. 133 (FAS 133), all companies that report under U.S. GAAP are required to recognize all derivatives as either assets or liabilities in the statement of financial position and measure those instruments at fair value. This is known as the obligation to "mark-to-market" derivatives positions. What does it mean? Let's assume that a company purchased one-year protection on Wal-Mart Stores Inc. at a price of 23 bps p.a. (i.e., 23 basis points per annum or 0.23 percent p.a.). At the time of each reporting period,

the market price of one-year protection on Wal-Mart Stores Inc. will have to be checked. If it is below 23 bps p.a., the company will have lost value and the company will have to reduce its position accordingly by recording a loss in its profit and loss statement. If, by contrast, the market price is above 23 bps p.a., the value of the swap will be increased and a gain will appear in the profit and loss statement. Thus, certain companies are not comfortable with the idea of exposing their bottom line to the volatility of the credit derivative market.

- Prices are based on the capital markets and are therefore sometimes viewed as expensive.
- The number of companies on which credit default swaps are sold is still relatively small. The trend is, however, clearly showing an increase in the number of companies as more and more participants are entering the market.
- Buyers of credit derivatives may take what is called "basis risk"—their exposures might not be fully covered, and gaps between the actual exposure and the protection offered by the derivative may exist. This may be particularly true for the amount of money that a buyer will receive with a cash or physically settled credit default swap. Also, in theory a customer could fail to pay certain of its obligations without creating a credit event.

HOW TO MAKE THE BEST USE OF THE CREDIT DERIVATIVE MARKET

Corporates can make the best use of the credit derivative market if they are proactively monitoring and managing their credit risk portfolio. Credit professionals concerned about a specific invoice or contract with a company already facing difficulties may not be able to use a credit derivative. Capital markets react quickly to negative news and prices increase quickly and sharply. For instance, the capacity available on certain energy companies after the bankruptcy of Enron has been reduced dramatically and prices have skyrocketed, often reaching up to 10 percent p.a. Instead, companies having a proactive approach will make the best use of the market. They will buy protection on their largest exposures before their counterparty credits deteriorate. They will buy either single-name credit derivatives or protection on a portfolio. Thus, if several companies were to default, they would be covered under the credit derivative contract.

Chapter 26

HOW TO WRITE A CREDIT ANALYSIS

Vigorous writing is concise. A sentence should contain no unnecessary words. A paragraph no unnecessary sentences, for the same reason that a drawing should have no unnecessary lines and a machine no unnecessary parts. This requires not that the writer make all his sentences short, or that he avoids all detail and treats his subject only in outline, but that every word tell.

– William Strunk, Jr., and E.B. White
THE ELEMENTS OF STYLE

THE ELEMENTS OF STYLE

In speaking, there is more being communicated than just the words. There is gesture, tone of voice, body language, and so on. Writers cannot see their audience, cannot respond to questioners who interrupt, and have to rely entirely on the printed page to convey their messages.

This chapter will discuss some principles of good writing, especially as they apply to an analysis. Also provided will be a standard outline to be followed when writing analyses.

SIX RULES FOR GOOD ANALYSIS

In business writing, it is customary to use words and phrases, which are not flowery but factual. That does not mean that business writing has to be dull and unimaginative.

Rule 1: Be an Analyst, Don't Just Quote Ratios and Numbers

This is the most important rule in writing credit analyses. What the reader wants to know about a company is not just a reiteration of calculated ratios but also how you perceive the company's strengths and weaknesses and how these affect the risk of repayment. Analysts should think about the facts, be selective of those facts, and then commit their factual interpretation to paper. The temptation is to present figures in quantity and leave the reader to judge which ones are relevant. This is a wrong approach. Make the figures speak for themselves, and be especially careful how they are presented.

Rule 2: Be Selective with the Numbers You Present

Just how detailed should the numbers be in an analysis? This is easily answered: keep to three figures! It is surprising how well this rule works. While we are on the subject of presenting numerical information, let's not forget the aspect of comparative analysis. You should ask, are the numbers above or below what you would expect compared to the company's past performance and current industry conditions? Are they above or below an average for the industry? If sales grow at 25 percent, is that good or bad, taking account of inflation and sustainable growth? Don't hesitate to use graphs where these will help convey the point dramatically. Graphs are especially useful when presenting comparative data.

Rule 3: Use Plain Words When You Can

A common error in business writing is using fancy language. Avoid the use of abstract words, long technical words, and other jargon. Official announcements are often good examples of these errors. "Would passengers about to board the train kindly allow arriving passengers to exit the train before attempting to board. Your cooperation is appreciated." It would have been easier to say, "Let them off first, please."

H. W. Fowler in an early twentieth century textbook, *The King's English*, laid down some simple rules for choosing words for good effect:

- Prefer the short word to the long
- Prefer the Saxon to the Romance (i.e., Latin or Greek)
- Prefer the familiar word to the farfetched
- Prefer the single word to the circumlocution
- Prefer the concrete word to the abstract

Fowler was laying the foundation for what later becomes described as "The Fog Factor" which leads us into the next rule.

Rule 4: Omit Needless Words

An inexperienced analyst is convinced that they must write long and serious-sounding analyses. It is the quality of the thinking which matters, not the quantity of words, which are written. A good analyst must be selective, but it is much harder to write a short analysis than a long one, since being selective requires judgment. Wordiness has been measured by something called "The Fog Factor." "To find your own Fog Factor, take a sample of your business writing. First, find the average number of words per sentence. Now count the number of words with three syllables or more (not including verbs ending in -ing or -ed). Add these two numbers and multiply by 0.4. The product is your Fog Factor. Readable prose has a Fog Factor of less than 12."

Rule 5: Present the Summary and Conclusion First

Don't forget, the reader wants to know what your decision is: do you recommend the proposal or don't you? If you leave that question to the end of the analysis, you may have a more logical order, but your reader will skip to the end anyway before reading the main text. It makes sense, therefore, to state your summary and conclusion at the start of the analysis. Of course, that does not mean that you actually write this part first! You should have an open mind as you work, making your conclusion only after careful thought. Work through your investigative process by first reading the owner or president's message about the past year and targets set for the coming year. Then turn your attention to the footnotes and accounting policies employed. Next, focus your attention on the Cash Flow Statement to see how successful the operation was and where the money went. You have not yet crunched one number but should have begun to form a picture and questions about where this company is headed. Now you are ready to crunch numbers, which will perhaps validate your assumptions. Make notes and highlight information presented as you go so that you can solve the mystery novel as to which direction the company is headed. No company is stagnant. They are either trending upward or downward. Your challenge is to figure out how steep the trend is and when to ask for security.

Rule 6: Following a Plan for the Structure

As stated earlier, make notes as you examine the evidence, whether working with financial statements or examining industry dynamics. Follow a plan for the main part of the analysis. Revise and rewrite something until you are happy with it. A basic structural design underlines every kind of writing, whether it is a letter or sonnet. Skill lies in executing the design without spoiling the general pattern.

Let's now consider a basic plan for a standard form of credit analysis.

OUTLINE FOR CREDIT ANALYSIS

Section I: Risk Analysis Summary and Recommendation, Risk Ratings

Here you should state the pros and cons of extending credit and evaluate the credit risks sufficiently to justify the credit decision. Apply a risk ranking to your recommendation based on information obtained from previous chapters and classify the risk as low, moderate, or high. A risk ranking may be supported by referring to the need for a guarantee, collateral, prepayment, or letter of credit.

Section II: Sources of Information

This section should give background information on your information sources:

- Indicate the type of financial statements, which are being analyzed (consolidated, parent company alone, or whatever).
- State whether the financial statements are audited or unaudited. If financial statements are not audited but prepared by an accountant or company official, make a statement about your confidence in the accuracy of such financials.
- Any change in accountants should be noted with an explanation of the reasons for the change.
- If the accounting firm auditing the company's financial statement is not generally recognized to be a leading public accounting firm, say something about the reputation and reliability of the auditors.
- Identify the various sources mentioned earlier that you have used such as newspapers, reporting agencies, magazines, and industry studies.

Section III: Business and Industry

This section should provide a concise yet meaningful description of the company's business and the industry in which it operates, focusing on industry dynamics, competition, current movements and changes, and so on. Try to avoid purely descriptive remarks without conclusions attached.

Explain the key management skills in this industry. To what extent does the company have those skills? What are their vulnerable points? Has management been around for a while and weathered a few business cycle storms? Think about worst-case situations and what could possibly happen then to your credit extension? What is the company's strategy in relation to its industry? Have they developed a market niche? Does the strategy make sense? What is the nature of the industry? Is it expanding? Is it high risk? What are the barriers to entry?

If the company has a complex corporate structure, you should explain how your exposure fits together and where the counterparty belongs in the structure. If dealing with a subsidiary, explain the relationships and whether this subsidiary is or is not a key element in its parent's strategy or chain of operations.

Section IV: Management

Any appraisal of management should include an evaluation of past strategies as measured by such factors as historical financing and operating results, accuracy of projections, and performance within the industry. Consider also the degree to which management owns the firm's equity. Is this a strength?

Section V: Source and Application of Cash

Spend some time summarizing the changes in the sources and uses of cash for the last three years by highlighting the major items.

Refer to our discussion on cash flow analysis and free cash flow for this discussion. This area is a look into the heart and soul of a company minus any accounting window dressing.

Section VI: Interpretation and Analysis of Financial Information

The written interpretation and analysis of financial information should reflect the understanding and resourcefulness of the writer. Trends are more important than single observations. Dynamic analysis is more important than static analysis. Financial information on spreadsheets should not be repeated in this section except as a reference to an analytical statement. The following categories are offered as samples of relevant areas of analysis:

- *Operations*. The past and projected operating performance should be analyzed as to significant trends and the major factors causing these trends. Special emphasis should be placed on the quality of earnings; that is, does the company's earnings reflect true performance and a source of cash flow or merely unique accounting, extraordinary items, or GAP (games accountants play).

Where a company has several lines of business, the contribution of each to the whole should be shown. The company's performance versus other similar firms should be compared and explained.

- *Cash Flow.* Past and projected cash flows should be analyzed in connection with expectations of future financial performance and ability to meet the cash requirements of the business. The company's capital expenditure program should be considered in the light of internal cash flow as well as the availability of external financing. Perhaps you would like to review the chapter on sustainable growth analysis. The debt repayment schedule should be analyzed in view of existing and new debt and in relation to past and projected cash flow. Review discussion on Cash Conversion Cycle (CCC) and Defensive Interval to see if significant cash is being generated to take care of daily and fixed business obligations.

- *Financial Condition.* This section should analyze changes in financial condition; working capital, and debt/equity ratios, and the reasons for such changes. The liquidity of the company should be noted. Special emphasis should be placed on the quality of current and fixed assets, with appropriate explanation of how the accounting principles affect recorded values. For instance, if LIFO is being used, is there a significant "inventory cushion" and does this overstate or understate profits? As stated in an earlier chapter, CCC will help uncover possible misleading signals presented by current and quick ratio calculations. Consider corporate structure, and contingent and other off-balance-sheet liabilities related to derivatives trading activity. Refer to the chapter on derivatives analysis.

SUMMARY

The best credit analyses are not the longest, but the most thoughtfully written. They follow a clear pattern. They focus on risk rather than general description. They place a company in the context of its industry. They identify both trends in markets and trends in the financial condition of the company under review. If done really well, they form a sound basis upon which credit decisions can be made and documented to file.

Chapter 27

AUTHOR'S VIEWPOINT

Choosing to grow and add value while facing tough challenges sums up the mindset that we all need in order to continue to be successful financial analysts and decision makers.

The downsizing years claimed many industry jobs. Managing operating costs is no longer a priority but has become our culture and a competitive imperative. How we came to our present state is understood. We've restructured around a whole new set of economic realities and have sustained our emphasis on financial performance in response to the rising expectations of our stockholders and investors.

What this means for the credit function is that the persistent focus on efficiency and cost reduction must continue—and at a faster pace.

With that in mind, it has always been of interest to me why corporations always seem to use outside consultants to assess a particular situation with regards to improving processes and operating more efficiently. It seems as though businesses feel they have to have third-party understanding and pay for it before they believe. We fail to realize that the information needed is just on the surface of every organization. As a result, it doesn't necessarily require the need to hire a consulting firm. Instead, transform yourselves into internal consultants. Our future business conditions will require that we rethink our current roles so why not take the approach that you already know your business better than a third party does and determine how you can contribute as an internal consultant?

You can make several contributions as an internal consultant such as:

- Make recommendations related to strategic and operational decisions being considered.
- Develop courses of action for the stated business objectives.
- Make recommendations that improve overall efficiency on a continuing basis.

Your input could be very valuable if timely and under the right conditions. You might ask what skills are needed to become an internal consultant. Some of the essentials are:

- Being sure to begin with a broad base of experience (including managerial accounting and industry trend knowledge).
- Developing a mind-set of starting your own consulting practice, and thinking like a professional consultant.
- Generating credibility with senior management if you don't already have it.
- Working to be perceived as a professional, or no one will seek out your advice.
- Being sure you have excellent communication skills and know what and when to communicate effectively.
- Thinking of co-workers and managers as clients who could easily outsource your services. Adopt a willingness and ability to respond to client (internal customer) needs.
- Being sure to have a strong sense of "value-added" in the performance of your duties.
- Beginning with the "olive branch" approach, rather than trying to "bull" your way in. Approach the process as a team player, rather than an intruder.
- Explaining what you can provide and how your services will add value to the organization.
- Being able to demonstrate some measurable improvement in the organization as a result of what you do or recommend.

OPPORTUNITIES TO SHINE

What kinds of results and benefits can you expect by setting yourself up as an internal consultant? You'll have the opportunity to "shine" in your organization. If you can show substantial bottom-line results, you may even be able to work your way into a different job title and promotion.

You may feel that you can do more than you have in the past in the role of consultant but perhaps still feel the need for a third-party consultant. After all, don't they bring a sense of objectivity to the table that internal people lack? I would disagree with this statement and say that the concern really boils down to communication or lack of it. Traditionally, we have difficulty finding the time to talk to one another even if separated only by a single floor. Something is not set up internally if it doesn't encourage a teamwork environment. Once you have established the proper infrastructure, you can accomplish just about anything—and you can do it by yourselves.

Chapter 28

HOW TO READ FINANCIAL STATEMENTS FROM AN INVESTOR'S VIEWPOINT

The fact is, too many investors don't pay enough attention to the fundamentals of a company's business. By using some of the techniques described in previous chapters and looking for common accounting tricks, you can be your own watchdog.

Selecting common stocks for investment requires careful study of factors other than those we can learn from financial statements. The economies of the country and the particular industry must be considered. The management of the company, as well as its plans for the future, must be assessed. Some of this information must be gleaned from the press or the financial services or supplied by some research organization.

When a company files an annual report with the SEC, it must contain three documents that the accountants produce: the balance sheet, the income statement, and the cash flow statement.

THE BALANCE SHEET

As stated in a previous chapter, the balance sheet is a snapshot of the company's overall financial health. So, what clues should investors look for? An easy way to get a feel for a company's health is by checking inventories and receivables (current assets and current liabilities). If either one is growing a lot faster than sales (or revenues) on the income statement, then trouble may be brewing. If inventories are rising, the company could be having trouble selling as much product as it forecasted. If demand is weakening, have the company's products lost customer acceptance in the marketplace? Has technology changed? Has a new competitor entered the marketplace? Is a general economic softness hurting the company?

If accounts receivable are growing faster than sales, has the company induced customers, using discounts and easy cancellation terms, to buy more goods than they really need?

When inventories are written down in value, investors should ask: What was the root cause? Did the company overestimate what it could sell? Is this a sign of poor sales forecasting, order management, or production quality controls? Normally, temporary reductions in revenues and profits do not result in assets being written down in value, under GAAP. Rather, write-downs are typically caused by long-term or permanent reductions in sales value. A write-down means that the company does not expect to recover the money it invested in inventory. Find an explanation as to why this took place in the section called "management's discussion and analysis."

It's vital to understand that a write-down is not just the one-time, historical event that analysts and corporate executives would have you believe. Instead, a write-down could indicate problems with the business strategy, product development, or marketing channels. Most importantly, it could be a distress signal about the company's future stock value.

THE INCOME STATEMENT

The Income Statement, sometimes called the profit-and-loss statement or the statement of operations, is a report on the company's business activities for one quarter or one year. While the balance sheet measures a company's overall health, the income statement measures its performance. It has two main components: revenues and expenses.

There are strict rules for when revenue can be recognized under GAAP. For example, revenue cannot be counted if the seller must provide a significant amount of services in the future to the buyer. Many companies abused the revenue recognition rules during the 1990s bull market.

At the end of the income statement are the earnings per share (EPS). This figure tells investors how much money the company earned for each share of stock outstanding. Again, be careful. The truer measure of how successful a company has been is the fully diluted EPS number, rather than the basic EPS number, which is the first one you see. The fully diluted figure takes into account stock options issued to managers but not yet exercised. It also figures in bonds, preferred shares, and stock warrants that can be converted to common stock, thus causing basic EPS to drop significantly.

One useful measurement is return on assets (ROA), which also connects the balance sheet to the income statement. Find the net income number on the income statement and divide that figure by the total assets number on the balance sheet. The higher the ROA, the better management is at using your capital to increase returns. A healthy company will have an ROA of at least 5 percent. Please refer to the chapter on profitability analysis and the discussion on how to figure what a good ROA and ROE number might be for a given company.

THE STATEMENT OF CASH FLOWS

To really understand the quality of a company's earnings, you need to analyze the cash flow statement. Please refer to the chapter covering cash flow analysis. As it implies, this statement shows the actual cash that came into the company and the actual cash that flowed out. Remember that the balance sheet reveals a company's assets, liabilities, and shareholders' equity at the close of the fiscal year or the most recent quarter. The income statement reflects the changes that have occurred in the balance sheet items, including promises of money that the company has made or received. The cash flow statement differs in that it reveals the changes in actual cash that the business has generated and the actual cash raised from creditors and investors. It also shows how the company invested that cash between the start of one fiscal year to the end of another. In short, cash flow shows where the money is coming from and how the money is being spent.

You may see negative cash flow from operations. While on its face that may seem like a bad sign, it isn't always a signal to sell. Fast-growing start-ups, which consume more cash than they can generate in the first few years of the business, will especially show negative cash flow. They cover the shortfall by borrowing money or issuing stock. But sometimes a negative operating cash flow indicates that a company is in serious trouble, especially if the company is disposing of asserts, such as by selling off pieces of the company because it can't persuade investors to buy its stock or bankers to lend it money.

If you look back at the balance sheet for the amount of cash the company has (listed under current assets) that figure comes from the final cash balance on the cash-flow statement.

When sifting for clues in the cash flow statement, it's sometimes necessary to examine cash flow side by side with the income statement, and also to examine both statements over multiple reporting periods. For example, if net earnings on the income statement have rocketed, but actual cash received from operations is much lower, that could be a sign that bad debts or obsolete inventories are piling up and next period's earnings could be lower.

To see if a company is playing the numbers game, compare the rate of growth in net income with the rate of growth in operating cash. If net income is growing at 10 percent but operating cash is growing at only 1 percent, while in years past the two numbers moved at a fairly even pace, that could signal that net income isn't as strong as it might appear. Or you can divide the net income figure into the total cash from operating activities. The closer the answer is to one, the higher the quality of the earnings.

It's far more difficult to manipulate the cash-flow statement than the income statement. Still, cash flow can be artificially inflated. Adding the tax benefits of stock options is one way companies improve cash flow. When employees exercise certain kinds of stock options, the difference between the grant price and the exercise price is counted as a deduction on the tax return, reducing the company's tax bill. With stock compensation, companies are giving employees something of value, the right to participate in the appreciation of the stock without having to pay a cent. But 99 percent of companies elect not to report an expense for that item on the income statement. That doesn't matter to the IRS. Companies can still deduct the "expense" for tax purposes when employees exercise their stock options. The refund from the U.S. Treasury boosts operating cash flows without ever having the fair value of the stock options recorded on the income statement. Sounds deceptive, but it's perfectly legal. But if you want a truer picture of operating cash flow, subtract the stock option tax benefit. Please refer to other adjustments, that were recommended to make to the cash flow statement, in the chapter covering cash flow analysis.

Enron's cash flow statement is worth examining. In 2000, Enron showed that cash provided by operating activities came to $4.8 billion. But investors who looked carefully at the balance sheet and its footnote 3C would have seen that the cash flow total includes $5.5 billion in customer deposits that Enron required of its California customers to make sure they didn't skip out on their bills during the state's energy crisis. So Enron's true operating cash flow was a negative $700 million. Enron also reported one-time asset sales of $1.8 billion on its cash flow statement. Without that, Enron's cash flow would have been a negative $2.5 million. Considering that Enron was showing total sales of $101 billion, a negative $2.5 billion cash flow is a sign that something is fundamentally wrong.

DON'T IGNORE THE FOOTNOTES

After plowing through the balance sheet, income statement, and cash-flow statement, you'll still need peruse the footnotes. The footnotes are important; they give you vital additional information, and they sometimes leave an entirely different impression from the rosy portrait the company may have painted in the financial statements. Too many companies would prefer that you not read the footnotes. The footnotes tell the story behind the numbers, and they may contain valuable information about risks and uncertainties that could affect future performance.

What little Enron told the world about its off-balance sheet shenanigans, for example, appeared in the footnotes. To maintain a high credit rating, Enron pushed loads of debt off its balance sheet and into so-called special-purpose entities. Enron did not report the financial details of these SPEs by consolidating them into its own statements, but instead revealed their existence in footnotes.

Footnotes typically start out with an explanation of the company's accounting policies, such as how and when it recognizes revenue. Footnotes reveal the number of stock options granted to executives and other employees, and how those options would affect earnings per share if they were included as an expense on the income statement. Those are important numbers, since many companies have showered their managers and employees with stock options. In doing so, companies are giving up the income they would receive if they sold these shares on the open market. And when those options are exercised, existing shareholders stakes decline in value.

Operating Leases

The footnotes also give you vital details on operating leases, the kind where a company makes monthly payments for the buildings it occupies but doesn't have a buyout at the end of the contract. Accounting rules say that operating leases are not assets to the company, so they can't go on the balance sheet. Still, leases are often a major liability that investors should know about, especially if the company operates a chain of retail stores and has hundreds of operating leases for its outlets.

Airlines use operating leases all the time to acquire rights to aircraft, but the rent payments on the leases don't show up on the balance sheet. A 1998 Morgan Stanley report showed that 42 percent of United Airlines' fleet did not appear on the balance sheet because of the heavy use of operating leases.

Pension Funds

A company's pension assets and liabilities won't appear on the balance sheet, either, but you'll find the details in a footnote. In bad times, underfunded pensions can cause net income to decline. The opposite is true in good times, when pension plans can be a significant contributor to net income. It was determined by a New York hedge fund Maverick Capital that in 2000, 30 percent of the companies in the S&P 500 used over-funded pension plans to bump up their net income figure. On average, they added a hefty 12 percent to pre-tax earnings. This is perfectly legal, but it obscures how much of the company's core operations contribute to net income.

Don't ignore the treatment given pension funds. A great example is Lucent Technologies Inc. Thanks to three benefit and pension funds that Lucent was born with when spun off from AT&T Corp. eight years ago, the big provider of telecom gear never had to dig into its own pocket to pay benefits for U.S. retirees. The funds paid every cent, both of pensions and of retiree's health care.

In addition, Lucent has been able to use assets in these funds to help it pay for repeated rounds of downsizing. Moreover, the benefit plans, thanks to accounting rules, have fed Lucent hundreds of millions of dollars of income. And through a separate accounting maneuver, the cuts that Lucent made in the benefit plans last fall will contribute hundreds of millions of dollars more in income over future years. In short, in most years the pension and retiree benefit plan have enhanced Lucent's earnings, not burdened them. But now that the surplus in the biggest fund is essentially gone, Lucent is faced with using some of its own cash to pay retiree benefits, and it is cutting those benefits.

The Lucent story is a case study of the often-bewildering world of retiree benefits. Contrary to a common perception, having a high ratio of retirees to employees doesn't necessarily raise a company's benefits burden. Lucent also shows the sundry ways companies can actually profit from their retiree plans, both to relieve demands on their cash and to produce new income that improves the bottom line.

Lucent says it adopted many techniques that other big companies, too, use to manage pension and benefits plans. But most companies imposing cuts are doing it to improve their performances or to better insulate themselves from health care inflation. Lucent was in an entirely different position. They couldn't generate the cash.

The pension plan served Lucent as a kind of piggy bank. From 1999 to 2001, Lucent withdrew about $1 billion from pension-plan assets to pay for retiree's health care. This is perfectly legal, although companies that do it face certain restrictions if they later try to cut those health benefits. Any cuts Lucent makes in its retirees benefits bring it accounting gains. The cuts lower a liability recorded earlier on Lucent's books. That generated an accounting gain, which adds to the company's income.

In summary, pay attention to under-funded pension plans, benefit cuts, and true cash flow from operations. The rich pension plan provided a valuable resource for the company in that it generated pension income when the return on assets in the fund exceeded their costs. The difference counts as company income. While the difference isn't spendable money, it fattens the reported profits that drive stock prices.

Taking the pension discussion a step further, pension plans consist of the actual assets that exist in the plan and estimates of future liabilities. Assets are maintained to match the timing and amounts of liabilities. These liabilities are estimated with many assumptions and they become cash draining events over time. Assumptions made are relative to healthcare inflation, future salary increases, discount rates, and costs to service the plan.

Please keep in mind that pension plans and other benefit plans are off-balance sheet items. The large potential liabilities generated by pensions are important considerations when assessing the credit of some firms. The firm should be making regular cash contributions to keep asset levels sufficient. Plan assets typically include:

- Cash
  - To pay short term liabilities and to provide liquidity
- Bonds
  - To provide income to pay liabilities over time
- Real Estate
  - To provide income to pay liabilities over time
  - To provide asset growth
- Stocks
  - To provide asset growth
- Alternative Investments
  - To provide asset growth without correlation to stocks

If we have another repeat of the 1970s stock market, firms could get caught if their plans call for heavy investments in stocks, not enough cash contributions and a management group that is more concerned with earnings than funding. So, pensions should be included in credit decisions when they are material in nature. To determine materiality, ask the question: Is the material relative to the company's size? Pensions are typically a material issue when dealing with old and large companies.

Pension information is included in the footnotes of the financial statement, or in the 10-K report in a series of tables. However, there are no conclusions drawn with this information. The best place to look for this information is under something labeled "Funded Status." This will give you the fair value of the plan assets minus projected benefit obligations. You will see "Cash Contributions" on the cash flow statement or in the footnotes. All assumptions the firm used and their portfolio composition will be in the footnotes.

Interpret the information provided by checking a few key assumptions:

- Discount rate: Make sure it is conservative (low) enough. If it's going up, ask why. (Is management managing earnings?)
- Expected return on plan assets: Is it conservative (low) enough? If it's significantly higher than the discount rate, be skeptical of the pension expense. (Is management managing earnings?)
- Rate of salary increase: Is it high enough? (Is management managing earnings?)
- Check the target/actual allocation of the pension plan: Is the company making sufficient use of bonds to fund the pension liability (conversely, are they overly exposed to equities?)

If you see firms making regular cash contributions, that's a good sign. Keep in mind that the firm's assumptions about the discount rate, rate of salary for compensation increases, expected return on plan assets, etc. have a direct effect on the plans performance and cost.

In summary, accounting practices will determine the firm's aggressive or conservative approach. An *aggressive* (dubious) accounting approach would consist of a high discount rate, an overly optimistic expected return on plan assets versus reality or the discount rate, and a low rate of salary increase. A *conservative* (good) accounting approach would consist of a low discount rate, an expected return on plan assets that is near the discount rate, and a high rate of salary increase. Look for firms to use bonds, and more bonds from an investing best practice standpoint. Also watch their good funding practices to see if they keep funding the plan each year. General Motors has had pension shortfalls that have materially hampered the health of the business. They have to make $8 billion a year in pension payments and they assume a 9 percent return on investments. GM's returns on stocks and bonds have been too low. In 2004, they reduced their reliance on stocks and bonds in favor of less conventional riskier alternatives such as junk bonds, emerging markets, real estate investment trusts and the slick science of arbitrage.

WRITE-DOWNS AND REVERSALS

When a company stockpiles equipment or other goods that it can't sell, and the value of that inventory declines below what it will be sold for, accounting rules require that the company write down, or reduce the value of, the inventory on the balance sheet. In a well-run company write-downs should be minimal; they happen rarely if managers are paying proper attention to the supply-chain signals of customers and inventory levels and to the timing of new product introductions. This is just something to keep in mind the next time you read about companies for example like Cisco Systems Inc.

GOODWILL GAMES

A company measures the value of an acquisition by forecasting the cash it expects the acquired company to generate. As a result of the Financial Accounting Standards Board finally challenging this accounting practice, many companies were forced to make huge write-offs of goodwill as a result of overvaluing themselves and causing shareholders to overpay.

The new FASB went into effect in 2001 and disallowed the "pooling method," but at the same time it lifted the requirement for companies to amortize goodwill. This means goodwill no longer will reduce earnings for years to come. Instead, companies must determine annually the value of the goodwill acquired, and must write down that value on their books if they determine that it has been "impaired," or lost value, since the purchase took place.

In the end, we investors must change our behavior. You should not follow the herd and grab for shares just because the headline on a press release trumpets an increase in pro forma earnings per share. Conversely, investors should not abandon ship just because a company fails to meet analysts' expectations. It's our responsibility to dig deeper to see what the company's true prospects are.

Nothing will change corporate managers, auditors and boards more than a change in investor expectations. If you demand more transparency and an end to the numbers game, and you back up those demands with your investment dollar, companies will have little choice but to change their behavior, too.

STOCK OPTIONS

Accounting rule makers unveiled that their long-awaited proposal to require that employee stock-option compensation should be treated as an expense on corporate financial statements starting in 2004.

The proposed rules by FASB promise to significantly alter investor perceptions of many companies' financial performance. The rules could also trigger sweeping changes in the way that many executives and rank-

and-file employees are paid for their work. The change, if made final pending a 90-day comment period, would bring U.S. rules on option pay in line with similar measures recently passed by the Internal Accounting Standards Board, the U.S. board's London-based counterpart that sets European accounting standards.

For decades, stock options—which give workers the right to buy shares of their company's stock at a fixed price within a defined period—have represented a free lunch of sorts for corporations large and small. The lack of any requirement to recognize stock-option pay as a corporate expense has often encouraged pay packages for their top executives, some of whom have collected hundreds of millions of dollars in option pay over the years.

FASB's move has been in the works for about two years and marks a response to longstanding investor criticisms that the current accounting rules for option pay have resulted in distorted corporate income statements that aren't comparable from company to company. Those criticisms began to accelerate shortly after Enron's collapse in late 2001 and spurred FASB to bring renewed focus to a number of thorny accounting controversies that had previously seemed untouchable.

This approach to compensation does come with costs—either in the form of dilution to current shareholders or through cash outlays by companies to repurchase their own stock in an effort to limit such dilution. However, the current accounting rules say that companies need not treat stock-option pay as an expense on their income statements, so long as they disclose estimates of option compensation in their financial statement footnotes.

According to Standard & Poor's, earnings for companies within the S&P 500 stock index would have been 10.6 percent lower in 2003, 19.2 percent lower in 2002 and 21.5 percent lower in 2001 if all the component companies had treated options as an expense.

Companies will now make significant changes to their options plans, including the number of options, the types of options and the methodology used to value them. For public companies, stock-option pay would be recognized as an expense when first granted to employees, based on their estimated values at the time. However, look for a fight against this ruling from Tec companies and venture capitalists.

SPECIAL PURPOSE ENTITIES (SPEs)

SPEs are referred to as off-balance sheet partnerships. Enron had hundreds of them that were used to hide its debt and book illusory profits. On Wall Street, they are known as special purpose vehicles or SPEs and you would be hard pressed to find a Fortune 500 company that doesn't use one. Are they all as bad as Enron's? Thankfully no. But they offer plenty of temptation for companies looking for legal ways to cook the books.

SPEs were created to perform a straightforward, necessary task, which was to isolate and contain financial risk. Businesses that wanted to perform a specialized task, such as an airline buying a fleet of airplanes or a company building a big construction project, would set up an SPE and offload the financing to the new entity. For example, a company looking to build a gas pipeline but not wanting to assume all the debt load would set up an SPE—essentially a joint venture with other investors—to build it. The SPE would own the pipeline and use it as collateral to issue the bonds to finance it. The sponsoring company would still operate the pipeline, with the revenues being used to pay back the bondholders.

In theory, an SPE protected both sides of the transaction if something went awry. If the project went bust, the company was responsible only for what it had put into the SPE; conversely, if the company went bankrupt, its creditors couldn't go after the SPE's assets.

Virtually every bank uses SPEs to issue debt secured by pools of mortgages. And companies as diverse as Target and Xerox use SPEs for factoring, the practice of generating cash by selling off receivables.

But SPEs also evolved into an effective scalpel for CFO's looking to perform cosmetic surgery on their balance sheets. That's because the accounting rules say that as long as a company owns less than 50 percent of an SPE's voting stocks, the SPE's assets and debt don't have to be consolidated on its books. As a matter of fact, the SPE's nominal owner can put up only 3 percent of the SPE's equity. The company establishing the SPE can contribute the remaining 97 percent and still qualify for off-balance sheet treatment. The reality of today with regards to SPEs is that they are not used to isolate risk but primarily to hide information from investors.

SPEs are also a good way to keep money from Uncle Sam. Most tax-avoidance techniques using SPEs cleverly exploit discrepancies between accounting rules and tax laws. Synthetic leases are a good example. These are transactions in which a company sells an asset to an SPE and then leases it back. The company gets to move the assets off its balance sheet yet for tax purposes it retains the ability to depreciate the assets as if it were still the owner.

One lesson learned from Enron relating to SPEs was that it was creating entities to give the appearance that the SPE investors and bondholders were assuming risks when, in fact, Enron retained most, and in some cases, all of it.

INVESTOR MEASURES

Earnings Per Share (EPS)

After-tax profit divided by number of shares in issue. The denominator is the average number of shares in issue throughout the year.

EPS shows the profit a company has earned on each ordinary share or unit of common stock it has in issue after allowing for all costs, expenses, financial charges, and tax.

Shareholders often make use of earning per share as a measure of the overall profitability of a company. EPS is to be found in the annual report either at the foot of the income statement or in a separate note giving earnings and share price movements. As with any pre-calculated ratio, you should try to discover precisely how the EPS number was derived. In most cases, it is probably worth doing the simple math yourself to ensure consistency in calculations if making comparisons with other businesses.

One problem with interpreting EPS can be the firm's treatment of extraordinary, or one-off, gains or losses that arise. For example, the sale or closure of part of a business which results in a dramatic improvement or fall in earnings per share.

Having arrived at the after-tax profit for the year, the next step is for the directors to declare the dividend they propose to be paid to shareholders. When the dividend per share is deducted from the earnings per share, what remains is the retained profit per share for the year. This number is an important element in the assessment of the financial performance and position of the firm. Key to any firm's financial strength is their ability to generate a significant source of funds from its ongoing operations and retained earnings is the self-generated financing of the firm.

Price/Earnings Ratio

Share price divided by earnings per share expressed as a multiple or number of times.

The Price/Earnings (P/E) multiple is one of the most widely-used multiples. Its calculation simplicity is attractive but tying it to a firm's financial condition is often ignored. Some analysts will use it in order to avoid having to be explicit about their assumptions related to the firm's risk and growth. Others use it because they think it reflects the market mood and perceptions. Thus, if investors are upbeat about a given stock, the P/E ratio will be higher to reflect this optimism. It becomes a financial status symbol. However, as we know, markets make errors in evaluating sectors. If the oil sector is overvalued on an average, for example, using the average P/E ratio will build in an error for a given firm's valuation.

Market Capitalization

Number of issued ordinary shares (common stock) times the share price.

If a company's shares are quoted on a stock exchange, there is a ready source of data upon which to base a valuation. The calculated number provides an indication of the firm's current stock exchange value. This is the market value, or the capitalization of the company. If the balance sheet shows the firm's equity of $10 million with a Market Cap of $30 million then you have a positive valuation. However, the Market Cap could be nearing $10 million which may indicate a negative trend and unfavorable market perceptions.

Beta Factor

Percentage change in share price over a period as multiple of percentage change in share prices generally. This measures the relative volatility of a share price performance.

For any given period, movements in both a company's share price and a selected stock exchange index can be plotted to give an indication of the sensitivity of the company's share price to general movements of the stock market. If it was found that for every 1% move in the stock market the firm's shares moved 1.5%, applying the 1.5 factor to the stock market index should provide an indicator of the likely price of that company's share. This is called the beta rating or beta factor.

A beta of 1.5 suggests that the firm's share price will on average move 1.5% with every 1% move in the market. A beta of 1 suggests the firm's share price moves precisely in tune with the market. If the buoyancy of the share market is linked to expectations of the company, companies with high beta values are likely to be directly affected by boom or doom. With a sound economy high beta firm's can be expected to generate extremely good returns, but in a recession they will probably be poor performers.

Dividend Yield

Dividend yield links the current share price to the dividend received.

Dividend yield equals 100 times (dividend per share divided by share price). It is expressed as a percentage of the current share price. It is income received per $100 of stock market value.

	A	B	C
Dividend per share	10	4	5.8
Share price	300	100	150
Dividend yield %	3.3	4.0	3.9

Changes in share price bring about a change in the dividend yield. As share price changes there is an automatic adjustment in dividend yield.

Shareholder or Stockholder Return

The return shareholders expect from their investment in shares is a combination of the capital gain flowing from an improvement in share price and income from dividends. If the shares in firm A increase in price by 10%, the total return to shareholders, ignoring tax, in the period is 30%: the dividend yield (20%) plus the capital gain (10%). Its significance is an indicator of the wealth generated for shareholders.

Dividend Cover

If after-tax profit attributable to ordinary shareholders is divided by the dividend, the result is the number of times the dividend was covered. As with interest cover, the higher the dividend cover ratio the better or safer is the position of a company.

$$\text{Dividend cover} = \text{after tax profit} \div \text{the dividend}$$
$$= \text{earnings per share divided by dividend per share}$$

	A	B	C
After-tax profit	75	25	175
Dividend	25	20	87
Dividend Cover	3.0	1.25	2.0

Levels of what is considered acceptable vary across business sectors. If a company is operating in a sector that is reasonably unaffected by economic downturns, such as food manufacturing and retailing, a lower dividend cover ratio is more acceptable because the risk is lower.

INVESTOR MEASURES

Indicator	Calculation	Significance
Earnings Per Share (EPS)	After-tax profit divided by number of shares in issue. The denominator is the average number of shares in issue throughout the year.	A measure of the overall profitability of a company.
Price/Earnings Ratio	Share price divided by earnings per share expressed as a multiple or number of times.	Financial status symbol.
Market Capitalization	Number of issued ordinary shares (common stock) times the share price.	An indication of the firm's current stock exchange value. This is the market value, or the capitalization of the company. Value is placed on equity by the financial markets.
Beta Factor	Percentage change in share price over a period as a multiple of percentage change in share prices in share prices generally.	The sensitivity of the company's share price to general movements of the stock market. This measures the relative volatility of a share price performance.
Dividend Yield	Dividend per share before tax expressed as a percentage of the current share price.	Income received per $100 of stock market value.
Shareholder or Stockholder Return	Change in the share price plus dividends received divided by the opening share price expressed as a percentage—usually on an annual basis.	Wealth generated for shareholders.
Dividend Cover	After tax profit divided by the dividend.	The higher the dividend cover ratio, the better or safer is the position of a company.

Appendix A

GLOSSARY OF LETTER OF CREDIT TERMS

Account party—Entity on whose behalf the *letter of credit* is issued. Same as *applicant*.

Advising bank—A bank that receives, *authenticates*, and delivers a *letter of credit* to the *beneficiary*.

Amendment—A change in the terms of a *letter of credit*, initiated by the *account party* and agreed to by the *beneficiary*.

Applicant—Same as *account party*.

Assignee—Party designated by the *beneficiary* of a *letter of credit* to receive a portion of the proceeds from the credit.

Assignment of proceeds—Method by which the *beneficiary* of a *letter of credit* designates another party, the *assignee*, as the recipient of a portion of the proceeds under the *letter of credit*.

Authentication—Verification of the genuineness of a document. If a *letter of credit* has been communicated electronically, the authentication process, called testing, consists of verifying that the message originated at the issuing bank.

B/A—Abbreviation for *banker's acceptance*.

Banker's acceptance—*Usance* (or time) *draft* or *bill* of acceptance *exchange* drawn on a bank and accepted by that bank. The *draft* is stamped "accepted" and signed by a bank officer. By accepting the draft, the bank agrees to pay the face value of the obligation at maturity if the issuer (the *drawer* of the draft) fails to pay.

Beneficiary—The party authorized to draw against a *letter of credit*, as designated by the *account party*.

Bill of exchange—Draft calling for payment in connection with a trade transaction.

Collecting bank—In a *documentary collection* transaction, the bank that receives the collection letter and documents from the remitting bank and that will collect the proceeds from the buyer in exchange for the documents.

Collection letter—In a *documentary collection*, the set of payment instructions and documents, including a *draft*, given by the seller to the remitting bank and relayed to the buyer by the *collecting bank*.

Commercial letter of credit—Letter of credit covering the movement of goods and requiring presentation of the related shipping documents.

Confirmation—The process whereby a second bank (usually the advising bank) adds its commitment to pay the *beneficiary* in case the *issuing bank* is unable or unwilling to honor its obligations.

Contract limit—Foreign exchange: the maximum dollar amount of all foreign exchange contracts that can be outstanding at any one time.

Correspondent—A bank acts as an agent for a local or foreign bank.

Country risk—Country risk includes political instability, currency fluctuation, and any of the variety of risks arising from a sovereign government's exercise of power.

D/A—Abbreviation for *documents against acceptance*, form of *documentary collection*.

D/P—Abbreviation for *documents against payment*, a form of *documentary collection*.

Discounting—The purchase of a *banker's acceptance*. The difference between what the seller receives and the face value of the draft is called the "discount," which reflects the time value of money.

Discrepancy—A disparity between the requirements of a *letter of credit* and the document package presented to the bank. The most common discrepancies are late shipments, late presentation of documents, and nonconforming descriptions of goods.

Documentary collection—Settlement of a trade transaction collection by the exchange through the bank of shipping documents against payment or acceptance of a draft drawn on the buyer by the seller. You make presentation of documents to the issuing bank in accordance with the letter of credit and receive payment directly from the customer's bank and not the customer.

Draft—Payment order in writing that directs a second party, the *drawee*, to pay a specified sum to a third party, the *payee*. The *payee* and *drawer* are often one and the same.

Drawee—Party that is expected to pay a draft when presented for payment.

Drawer—Party making demand for payment by drawing a draft.

Export Import Bank of the United States—National export financing agency created by executive order in 1934. The bank provides loans, working capital guarantees, export insurance, and guarantees. The bank is funded through financing extended by the U.S. Treasury, loan repayments and fees.

Ex-Im Bank or Ex-Im—Short name for the Export Import Bank of the United States.

Formula exposure limit—Foreign exchange: maximum *market risk* that the bank is willing to take.

Forward contract—Foreign exchange: A forward contract is virtually identical to a spot contract, except that the *value date* is more than two business days. Forward contracts allow customers to secure a price today for currency to be bought or sold in the future.

Forward points—Foreign exchange: Difference between the price of a currency for delivery in two business days (*spot*) and the price of the same currency for delivery beyond two business days (*forward contract*).

GSM-102/103 Programs—Commodity Credit Corporation's guarantee programs covering commercial bank loans made for the export of U.S. agricultural products.

Issuing bank—The bank that issues or opens a *letter of credit* on behalf of the account party.

LC—Abbreviation for letter of credit.

Letter of Credit—Letter from a bank committing to pay a specified amount against presentation of stipulated documents.

Market risk—Foreign exchange. Risks arising from exchange rate fluctuations.

Negotiation—Review and payment of documents presented to the bank under a *letter of credit*.

Paying bank—A bank that pays the proceeds of a *letter of credit to the* beneficiary.

Political risk—Includes war, insurrection, civil instability, or any event resulting from a government's inability or unwillingness to pay claims of foreigners.

Presenting bank—In a *documentary collection* transaction, the bank that presents the documents to the buyer.

Remitting bank—In a *documentary collection*, the bank that remits payment to the seller.

Second beneficiary—Transferable *letter of credit*: the third party to whom the *beneficiary* transfers part, or all of the credit.

Settlement cycle—Wire payment: Time that elapses between the moment when the payment instructions are sent and when the funds are available to the beneficiary.

Settlement limit—Foreign exchange: Dollar value of all commitments that can be settled within two consecutive business days.

Settlement risk—Foreign exchange: refers to the possibility that the customer will default during a *settlement cycle*, exposing the Bank to a loss if it has already delivered the currency but has not yet received value in return.

Sight credit—A *letter of credit* that calls for the presentation of a draft payable at sight.

Sight draft—A draft that is payable upon presentation to the *drawee*.

Spot contract—Involves the commitment by one party to deliver a specified quantity of one product against the other party's delivery of a specified quantity of a second product, generally within two business days of the date of contract.

Standby letter of credit—A *letter of credit* that represents an obligation by the issuing bank to pay the *beneficiary* upon presentation of certain documents, generally a *draft* and a statement indicating that the *account party* has failed to perform under the terms of a contract with the beneficiary or has failed to honor his financial obligation to the beneficiary. If the standby credit only calls for the presentation of a *draft*, it is referred to as a clean credit. A standby letter of credit is usually issued with the understanding that, in most cases, it will never be drawn against.

Time (usance) draft—A *draft* payable at a future date.

Trade acceptance—Typically in connection with *documentary collection*, a draft drawn on and accepted by a *drawee* other than a bank. The *drawee* is usually the buyer of goods.

Transferable—A *letter of credit* that allows the *beneficiary* to transfer part, or all, of the letter of credit rights to a third party. The party receiving the transfer is called the *second beneficiary*.

Usance draft—A draft payable at some future date, typically 180 days or less; same as *time draft*.

Usance letter of credit—A letter of credit that calls for presentation of a *usance draft*.

Value date—Foreign exchange: date on which the currency bought or sold must be delivered.

Working Capital—Ex-Im Bank loan guarantee program designed to provide eligible exporters with Guarantee Program access to working capital loans from commercial lenders.

Appendix B

EXPORT LETTER OF CREDIT CHECKLIST

Letter of Credit # _____   Reference # _____

Date Received: _____

Issued By: _____   Confirmed By: _____

1. Is the LC irrevocable?
2. Is the LC addressed properly? Has the original operative letter of credit been received?
3. Is the LC confirmed or unconfirmed?
4. Does the merchandise description agree with invoice or contract?
5. What are the shipping terms (FOB port, CFR, CIF, etc.) and do these agree with the quote or contract?
6. What are the terms of the draft for payment (i.e., sight or time)? If a time draft, who pays discount charge? If sight, where?
7. What is the latest shipping date? Can this date be met?
8. What is the expiration date? Can this date be met?
9. Is the amount of the LC sufficient?
10. What are the documents required? Can these documentary requirements be met?
11. Are partial shipments permitted? Not permitted?
12. Is transshipment permitted?
13. What is the port of exit? Discharge? Can you comply?
14. Are transportation charges collect or to be prepaid? Does this comply with the shipping terms?
15. If insurance documents are not required, do you have evidence the buyer will insure?
16. Are there LC terms and conditions, which need clarification?
17. Do the unit prices agree with proforma invoice, quotation, or contract?
18. Is the LC payable in U.S. dollars or another currency?
19. Has the LC been circulated through sales, credit, production, traffic, treasury, billing, and other departments?
20. Is an amendment in order?

References Useful for Further Reading

Altman, Edward I. *Corporate Financial Distress and Bankruptcy.* Hoboken, NJ: Wiley & Sons, Inc., Second edition, 1993.

Brigham, Eugene F. *Financial Management: Theory and Practice.* The Dryden Press, Eighth edition, 1997.

Gallinger, George W. and P. Basil Healey. *Liquidity Analysis and Management.* Boston: Addison Wesley, Second edition, 1991.

Hale, Roger H. *Credit Analysis.* Hoboken, NJ: John Wiley & Sons, Inc., 1983.

Jorion, Philippe. *Value at Risk.* Toronto: Irwin Professional Publishing (McGraw-Hill Companies, Inc.), 1997.

Maness, Terry S. *Short-Term Financial Management.* Eagan, MN: West Publishing Company, 1993.

O'Glove, Thornton L. *Quality of Earnings.* The Free Press (a division of Macmillan, Inc.), 1987.

Special Thanks

To Mr. James S. Carr, Bankruptcy Attorney, Partner with Kelly Dry & Warren LLP, 101 Park Avenue NY, NY for his review and advisements related to Chapters 3, 14, 22, and 23.

Index

<u>A</u>

accounting
  full cost method, 11
  loss, 180
  policy, 3, 209, 214, 251, 254, 262
  rules, 262-263, 265-266, 267, 268
accrual(s), 36, 41, 45, 51, 52, 53-56, 60, 63, 209-213
  accounting, 49, 50, 51-56, 210-211, 213
acid test ratio, *see* quick ratio
activity ratios, *see* balance sheet ratios
adequate assurance clause, 91
administrative expense claim, 218-219
agency ratings, 18-19, 23, 91-92, 93, 140-142, 144, 152-159, 170-171, 175, 245
Altman, *see* Z score
American Bar Association (ABA), 115-116
amortization, 44, 51-52, 53, 57, 111-112, 181-182, 211, 266
asset backed securities (ABS), 241
asset intensity ratio, 188-191
asset to equity ratio, 65
assets, 3, 10-15, 16, 25-31, 44, 46, 52-53, 71-72, 96-97, 111, 122-123, 146, 150, 152-159, 185, 198, 209-216, 241, 258-268
  as collateral, 111, 112, 230-232, 245
  in bankruptcy, 220-222, 225
  current, 21, 25, 26, 30, 34, 35-36, 39, 210, 258
  defensive, 38-41
  fixed, 10-15, 21, 26-27, 57, 111, 187-188, 189, 254
  growth, 185-192, 264
  intangibles, 1, 9, 10, 17, 18, 25, 111-112
  liquid, 17, 38, 39, 160, 230-232
  liquidation, 36, 220-221, 227, 229
  management, 63-70, 202
  oil and gas reserves, 11-14
  overstating/understating, 3, 4
  pledged, 230-231
  quick, 40-41
  settlement, 245
  total, 58-59, 61, 73-77, 123, 146, 150, 151, 187-188, 215
  turnover, 27-29, 32, 58-59, 63-70, 71, 73-74, 191
  value, 153-155, 159, 205

volatility, 78-79, 90, 96-97, 99, 155, 160-162, 164-165, 166-167, 168, 204, 205, 270
at-the-money, 103
auditor, 182, 210-211, 252
  opinion, 1, 4, 5, 266
author's viewpoint, 255-257
Automatic Reduction Clause, 131
automatic stay, 131, 221, 222, 225

B

balance sheet, 44-47, 49, 53, 76, 116, 181, 182, 187-189, 194, 197, 202, 211, 213, 240, 258-259, 260, 268, 270, *see also* off-balance sheet
  assets, 15, 35-41, 44, 46, 111, 159, 188-189, 198, 215, 216
  book net worth, 8-11
  equity, 8-11, 44, 46, 65
  financing, 65-66
  fixed assets, 10-12, 111, 187-188, 254
  intangibles, 10, 18, 24-25, 111
  inventory, 8, 266
  liabilities, 9, 44, 46
  ratios, 23-24, 25-26, 32, 33, 34-35, 36-41, 136, *also see* liquidity ratios
  risk, 149, 159, 268
  sources and uses of funds, 44-45, 52
bank, 19, 110, 125, 127, 129, 130, 237-240
  advising, 132, 226, 238, 273
  analysis/evaluation, 122-124, 205
  confirming, 131
  guarantee, 174-175, *also see* letter of credit
  issuing, 126, 131-132
  reference information, 3, 18-19, 21, 120-121
  risk, 100, 122-124
bankruptcy, 16-17, 64, 93, 116, 131, 182, 217-229, 232, 234, 241, 244
  administrative expense claim, 218-219
  administrative priority, 219, 220
  automatic stay, 131, 221, 222, 225
  Chapter 7, 7, 16-17, 131, 220-221, 224
  Chapter 11, 217-220, 221-224, 225, 226-229
  Code, 217-225, 236
  creditors' committee, 218, 221, 223, 225, 226-229
  debtor, 17, 131, 217-219
  debtor-in-possession (DIP), 219, 220, 221, 225
  fraudulent conveyances, 143, 219
  glossary of terms, 225
  ordinary course of business, 218-219, 220, 225

petition, 145, 171, 218-219, 220, 221, 222, 225
plan of reorganization, 219, 220, 221-224, 225, 227-229
prediction, 35, 68, 110-111, 140, 145-151, 207-216
preference rule/preferences, 113, 131, 220, 224-225, 227
Proof of Claim, 223
reclamation, 218-219, 222
trustee, 17, 218, 220-221, 225, 227
unsecured creditors, 16-17, 111, 221, 223, 226-229
Bankruptcy Abuse Prevention and Consumer Protection Act of 2005, 217-220
basis risk, 94-96, 99, 248
before-tax return on assets ratio, 63-64, 66
beta factor, 270, 272
bill of lading, 127, 129, 130
Black-Scholes Model, 157-159
Black-Scholes-Merton (BSM) Model, 154, 157-159
bond rating, 150, 151, 152
bond spread, 144
book net worth, 8-10
book value, 156, 194, 205
  automobile, 17
  debt/equity, 146, 151, 194, 205
  fixed assets, 10-15
  home, 16-17
  intangible, 111-112, 114
  liabilities, 146, 151, 153, 155
  personal items, 17
break even analysis, 183-185
Brent, 99, 102
brokerage/bank risk, 100
business, forms of, 107-117

C
C corporation, 107-108, 115
Cs of credit, 1, 2
calendar risk, 95
capacity, 1, 2, 16, 52, 122-124, 170-171, 188, 191
capital, 1, 2, 26, 59, 116, 122-124, 193-206, 248
  allocation of, 165-168
  cost of, 42, 64, 68, 193-206
  risk, 162, 163, 203-206
  working, 8-9, 21, 26, 27, 35-36, 146, 148-149, 151, 187-189, 208, 229, 274, 276
Capital at Risk (CAR), 161-166, 167-168
Capital Value at Risk (CVAR), 166-167

cash, 17, 34-56, 60, 72, 78-106, 111-112, 175, 194, 215, 241, 245, 253, 263, 264-265
   as collateral in bankruptcy, 222, 230-231
   converting from receivables, 28-29, 198-199
   market, 78-106
   settlement, 233, 245
   source and application, 253
Cash Conversion Cycle (CCC), 35-38, 40, 254
cash flow, 1, 5, 11, 13, 34-56, 108, 110-111, 112-113, 114, 138-151, 156, 184-192, 199-200, 209, 216, 253-254, 260-261, 264-265
   adjustments to CFFO, 51-52
   analysis, 42-56, 110-111, 148-150, 254
   break even, 184-185
   defined, 42
   financing, 49, 52-53
   forecasting, 156
   from operations, 35, 36, 39, 43-48, 49-50, 51-55, 110-112, 114, 149-151, 211, 215, 260-261, 263
   investing, 49, 52, 265
   ratios, 47-48
   sources and uses, 44-45, 47, 48, 53-54, 71, 253
   statement, 1, 5, 29, 36, 39, 40, 43-56, 110-111, 149, 251, 260-261
CCC, *see* Cash Conversion Cycle
Chapter 7, 7, 16-17, 131, 220-221, 224
Chapter 11, 217-220, 221-224, 225, 226-229
character, 1, 2, 20-21, 41
collateral, 1, 2, 19, 21, 25, 89, 90, 110, 111, 112, 122, 132, 171, 175, 180, 222, 230-242, 252, 268
collection effectiveness index (CEI), 28-29
commercial invoice, 126-132, 136, 239, 277
commissions, 158, 183, 184
commodities, 78, 82, 234-236
common-size analysis, 215
common-size income statement, 61-62, 64
communication/communication skills, 21, 113, 114, 224, 228, 229, 256-257
community property, 134, 232-233
comparative analysis, 2-3, 250
conditions,
   economic, 113, 170, 171, 214
   financial, 1, 2, 4, 21, 48, 58, 73, 91, 113-114, 119, 122, 254, 269
consultants, 218, 229, 255-257
corporations, 5-6, 107-108, 109, 115, 133, 145, 186, 202, 210, 213, 244, 255, 267, 275
   analysis, 110-114, 116-117

C, 107-108, 115
close/closely held, 6, 107
public, 107, 112
Subchapter S, 108, 115, 116-117, 186
counterparty risk, 85, 87, 89-90, 92-93, 94, 96, 97, 98-102, 144-145, 155-157,
168, 175-178, 230, 237-239, 242, 247
country risk, 118-121, 274
credit, 1-77
agency reports, 3, 18, 120
analysis, 34-77, 107-117, 183-206, 249-272
default pricing, 145
default swap, 143, 145, 242, 243-248
derivatives/derivatives contract, 98, 99, 155-156, 168, 219, 242, 243-248
events, 91, 160, 162, 223, 242, 243-248
how to write analysis, 249-254
insurance, 98, 112, 121, 136, 175, 241, 244, 246, 247
international, 118-121
rating (and agencies), 18-19, 23, 91-92, 93, 140-142, 144, 152-159, 170-171,
175, 245
spreads, 144-145, 155
terms, 91-93, 113, 114, 125-137, 230-242, 273, 276-277
credit limit, 1-24, 41, 133
determining, 16-24, 138-139
formula, 24
value judgments, 20-21, 41
worksheet, 23
credit risk, 97-102, 107-182, 207-225, 230-248, 252
categories, 169
exposure, 78, 85-86, 90, 97-100, 113, 122, 125, 139-140, 160-178, 205, 230,
242-248
exposure measurement, 160-182
group concentration, 180
mitigation strategy, 175-177
credit scoring, 138-151, 155-159, 230
bond rating, 150, 151, 152
Altman Z Score, 145-147, 151, 157
Lambda, 147-150, 151, 156, 157
model formats, 151, 157-159, 174-175
parameters, 140-144
spread types, 144-145
creditors,
secured, 20
unsecured, 16-17, 111, 221, 223, 226-229
creditors' committee, 218, 221, 223, 225, 226-229

cross-default clause, 93
current
   assets, 21, 25, 26, 30, 34, 35-36, 39, 210, 258
   debt/liabilities, 21, 25, 26, 27, 34, 35-36, 39, 44, 46, 47, 258
current debt to tangible net worth ratio, 21, 27
current ratio, 21, 23, 26, 30, 33, 34-36, 37, 38, 39, 40, 41, 254

D

D&B, 5, 18, 20, 23, 120
   industry norms, 34
days sales outstanding (DSO), 28-29, 36-37, 38
DDA balance, 19
debt, *see* liability
debt to equity ratio, 24, 34, 65, 67, 71, 191, 204
debtor-in-possession (DIP), 219, 220, 221, 225
deductions, 10, 16, 115, 117, 261
default, 93, 135, 233-236, 242
   pricing, 145
   probability/rate, 143-144, 152-159, 168, 177, 230
   risk, 78, 152-159, 174-175, 223-224, 244-248
default model paradigm, 168-171
Defensive Interval (DI), 35, 38-41, 254
depreciation, 3-4, 22, 46, 51-53, 57, 211, 214
derivatives, 78-106, 172-173, 181, 216, 237, 243-248
   categories and definitions of risk, 96-97
   certificate of eligibility, 92
   contract, 78, 97-102, 181, 243-248
   credit, 98, 99, 155-156, 168, 219, 242, 243-248
   definition, 78
   forwards/forward contract, 79, 80-85, 103, 172-173, 217-218, 219, 228, 244
   futures/futures contracts, 80-83, 102-106, 179, 216
   hedging, 78-79, 94-96, 181, 237
   margin calls, 81, 100
   options, 102-106
   performance risk, 80, 89, 97-99
   risk analysis, 78-106
   risk tracking report, 88
   settlement, 245-246
   suggested principles for risk analysis, 97-99
   swaps, 83-89, 90-94, 96, 102-106, 145, 172-173, 217-218, 219, 242
   VAR (Value at Risk), 96, 97, 99, 160-161, 162, 166-167, 168, 204, 205
DI, *see* Defensive Interval
digital settlement, 245

Direct Statement of Cash Flow, 54-56
disclosures, 142, 179, 180, 209
  oil and gas reserves, 12-14
dividends, 47, 48, 49, 53, 55, 68, 71, 73, 76, 77, 108, 157, 159, 186, 187, 189, 190, 192, 270-271, 272
documentary letter of credit, 126, 127-130, 237, 238
Dominion Bond Rating Service, Ltd., 152
DSO, *see* days sales outstanding
Dun & Bradstreet, *see* D&B
DuPont Model/Extended DuPont Model, 57-70, 76, 191-192, 203, 204
  analysis, 74
  modified formula, 203, 204

E

earnings, 3, 42-56, 57, 58-59, 60, 61, 67, 73, 75-77, 116, 146, 151, 194, 209-216, 260, 265, 269-270
earnings before interest and taxes (EBIT), 61, 62, 65, 113, 146, 204
earnings before interest, taxes, depreciation and amortization (EBITDA), 57
EBITA (operating return on sales), 61, 62, 63-64
earnings per share (EPS), 48, 181, 194, 199, 200, 259, 262, 266, 269, 272
economic
  conditions, 113, 170, 171, 214
  risk, 120
Economic Value Added (EVA), 193-203, 205-206
Emery, Gary, *see* Lambda
Enron, 102, 182, 209, 215-216, 236, 248, 261, 262, 267-268
equity, *see* assets
estoppel, 134-135
exchange for physical (EFP), 95-96
Export Import Bank of the United States (Ex-Im), 121, 274
exposure, maximum potential, 166-167
Expected Default Frequency (EDF), 154-155, 159
expected loss modelling, 177
expected value of credit exposure, 164-165
Extended DuPont Model, *see* DuPont Model
Eye-ball analysis, 1, 21-22

F

FAS-105, 179
FAS-133, 181-182, 247
FCIB, 120
Financial Accounting Standards Board (FASB), 49-50, 53, 54, 179-182, 247, 266-267

financial
  crisis event response plan, 182
  distress warning signs, 207-216
  financial information analysis, 110-111, 114, 253-254
  indicators checklist, 32-33
  planning, 71-72, 183-192
  review, 1-124, 142
  shenanigans, 213-216, 268
  structured, 212
financial leverage, 64-67, 70, 153, 191
  favorable and unfavorable, 66-67
  multiplier, 59, 64-65, 70
financial statement, 1-7, 16-17, 20, 73, 153-156, 179-182, 210, 252
  adjustment of items, 4, 8
  audited, 5, 11, 12, 14, 142
  certification, 14
  compiled, 6
  cost, 5, 6
  disclosures, 12-14, 142, 179-180
  footnotes, 3, 8, 11, 18, 251
  how to read, 258-272
  management prepared, 6
  monitors, 142
  notes, 10, 11, 149, 180
  personal, 16-17, 133, 134, 231, 232
  preliminary review, 1-7
  reviewed, 1-7
  tax returns, 6-7
  in writing credit analysis, 210, 252
financing activities, 49, 52-53, 185-192, 209-216
first in, first out (FIFO), 3, 8-9, 200, 214
Fitch, Inc., 140, 152
fixed assets to tangible net worth ratio, 21, 26-27
fixed costs, 30, 183-184
Fog Factor, The, 250-251
footnotes, 1, 3, 8, 12, 18, 29, 202, 214, 251, 261-265, 267
forwards/forwards contract, 79, 80-85, 103, 172-173, 217-218, 219, 228, 244
full cost accounting method, 11
funded debt to net working capital ratio, 27
funds
  needed to sustain growth, 185-192
  sources and uses, 44-45, 47, 48, 53-54, 56, 71, 185, 253
futures/futures contract, 80-83, 102-106, 179, 216

G

games accountants play (GAP), 214, 253
gas reserves, 11-14
general partnership, 108, 109, 116, 117
generally accepted accounting practices (GAAP), 4, 5, 6, 35, 120, 179, 181,
  194, 210, 211, 214, 247, 259
goodwill, 10, 25, 53, 111-112, 114, 181-182, 266
gross margin, 32, 69
guarantee(s), 109, 132-136, 179, 220, 229, 252
  bank, *see* letter of credit
  corporate/parent, 20, 132-133, 175, 231
  personal, 16, 19, 117, 133-135, 231-233
  personal signature, 134-135

H

hedge/hedging, 78-79, 94-96, 181, 237
highly leveraged companies (HLC), 110-111, 237
homestead states, 17, 134

I

ICC Publication No. 500, 127, 128
in-the-money, 103-105, 167
income
  from operations, 30-31, 43-44, 48, 49-52, 54, 67
  statement, 29, 39, 45-46, 47, 49, 54, 56, 57, 61, 62, 66, 76, 194, 211-212,
    258-262, 267, 269
  tax, 10, 11, 18, 29, 67, 108, 116-117, 232
Indirect Statement of Cash Flow, 49-54
industry standards, 2, 14, 34, 210
insurance, 79, 98, 112, 121, 136, 175, 241, 243, 244, 246, 247
interest
  expense, 48
  income, 30-31, 50-51
  pooling, 181-182
  rate risk, 55, 78, 158-159
interest coverage ratio, 30, 110, 150, 191
interest expense/operating earnings, 47, 48, 50-52, 58, 59-62, 65, 66, 110, 184,
  210
internal analysis, 2, 4, 21-22
internal consultant, 255-257
international credit risk, 118-121
interpretation of financial information, 253-254
inventory, 3, 8-9, 21, 26, 28, 34, 37-40, 51-52, 194, 197, 198, 208, 210, 214,
  258-259, 265-266

investing activities, 45-46, 49, 50, 52, 53, 149, 191-192, 213, 269-272
investor
  measures, 269-272
  viewpoint, 258-272
invoice net out, 135
irrevocable standby letter of credit, 126-127, 136, 239, 240, 277
ISDA Agreement, 191, 242
ISDA Credit Support Annex, 237

J
joint interest and financial leverage multiplier, 61, 66

K
Kaplan-Urwitz, 150-151
KMV scoring model, 143, 144, 154-157, 159, 174-175

L
Lambda, 147-150, 151, 156, 157
last in, first out (LIFO), 3, 8-9, 29, 194, 200, 214, 254
LBO, *see* leveraged buyout
letter of credit (LC), 90, 122, 123-124, 125-132, 136-137, 168, 174, 175, 179,
  223, 237-240, 254, 273
  account party, 237-238, 239
  advisements, 132, 226, 238, 273
  Automatic Reduction Clause, 131
  beneficiary, 125, 126, 128-130, 131, 136, 238-240
  checklist, 128-130, 277
  confirmation, 4, 131, 238, 239, 274
  discrepancies, 125-126, 128, 132, 274
  documentary, 126, 127-130, 237, 238
  glossary of terms, 273-276
  expiration, 133, 136
  export checklist, 230
  format, 133, 136-137
  irrevocable standby, 126-127, 136, 239, 240, 277
  issuing bank, 126, 131-132
  letter of indemnity (LOI), 130
  revocable, 126, 239
  sight vs. time, 239
  standby, 126-127, 133, 229, 239
  terms, 130, 273-276
letter of indemnity (LOI), 130
leverage, *see* financial leverage
leverage ratios, 27, 30, 33, 74-77, 191

leveraged buyouts (LBO), 109, 111-114
liability, 34-38, 71, 108, 109, 111, 115, 116, 117, 153-155
  balance sheet, 9, 44, 46
  book value, 146, 151, 153
  current, 21, 25, 26, 27, 34, 35-36, 44, 46, 47, 49, 191, 258
  lease, 18, 262, 268
  long-term, 22, 25, 27, 32, 36, 46-48, 51, 55, 60, 63, 152-154, 210
  pension, 9, 18, 261-265
  short-term, 25, 27, 32, 33, 48, 55, 108, 115, 153-155
libor spread, 144, 145
life insurance, 17, 135
LIFO, *see* last in, first out
limited liability company (LLC), 108, 109-110, 115-116
limited partnership, 109, 115
liquid accessible net worth (LANW), 232
liquidity, 35-38, 47, 110, 142, 147-150, 160, 254
liquidity ratios, 21, 26-27, 30, 32, 33, 37-41, 145-147, 254
  current debt to tangible net worth, 21, 27
  current ratio, 21, 23, 26, 30, 33, 34-36, 37, 38, 39, 40, 41, 254
  fixed assets to tangible net worth, 21, 26-27
  funded debt to net working capital, 27
  Lambda, 147-150, 151, 156, 157
  quick ratio, 23, 26, 30, 33, 34-36, 40, 41, 254
liquidity risk, 78, 162
loans, 19, 111, 116, 117, 123-124, 159, 166, 200, 215, 241, 245
location risk, 95
long-term sustainable growth rate (LTSGR), 71-72, 186
losses, 183-185, 204-205
  expected, 108, 115, 144-145, 160-161, 163, 166-170, 177, 204-205
  unexpected/unrealized, 162, 163, 165
Lucent Technologies Inc., 263

M
managerial signals of financial distress, 208, 209
market,
  appraisals, 15
  capitalization, 270, 272
  information, 142-143, 144
  over-the-counter, 82, 83, 104
  price of debt and equity, 153-154
  risk, 78, 95, 96, 97, 105-106, 144-145, 160-161, 162, 180
  spot, 84, 105
  values, 8-9, 11-12, 83, 87, 146-147, 153, 156-159, 172-173, 177, 193-203, 270

mark-to-market (MTM), 80-82, 88-90, 98-99, 100, 160, 167, 171-173, 181, 247
Marking Swaps to Market, 86-87, 89
master netting agreement, 218, 220, 234-237
Master Trade Agreements (MTA), 91-93, 97-98
material adverse change (MAC), 91-92, 93
Monte Carlo simulation, 160, 172, 176, 177, 184-185
Moody's, 92, 140, 152, 157, 174, 245
multiple discriminant analysis (MDA), 145-147

N

Nationally Recognized Statistical Rating Oranizations (NRSROs), 152
Net Fair Value, 111
net income, 29, 44, 49-51, 53, 58-59, 68, 73-76, 116, 150, 186, 189, 194, 259,
    260-261, 262-263
net income ratio, 29
net-out agreements, 98
net operating profit after taxes (NOPAT), 50-52, 193-203
net present value (NPV), 87, 138, 194, 197, 201-202, 203, 206
net profit margin (NPM), 58-59, 68-70, 190
net sales to inventory ratio, 21, 28
net sales to net working capital ratio, 21
net sales to tangible net worth ratio, 21
net sales to total assets ratio, 27-28, 74-77
net worth, 4, 8-15, 16-17, 18, 21-23, 25-27, 113, 114, 232
netting (set-off), 93, 168, 175, 218, 220, 224, 230, 233-237
non-sufficient funds (NSF), 19, 207
NOPAT, *see* net operating profit after taxes
notes, financial statement, 10, 11, 149, 180
notes payable/receivable, 16, 25, 47
number crunching, 5, 31, 251
NYMEX, 80-81, 83-85, 102, 103, 105-106

O

off-balance sheet, 15, 142, 155, 156, 179, 209, 213, 224, 240, 262, 264, 267-268
oil and gas, 86
    futures, 80-86
    markets, 102
    reserves, 11-14, 18
operating
    activities, 26-27, 32, 46, 49-50, 52, 53, 61-62, 192, 211, 216, 222, 253-254,
        259, 261
    break even, 184
    cash flow, 35, 36, 39, 43-48, 49-50, 51-55, 110-112, 114, 149-151, 211, 215,
        260-261, 263

cost, 33, 185, 215, 255, 262
cycle, 36-37, 38
earnings, 60, 62, 269
effects, 186
expenses, 30, 39, 40, 43, 60, 69
income, 30
leases, 194, 262
margin, 32, 69
obligations, 39
performance, 75, 76-77, 110, 253
profit/net profit, 32, 33, 195, also see Economic Value Added
risk, 64-65, 78, 96, 162
operating cash to total debt ratio, 48
operating return on sales (EBITA), 60, 61, 62, 63-64
operational signs of financial distress, 208, 209
opinion,
accountant's, 108, 115
auditor, 1, 4, 5
management's, 4-5
options, 83-85, 102-106, 156-158, 159, 181, 219, 262, 266-267
call, 83, 98, 99, 101, 103, 157-159
out-of-the-money, 103-104
over-the-counter (OTC), 82, 104, 105-106, 237
Overdrafts (ODs), 19, 207

P

payment
risk, 80, 97-98, 107-117, 125-137, 138, 230-242
terms, 54, 105, 118, 125-137, 230-242
payment pattern analysis, 28-29
pensions, 9, 18, 210, 262-265
performance
measurement, 68-69, 193-206, 259-260
risk, 57, 98-100
personal
guarantee(s), 16, 19, 117, 133-135, 231-233
net worth analysis, 16-17
retirement accounts, 17, 134
political risk, 78, 119, 227
portfolio
risk, 89, 160-178
transactions, 246-247
Potential Future Exposure (PFE), 162, 171-177
preference rule/preferences, 113, 131, 220, 224-225, 227

prepayment, 175, 230-231, 252
price/earnings ratio, 269-270, 272
price risk, 78-79, 82, 85, 89, 96, 101, 102, 143
Principal Component Analysis (PCA), 176
Pro Forma Financial Statement, 111, 114, 192
probability distribution, 162-164
profit, 71
   break even, 184
   levels, 183-185
   retention ratio, 186-191
profit before interest and tax ratio, 32
profit-and-loss statement, *see* income statement
profit margin, 23, 58-59, 68-70, 74-77, 190
profitability analysis, 57-70, 183-192
   of banks, 122-124
profitability ratios, 29-31, 32, 57-70, 68-69, 145, 150
   interest coverage, 30, 110, 150, 191
   net income/sales, 29-30
Proof of Claim, 223
property, plant and equipment (PP&E), 49, 53, 210

Q

quality risk, 12, 95, 122
quick ratio, 23, 26, 30, 33, 34-36, 40, 41, 254

R

ratios, *also see* specific ratio name
   acid test ratio, *see* quick ratio
   activity/balance sheet, 23-24, 25-26, 32, 33, 34-35, 36-41
   appraising the use of, 34-41
   asset intensity, 188-191
   asset to equity, 65
   asset turnover, 27-29, 58-59, 63-70, 71, 73-74, 191
   before-tax return on assets, 63-64, 66
   cash flow, 47-48
   current, 21, 23, 26, 30, 34-36, 37, 38, 39, 40, 41, 254
   current debt to tangible net worth, 21, 27
   debt to equity, 24, 34, 65, 67, 71, 191, 204
   DSO, 28-29, 36-37, 38
   fixed assets to tangible net worth, 21, 26-27
   funded debt to net working capital, 27
   interest coverage, 30, 110, 150, 191
   Lambda, 147-150, 151, 156, 157

leverage, 27, 30, 33, 74-77, 191
liquidity, 21, 26-27, 30, 32, 33, 37-41, 145-147, 254
net income to sales, 29-30
net sales to inventory, 21, 28
net sales to net working capital, 21
net sales to tangible net worth, 21
net sales to total assets, 27-28
operating cash to total debt, 48
price/earnings, 269-270, 272
probit before interest and tax, 32
profit margin, 74-77
profitability, 29-31, 32, 57-70, 145, 150
quick, 23, 26, 30, 33, 34-36, 40, 41, 254
retention, 68, 72, 75-77, 186-191
total debt to net working capital, 27
total debt to tangible net worth, 22, 27
turnover/productivity, 21, 22, 27-29, 63, 71, 74-77, 191, *also see* assets
    turnover
receivables, 9, 16, 21, 25, 26-30, 32, 36, 37, 38-29, 53, 63, 197-202, 210, 233-
    234 258
trade, 241-242
turnover of, 198-202
refineries, 10-11, 80-85, 111
reorganization, *see* bankruptcy
reserves, 11-14, 147, 194, 204
retention ratio, 68, 72, 75-77, 186-191
retirement accounts, 9, 17, 18, 134, 210, 262-265
return on assets (ROA), 48, 58-59, 63-64, 66, 68-70, 199-200, 205, 259-260
return on equity (ROE), 58-61, 66-70, 71-72, 74, 186-187, 191, 192, 205
return on investment (ROI), 59, 201, 265
return on sales, 55, 60, 61-62, 63-64, 183-184, 185, 211, 216, 258, 259-260
revenues, 30, 40, 42, 44, 50
revocable letter of credit, 126, 239
risk, *also see* specific type of risk
    analysis, 160-178
    management, 80-85, 99-102, 160-182
    measurement, 161, 205
    ranking, 155, 159, 170-171, 252
    transferring of, *see* derivatives
risk-adjusted return on capital (RAROC), 203-207
Robert Morris Associates (RMA), 34
ROA, *see* return on assets
ROE, *see* return on equity
rumor mill, 143-144

S

sales, 21, 26, 27-29, 32, 36-41, 50, 54, 55, 56, 59, 60, 62, 63, 67-69, 71-77, 84, 118, 146, 182-192, 204, 208, 215
Sarbanes-Oxley Act, 14, 182
SEC, 12-14, 142, 152, 211, 258
security instruments, 20, 98, 111, 125-137, 180, 217-218, 220, 223, 230-242
set-off, *see* netting
shareholders, 6, 33, 36, 59, 67, 71, 107-108, 109, 111, 116, 117, 157, 185-196, 189, 193, 196-197, 201, 202-206, 213, 216, 260, 262, 266, 267, 271, 272
    value analysis (SVA), 206
shenanigans, financial, 213-216, 268
Sheshunoff, 122, 123, 124
social risk, 119-120
sole proprietorship, 109
sources and uses of funds, 44-45, 47, 48, 53-54, 71, 253
sovereign risk, 97, 118, 131, 162
special-purpose entities (SPEs), 209, 212, 216, 262, 267-268
special-purpose vehicles (SPVs), 241
speculation, 76, 78-106, 170
speculators, 82
spreads, 143, 144-145, 155, 156
Standard & Poors (S&P), 91-92, 120, 152, 245, 267
    default rates, 168, 178
    rating definitions, 169, 170-171
standard deviation, 90, 95, 96-97, 150-151, 159, 162, 164-165, 167
Standard Industrial Classification (SIC), 28
standby letter of credit, 126-127, 133, 229, 239
Statement of Cash Flows, 1, 5, 29, 36, 39, 40, 43-56, 110-111, 149, 251, 260-261
stock/stock market, 32, 45, 46, 51, 60, 61, 78, 103, 148, 157-159, 193, 195, 200, 215-216, 206, 264-265, 270-271, 272
    company, 16, 17, 147, 203
    investing in, 258, 259
    options, 159, 214, 259, 261, 262, 266-267
    preferred, 10, 65, 146, 150
    warrants, 157-158
stockholders, 4, 10, 16, 46, 59, 115, 116-117, 123, 133, 196, 201, 209, 271, 272
Subchapter S Corporation, 108, 115, 116-117, 186
successful efforts accounting method, 4, 11
surety bonds, 175, 230, 233
sustainable growth, 60, 61, 67-69, 71-77, 183, 185-192
    analysis, 67-69, 74-77
    DuPont Model, 57-70, 76, 191-192, 203
    formula, 68, 71-72

long-term (LTSGR), 71-72, 186
predicting, 73-77
rate, 188-191
swaps, 79, 85-89, 97, 98, 101, 102-105, 106, 172, 173, 179, 217-218, 219, 246-247
credit default, 145, 242, 243-248
credit risk, 86-87, 89, 93-94
flexibility, 85, 93-94
ISDA, 91-93, 237
margin/collateral, 90
risk, 85-86
trading limits, 89-90
systemic risk, 96

T

tangible net worth, 21, 22, 25-27, 34, 112, 114
tax, 10, 32, 33, 51, 60, 69, 46, 50, 57, 63-64, 65-67, 71, 73, 107-108, 115-117, 120, 146, 189, 193-203, 204, 232, 261, 268, 269, 272
income, 10, 18, 29, 30, 67, 108, 116-117
returns, 6-7
term finance certificates, (TFC), 241
terms
credit, 91-93, 113, 114, 125-137, 230-242, 273, 276-277
letter of credit, 130, 273-276
payment, 54, 105, 118, 125-137, 230-242
of sale, 20, 23, 97, 118, 136
total debt to tangible net worth ratio, 22
total debt to net working capital ratio, 27
trade credit insurance, 241
trade receivables, 241-242
trade references, 19-20, 112, 114
trading companies, 82, 83, 85-90, 102, 174-175, 205, 216, 235-236
trading limits, 89-90
trust, 109
turnover ratios, 21, 22, 32, 63, 71-72, 74-77, 191, *also see* assets turnover
DSO, 28-29, 36-37, 38
net sales to total assets, 27-28, 74-77
net sales to inventory, 21, 28

U

Uniform Commerical Code, 125, 130
UCC-1, 20, 231
Urals, 99
U.S. Commodity Futures Modernization Act, 92

U.S. Trustee, 17, 218, 220-221, 225, 227
uses of funds, *see* sources and uses of funds

V

Vasicek-Kealhofer Model, 154, 157
Value at Risk (VAR), 11, 90, 96, 99, 160-161, 162, 166-167, 168, 204, 205
variance analysis, 29
volatility, *see* assets

W

warning signs of financial distress, 207-216
weighted average cost of capital (WACC), 64, 196
working capital, 8-9, 21, 26, 27, 35-36, 146, 148-149, 151, 187-189, 208, 229, 274, 276
write-downs, 265-266, 259
writing a credit analysis, 249-255

Z

Z score, 145-147, 151, 157
zero sum game, 73